Jesus

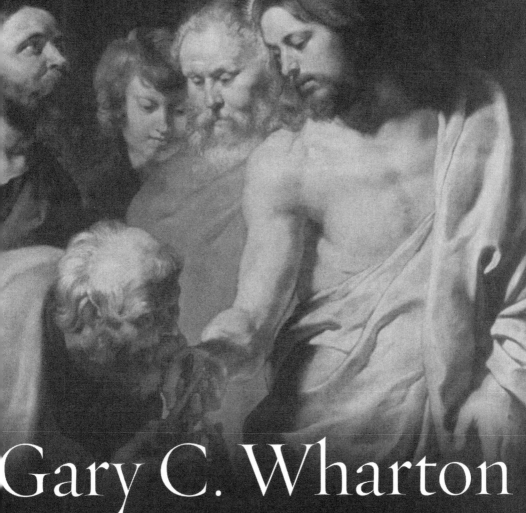

THE AUTHORIZED BIOGRAPHY

Gary C. Wharton

PRESENTED TO

_____

_____

FROM

_____

_____

Jesus

THE AUTHORIZED BIOGRAPHY

The Eyewitness Accounts by Those Who Personally Knew Him

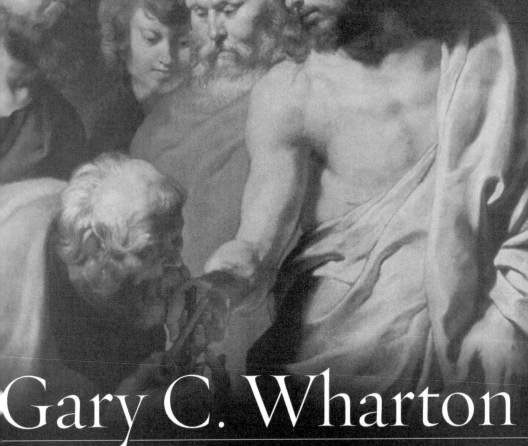

Gary C. Wharton

The Eyewitness Accounts by Those Who Personally Knew Him

First printing: February 2005

Copyright © 2004 by Gary C. Wharton. All rights reserved. No part of this book may be used or reproduced in any manner whatsoever without written permission of the publisher, except in the case of brief quotations in articles and reviews. For information write New Leaf Press, P.O. Box 726, Green Forest, AR 72638.

ISBN: 0-89221-618-2
Library of Congress Number: 2004118189

Cover by Left Coast Design, Portland, Oregon

Printed in the United States of America

Please visit our website for other great titles:
www.newleafpress.net

For information regarding author interviews,
please contact the publicity department at (870) 438-5288.

JESUS: THE AUTHORIZED BIOGRAPHY

first and foremost
is dedicated to
Jesus, the Christ, the Messiah
my Savior and my Lord,
the Almighty,

who, through His amazing birth, life, and death,
and His resurrection and ascension,
as recounted here entirely from the Scriptures,
indeed changed the world
and redirected my life
forever!

and to each of you who,
by your example and by your encouragement,
or by your opposition,
by the grace of God
contributed to the production of this book;

and to each of you who reads this amazing account
of this most amazing life,
that you may be challenged and changed forever!

THE FOUR GOSPEL WRITERS — Matthew, Mark, Luke, and John, along with the apostle Paul — introduce Christ and tell of his birth, childhood, and amazing life story through his triumphal entry into Jerusalem and the eventful week leading to his crucifixion, resurrection, and ultimate ascension. The following account presents this narrative in chronological order.

When *anno Domini*, the Year of our Lord, A.D., was first established, the chronologicalers were off five years. As a result, the Messiah was born, not in zero or A.D. 1, as one might suppose, but rather in A.D. 5, as chronicled here.

CONTENTS

Preface.. 13

Introduction... 15

Psalm 22 17

Section 1
The Advent of Messiah: The First Christmas 18

  1 **IN THE BEGINNING**... 19
    Introduction; Prologue: Messiah's Pre-Existence

  2 **BEFORE JESUS' BIRTH** (6 B.C.) 21
    The Announcement of John's Birth; The Angel's Announcement to
    Mary; The Angel's Announcement to Joseph; Elizabeth's Song; Mary's
    Song; The Birth of John the Baptizer

  3 **THE BIRTH OF JESUS** (6–2 B.C.) 31
    Jesus' Birth; The Proclamation by the Angels; The Visit by the
    Shepherds; The Temple Visit; The Testimony of Simeon; The Testimony
    of Anna; The Visit by the Magi; The Escape to Egypt

  4 **THE BOYHOOD OF JESUS** (2 B.C.-A.D. 9) 39
    Home to Nazareth, Jesus in the Temple; Back in Nazareth

Section 2
Messiah's Ministry Begins: Going Out into the Harvest 42

  5 **THE INAUGURATION** (A.D. 27) 43
    The Messenger and His Message; Questions from the Crowds;
    Questions from the Heart; The Baptism of Jesus; The Ancestry of Jesus
    through Joseph; The Ancestry of Jesus through Mary; The Temptation
    of Jesus; Jesus, The Lamb of God; Jesus' First Followers

6 FIRST JUDEA (8 months, A.D. 27) 55
The First Miracle, at Cana; The First Cleansing of the Temple;
Miraculous Signs at His First Passover; By Night; The Groom's Best
Man

7 THEN SAMARIA (A.D. 27) 61
Jesus Departs Judea for Samaria; The Samaritan Woman at the Well; A
Spiritual Harvest; Ministering in Sychar; Back Home to Galilee

Section 3
The Great Galilean Ministry: Acceptance and Rejection 66

8 HOME IN GALILEE (22 months, A.D. 27-28) 67
The Great Galilean Ministry Begins; Healing the Cana Official's Son;
Rejected at Nazareth; A New Home in Capernaum; The First Four
Fishers of Men; Healing in the Synagogue on the Sabbath; Peter's
Mother-in-Law is Healed; The Great Galilean Ministry Goes on Tour;
Healing a Leper; Healing a Paralytic; The Conversion of Matthew;
Feasting, Not Fasting

9 THE SECOND PASSOVER (A.D. 28) 77
In the Pool on a Sabbath; The Persecution Begins; The Son Is Equal to
the Father

10 BACK TO GALILEE (A.D. 28) 81
Against the Grain on a Sabbath; Do Good on the Sabbath;
Healing the Multitudes; Choosing the Twelve

11 THE SERMON ON THE MOUNT (A.D. 28) 85
The Beatitudes; The Least and the Great in the Kingdom; Superior to
the Law; Real Righteousness; Devotion to God; The Blind Leading
the Blind; Pearls, Pigs, and Prayer; Personal Righteousness; Amazing
Authority

12 GROWING FAME (A.D. 28) 99
A Centurion's Faith; A Widow's Only Son; A Baptist's Doubts; The
Cities Reproached; The Son's Invitation; The Messiah Anointed

13 FIRST PUBLIC REJECTION (A.D. 28) 107
The Second Great Galilean Tour; Jesus and Beelzebub; The Sign of
Jonah; Woe to You, Pharisees!; The Danger of a Spiritual Vacuum; The
True Family of Jesus

14 SECRETS OF THE KINGDOM (A.D. 28) 115
The Setting by the Sea; The Soil; The Seeds; The Weeds; The Mustard
Seed; The Leavened Loaf

15 THE KINGDOM SECRETS REVEALED (A.D. 28) 123
The Weeds Explained; The Hidden Treasure and Priceless Pearl; The
Dragnet and the Storeroom

16 CONTINUED OPPOSITION (A.D. 28) 127
Calming the Storm; Curing the Demoniac; Healing a Woman and Raising a Daughter; Healing the Blind and the Mute; Last Visit to Nazareth

17 FINAL GALILEAN CAMPAIGN (A.D. 28) 133
Shortage of Workers; Commissioning the Twelve; The Disciples Deputized; Jesus Mistaken for John; John the Baptizer Beheaded

Section 4
Training the Twelve: Lessons on Discipleship 138

18 LESSONS ON THE BREAD OF LIFE (A.D. 28) 139
The Capernaum Retreat; Feeding Five Thousand; The Crowds Dispersed; Jesus Walks on Water; Triumph at Gennesaret; The Bread of Life; Disciples Defect

19 LESSONS ON LEAVEN (6 months, A.D. 28-29) 149
Ceremonial Defilement; Internal Defilement; Rewarding a Syrian Mother's Faith; Healing the Impaired; Feeding Four Thousand; Demand for Miraculous Proof Denied; Admonition against Hypocrisy; Admonition to Fear God Only; Admonition against Materialism; Healing the Blind at Bethsaida

20 LESSONS ON MESSIAHSHIP (same 6 months, A.D. 29) 159
Peter's Proclamation: Jesus is the Messiah; Jesus' First Prediction: Rejection, Crucifixion, and Resurrection; Jesus' Promise: The Coming Kingdom of the Son of Man; Jesus' Transfiguration: The Chosen One, the Beloved Son of God; Jesus' Descent: The Return of Elijah and the Suffering of Messiah

21 LESSONS ON RESPONSIBILITY (same 6 months, A.D. 29) 165
Healing the Demonic Boy: Unbelief Rebuked; Jesus' Second Prediction: Death and Resurrection; Jesus' Contribution: Payment of the Temple Tax; The Disciples' Contention: The Greatest in the Kingdom; Jesus' Admonition: Anyone Not against Us Is for Us; Dealing with Sin against You: There I Am in Your Midst; Forgiveness: The Parable of the Contemptible Slave

22 LESSONS ON COMMITMENT (3 months, A.D. 29) 173
Listen for the Lord's Timing: Rejecting Brotherly Advice; Look for the Lord's Direction: Rejection in Samaria; Count the Cost of Complete Commitment: True Total Discipleship

Section 5
Messiah's Final Missions: The Judean and Perean Ministries 176

23 LAST JUDEAN MINISTRY (A.D. 29) 177
The Feast of Tabernacles: Jesus Teaches at the Temple; Forgiveness of an Adulteress: Cast the First Stone; The Light of the World: Conflict

with the Pharisees; The Prophecy Test: Relation to the Father God; The Prophecy Test: Relation to the Father Abraham; The Man Born Blind: Healing and Consequences; Parable of the Good Shepherd: Further Conflict among the Jews

24 LESSONS ON LOVING SERVICE (A.D. 29) 193
Commissioning the Seventy; Celebrating the Seventy; The Good Samaritan; Hospitality of Mary and Martha; A Model Prayer

25 ACCUSATIONS AND WARNINGS (A.D. 29) 197
Do Not Worry: Your Treasure Is in Heaven; Always be Vigilant: The Son of Man Will Come Unexpectedly; Sorrow Ahead: Not Peace but Division; Discern the Times: Judge What Is Right

26 REPENT OR PERISH (A.D. 29) 201
Great Calamities: Not the Result of Greater Sins; The Fruitless Fig Tree: One More Year; Healing on the Sabbath: Humiliating His Opponents; The Festival of Hanukkah: Accusation of Blasphemy

27 PRINCIPLES OF DISCIPLESHIP (A.D. 29–30) 205
Beyond Jordan: Jesus Withdraws to Bethany; Warnings about Salvation: Enter through the Narrow Door; Warnings about Herod and against Jerusalem; Healing on the Sabbath without Response; Parable of the Ambitious Guests and the Best Seats; Parable of the Great Banquet and the Cost of Being Too Busy; The Cost and Demands of Discipleship; Parables of Associating with Sinners: The Lost Sheep, the Lost Coin, and the Prodigal Son; Parable of the Dishonest Manager: You Cannot Serve God and Worldly Wealth; Rebuking the Pharisees: God's Law Cannot Be Altered; Parable of the Rich Man and Lazarus: The Danger of Wealth; Lessons on Discipleship: Forgiveness, Faith, and Duty; The Death of Lazarus: Victory over Death; The Fallout: The Plot to Kill Jesus

28 TO JERUSALEM (A.D. 30) 219
Healing Ten of Leprosy: Only One Shows Gratitude; The Suddenness of the Coming Kingdom: Those Not Prepared Will Be Left Behind; Two Parables on Prayer: The Persistent Widow and the Pharisee and the Tax Collector; Conflict with the Pharisees: Teachings on Divorce; Christ and the Children: For of Such Is the Kingdom of Heaven; The Rich Young Official: The Possession of Possessions; Sovereignty of the Estate Owner: Parable of the Vineyard Laborers; Jesus' Third Prediction: His Death and Resurrection; Leadership and Service: Warning against Ambitious Pride

Section 6
Jerusalem: The Final Countdown —
The Week That Changed the World 230

29 SEVENTH DAY BEFORE PASSOVER (9th of Nissan A.D. 30) 231
Healed by Faith: Two Blind Men Receive Their Sight; Preparing for
Passover: Looking for Jesus; Zacchaeus at Jericho: Seeking and Saving
the Lost; The Minas Touch: To Everyone Who Has, More Will be
Given

30 SIXTH DAY BEFORE PASSOVER (10th of Nissan A.D. 30) 235
Jesus Anointed by Mary

31 FIFTH DAY BEFORE PASSOVER (11th of Nissan A.D. 30)................ 237
The Donkey and Her Colt; The Triumphal Entry

32 FOURTH DAY BEFORE PASSOVER (12th of Nissan A.D. 30)........... 241
The Fig Tree; Jesus Clears the Temple

33 THIRD DAY BEFORE PASSOVER (13th of Nissan A.D. 30) 243
Faith That Moves Mountains; Jesus' Authority Challenged; The Two
Sons; The Wicked Tenants; The Wedding Feast; The Pharisees' Tax
Trap; The Sadducees' Trick Resurrection Question; The Greatest
Commandment; Messiah, Son of David; Denunciation of the
Pharisees; Hypocrisy of the Pharisees; Jesus Mourns over Jerusalem;
The Widow's Penny; The Messiah Glorified; The Great Temple
Prophecy; Jesus' Daily Practice; Jesus Forecasts the Future: The "Olivet
Discourse"; Ten Bridesmaids; Five Hundred Thousand Dollars; Day of
Judgment; Jesus Forecasts His Own Crucifixion

34 SECOND DAY BEFORE PASSOVER (14th of Nissan A.D. 30)........... 265
The Reanointing of Jesus; The Ultimate Betrayal; Preparation for
Passover

Section 7
Last Days of Messiah: The Weekend That Changed the World 268

35 THE DAY BEFORE PASSOVER (15th of Nissan A.D. 30) 269
Jesus' Lesson in Humility; The Leader as Server; Jesus Reveals His
Betrayer; The Lord's Supper Instituted; Jesus Predicts Peter's Denial;
The Disciples' First Commission; Conversations in the Upper Room;
The Last Conversation on the Way to Gethsame; Last Words about the
Future; The Intercessory Prayer of Messiah; Peter's Desertion Predicted
Again; The Grief of Gethsemane; The Betrayal and Arrest; The Night
Trial by Annas; Peter in the Courtyard of the Chief Priest; The Night
Trial by Caiaphas; The Three Denials of Peter; The Condemnation by
the Council; Judas Commits Suicide; The Messiah Before Pilate; The
Messiah Before Herod; The Messiah Back Before Pilate; The Messiah or

Barabbas; The Message from Pilate's Wife; Crucify Him!; The Messiah Mocked; No Case against Him; No Friend of Caesar; No King but Caesar; Capitulation; The Soldiers Mock Jesus; To Golgotha via Dolorosa

36 SIX HOURS ON THE CROSS (15th of Nissan, A.D. 30) 301
Crucified with Criminals; The Notice; Gambling for Garments; Jeering at Jesus; Entrusting Mary; The Enveloping Darkness; The Centurion; No Broken Bones; Watching from a Distance

37 PASSOVER SABBATH: MESSIAH'S BURIAL
(16th of Nissan A.D. 30) 309
Joseph's Tomb; The Sepulcher Secured

38 THE FIRST DAY OF THE WEEK (18th of Nissan A.D. 30) 311
The Women Visit the Tomb; An Angel Opens the Tomb; Visitors in the Empty Tomb; The Message from Beyond; Jesus Meets the Women; The Women Talk Nonsense; Bribing the Soldiers; The Empty Shroud; Stop Holding On!; The Couple from Emmaus

39 THE NEXT DAY AND ONE WEEK LATER
(19th & 26th of Nissan A.D. 30) 317
Behind Locked Doors; Doubting Thomas; No Doubt about It!

40 FROM GALILEE TO GLORY: THE ASCENSION (A.D. 30) 321
Breakfast with Jesus; The Demands of Dedication; Pay Your Own Price; The Great Commission; The Ascension; Many Appearances; True Testimony

41 MESSIAH GLORIFIED 327
From Empty to Exaltation; Stephen's Vision of Jesus; Paul's Vision of Jesus; John's Vision of Jesus

Isaiah 53 334

Index of Ancient Prophecies from the Old Testament Fulfilled
in the Life of Jesus 336

Synoptic Index 338

Scripture Index 340

Subject Index 345

PREFACE

JESUS CHRIST, the Messiah, is the single most important and influential person in history. Everything, including our yearly calendar, focuses on him.

The biography of Christ's life is carefully preserved for us by the compilers of the first four books of the New Testament — Matthew, Mark, Luke, and John — with later references by the apostle Paul.

Jesus: The Authorized Biography offers a synthesis of the gospel accounts, with excerpts from Paul, taken entirely from the Scriptures. Believing that God, through his Spirit, inspired every single word of the original texts, *Jesus* recounts this incredible life, word for word from the Bible, without embellishment, which is why this is his "authorized" biography.

Different translations in today's vernacular have been blended together to form one narrative. Only where there is redundancy between the gospel writers have words been omitted. And only where verb tense or other clarification is required have modifications been made.

As much as has been possible, *Jesus: The Authorized Biography* offers a pure chronological recounting of his most amazing life.

Contemporary language is used throughout, including the personal pronouns for deity (*you* instead of *thee*, for example). "Holy Spirit" rather than "Holy Ghost" is consistently used. Poetry, prose, and prophecy are presented in open verse for clarity and beauty. The very words of Jesus, and the voice of God in Old Testament references, are emphasized in bold print. And the Hebrew word "Messiah" is selected over the Greek synonym "Christ," as often as considered appropriate.

Relevant Old Testament prophecies are included to demonstrate the absolute marvel of this miraculous account.

The Birth of Jesus, The Story of Christmas, and *The Last Days of Messiah,* companion Cumberland House and Meridian Publishing books, also recount the beginning and ending, the alpha and the omega, of Christ's life among us.

It is our prayer that this "authorized" contemporary narrative will not only help us more completely understand the full gospel record, but also help us more fully celebrate his true life story and its impact in our own lives today.

INTRODUCTION

J*esus: The Authorized Biography* uniquely syntheses all the gospel writings, along with portions of the New Testament letters, incorporating every word of Scripture about the life of Jesus. Not one new word or embellishment is introduced to "enhance" or even "clarify" the account. Nor are any words omitted, except where two or more of the gospel writers recount the same incident, and then only to eliminate duplication.

All the words spoken by Jesus, and by God in the Messianic prophecies, are emphasized in bold print.

All current translations — over three dozen of them — as well as references to the New Testament Koine Greek — have been consulted to provide the most accurate, contemporary reading of this amazing life story.

All the Messianic prophecies fulfilled by Jesus throughout his life, as recorded by the gospel writers, are included.

Jesus: The Authorized Biography is not the first effort to synthesize the accounts of the life of Jesus. The original of course was Luke who began his Gospel:

> Following what was heard by the original eyewitnesses and servants of Jesus Christ, the Messiah, who is the Word, many have undertaken to compile a narrative of the events that happened among us. For this reason, I have carefully checked everything from the beginning, and present it here in proper chronological order for you, so that you may be assured that what you have been taught is indeed true.

One of the first "modern" attempts to synthesize the four gospel accounts was *The Compendium of the Life of Jesus Christ,* compiled by Blaise Pascal about 1650. When the Gospels were written, Pascal noted in his preface, "Everything was done so that we would believe that Jesus is the Son of God and in believing would have eternal life thanks to him."

Pascal then continues, in words also reflecting our own present intentions:

> Since, for motives perhaps in part unknown, the holy evangelists wrote following an order which does not always respect chronology, we

will present it chronologically, placing every verse of each evangelist in the order in which the recorded event occurred, to the extent that our frailty has allowed us.

He then concludes, also expressing our own intent:

If the reader finds anything good, then give thanks to God, the only author of all good. Anything found bad can be attributed to my own weakness.

PSALM 22

My God, my God. Why have you abandoned me?
Why are you so far from helping me,
    and from the words of my roaring?
O my God, I cry in the daytime, but you hear not,
    and in the night seasons and I am not silent. . . .

All they that see me laugh me to scorn;
    they insult me with their lip,
    they shake their head, saying:

        He trusts in the Lord Jehovah,
        let him deliver him;
        seeing he delights in him. . . .

They gape on me with their mouths,
    as a ferocious and roaring lion.
I am poured out like water;
    and all my bones are out of joint.
My heart is like wax; it is melted within me.
My strength is dried up like broken pottery;
    and my tongue cleaves to my jaws;
    and you have brought me into the dust of death.
Dogs have surrounded me;
A wicked mob has encompassed me;
They pierced my hands and my feet.
I can count all my bones;
They look and stare upon my nakedness.
They divide my garments among themselves,
    and for my clothing throw dice. . . .

They will come and declare his righteousness
    to people that are yet to be born
That it is finished —
That he has finished it!

Written by King David, year c. 1000 B.C.
Psalm 22:1-2, 7-8, 13-18, 31

THE ADVENT OF MESSIAH:

THE FIRST CHRISTMAS

1

SECTION ONE

ONE

INTRODUCTION

FOLLOWING what was heard by the original eyewitnesses and servants of Jesus Christ, the Messiah, who is the Word, many have undertaken to compile a narrative of the events that happened among us.

For this reason, I have carefully checked everything from the beginning, and present it here in proper chronological order for you, so that you can be assured that what you have been taught is indeed true.

Luke 1:1–4

PROLOGUE: MESSIAH'S PRE-EXISTENCE

BEFORE TIME BEGAN, Jesus Christ lived. In fact, he has always been. In the beginning he was the Word, and as the Word he was with God and he was also God. He was in the beginning eternal with God.

Everything that was created came into being by him and there is nothing in existence that he has not created. In him was life and that life brought light to men. His light shines brightly in the darkness and the darkness cannot snuff it out.

There was a man, sent from God, named John. John came to announce to everyone that this unquenchable light was even then, at that very moment, coming into the world. His purpose in coming was that everyone might believe through him. John was not that light, but he was the announcer of the light's coming.

Jesus Christ is the true light, who, coming into the world, enlightens every man. He was in the world, and even though he had created the world, it did not recognize him.

He came to his own people, and even they did not receive him. But to others who did receive him — those who believed and put their faith in him — to them he gave the right to become children of God. This did not happen through ancestry, nor sexual passion, nor by willing it to be, but by God.

The Word, Jesus, became a human being and lived very briefly among us. We actually saw his glory, the splendor of the only Son God ever fathered, the embodiment of all grace and truth.

When John had announced his coming he said, "This was he of whom I said: He who succeeds me has a higher rank than I, for he existed before me."

And from his fullness we have all received bounty heaped upon bounty, because while the Law has come to us through Moses, grace and truth came through Jesus Christ, the Messiah.

No man has ever seen God, but he has been revealed to us through the only fathered Son, who has now returned to his Father's side.

John 1:1–18

The Announcement of John's Birth *circa 6 B.C.*

DURING THE REIGN of Herod the Great, who was then king of the Jews, there lived in the province of Judea a priest of the order of Abijah, whose name was Zacharias.

His wife was called Elizabeth, and they shared a common ancestor, the High Priest Aaron. They were a deeply religious couple, devout and zealous in the practice of their faith.

The major disappointment in their lives was that they were childless because of Elizabeth's infertility, and both were now well advanced in years.

It was common practice among the Abijah priests, when it was their turn to serve in the temple, to draw lots determining which duties each would undertake. On this particular day, it was Zacharias's responsibility to go into the temple to burn incense. The usual crowd of worshipers remained outside, praying.

In the midst of his duties, Zacharias was suddenly startled with terror. To the right of the altar he saw an angel, the angel of the Lord, who spoke to him!

"Do not be afraid, Zacharias, your prayers have been heard. Elizabeth, your wife, is going to have a son and you are to name him John.

> He will be your joy and delight;
> His birth will be a time of great celebration,
>> because he is destined to become
>> one of God's great men.
> He will never touch wine or liquor:
> Instead he will be filled
>> with the Holy Spirit,
>> even in his mother's womb,
>> before he is born!

He will be a messenger of God,
    a forerunner of the one
    who is promised to come,
    with the strength and power
    of the prophet Elijah.
He will return many of Israel's children
    to the Lord their God,
And reconcile parents and their children,
    and restore the rebellious
    to the wisdom of the righteous
    to thoroughly prepare his people
    for the coming of the Lord.

"But I am an old man," Zacharias said, "and Elizabeth is getting on in years. How can I be sure this is true?"

"I am Gabriel," the angel replied. "I come directly from standing in the presence of God. I have been sent to speak to you and to bring you this good news. But you do not believe me!

"So from now until all I have said has happened, you will lose your ability to speak, and will remain silent. Put your faith in God, Zacharias. Everything I have told you will come true, at the proper time."

In the meantime, the crowd waiting outside for Zacharias was growing impatient, wondering why he was delayed so long in the sanctuary. When he finally did come out, they immediately realized he had seen a vision. He was unable to speak a word! When he tried to speak, no sound came out. He just stood there, communicating with gestures, but unable to say a word.

So when his duties in the temple were over, he went home. Soon after this, Elizabeth became pregnant, but she did not show herself in public, or tell anyone, for five months.

When she did make the announcement, she said, "This is what the Lord has done for me! God has shown me his favor. He has removed the embarrassment I felt for being childless, and I no longer have to feel ashamed any more."

Luke 1:5–25

Behold, I will send you Elijah the prophet
    before the great and dreadful day of the Lord comes.
And he will restore the heart of the fathers to the children,
    and the heart of the children to their fathers,
Lest I come and smite the land with a curse of utter destruction.

Recorded by the prophet Malachi, year c. 425 B.C.
Malachi 4:5–6

THE ANGEL'S ANNOUNCEMENT TO MARY *circa 6 B.C.*

A T THE SAME TIME, a virgin whose name was Mary lived in the town of Nazareth, in the province of Galilee. Mary was Elizabeth's cousin, and was engaged to Joseph, a direct descendant of David, the ancient king of Israel.

When Elizabeth was in the sixth month of her pregnancy, God sent the angel Gabriel to Mary. Gabriel entered Mary's room.

23

"Greetings, Mary," the angel said. "How favored you are! The Lord is with you!"

Startled, Mary tried to comprehend just what such a greeting meant.

"There is no need to be frightened," the angel said. "God loves you very much, and he has chosen you! You are going to have a baby! A son! You are to name him Jesus.

> He will be great:
>> and he will be called
>> the Son of the Most High God!
> And the Lord God will place him
>> on the throne of his ancestor David.
> He will reign
>> over the house of Jacob forever;
>> and there will never be an end to his reign."

"How can that be?" Mary asked. "I am not married, and I am a virgin."

The angel answered her:

> God's Holy Spirit will envelope you;
>> and the power of the Most High God
>> will overshadow you;
> And your child shall be called the Son of God!
> Consider your cousin, Elizabeth,
>> the one they called the Barren One!
> She has conceived in her old age
>> and is now pregnant in her sixth month!
> God's promises can never fail!
>> There is nothing that God is unable to do.
>> Nothing is impossible with God!
>> God can do anything!

"I am the Lord's servant," Mary replied. "Let it happen as you have said."

At that, the angel left her.

Luke 1:26–38

BEFORE JESUS' BIRTH

The Lord himself
    will give you a sign;
Behold, a virgin shall conceive,
    and bear a son,
    and shall call His name
Immanuel,
    (meaning God with us).

Written by the prophet Isaiah, c. 700 B.C.
Isaiah 7:14

And when the days are fulfilled
    and you shall sleep
    with your fathers;
I will set up your seed after you,
    which shall proceed
    out of your bowels,
And I will establish
    his kingdom.

He shall build a house
    for my name,
And I will establish the throne
    of his kingdom for ever.

I will be his father
    and he shall be my son.
And your house and your kingdom
    shall be established for ever
    before you.
Your throne shall be established
    forever.

Recorded by the prophet Nathan to King David, c. 1000 B.C.
2 Samuel 7:12–16

He shall build me a house,
　　and I will establish his throne forever.
I will be his father,
　　and he shall be my son:
And I will not remove
　　my mercy from him,
　　as I removed it from those
　　that were before.
But I will establish him
　　in my house
　　and in my kingdom forever:
And his throne shall be established
　　for evermore.

25

Recorded by the prophet Nathan to King David, c. 1000 B.C.
1 Chronicles 17:12–14

THE ANGEL'S ANNOUNCEMENT TO JOSEPH

MARY HAD PROMISED to become Joseph's wife. In fact, they were engaged. But before they were married, before they lived together, Joseph learned that Mary was pregnant (by the Holy Spirit). Being a man of principle, and at the same time not wanting her to be publicly disgraced, Joseph resolved to discreetly break off their engagement.

While Joseph was tossing in bed one night, contemplating the best course to follow, an angel of the Lord appeared to him in a dream.

"Joseph, son of David," the angel said, "do not be afraid to make Mary your wife. The baby in her was conceived by the Holy Spirit of God. It is a boy! A son! You are to name him Jesus (which means *Savior*), because it is he who will save his people from their sins."

All of this occurred fulfilling a prediction that the Lord God made through the prophet Isaiah, hundreds of years earlier:

Behold, a virgin shall be with child and shall bear a son,
　　and they shall call his name Immanuel.

Immanuel translated means *God with us.*

So when Joseph awoke from his sleep, he did exactly as the angel of the Lord commanded him. He took Mary as his wife. But he did not sleep with her until after she gave birth to her first son. And he named the baby Jesus.

Matthew 1:18–25

ELIZABETH'S SONG

AT A TIME early in her pregnancy, Mary got her things together and hurried away to the hill country, to a town in Judea. There she went to the home of Zacharias, and greeted her cousin Elizabeth.

At the instant Mary greeted her, Elizabeth felt her unborn baby virtually leap within her, and she herself was filled with the Holy Spirit.

Elizabeth cried out:

> Oh, Mary, how marvelously God
>   has blessed you!
>   singling you out
>   from all the women in the world!
> And how specially blessed is the child
>   who will come from your womb!
> What an honor it is for me
>   to have the mother of my Lord
>   visit my home!
> For the instant you greeted me
>   my baby leaped for joy within me!
> How specially blessed is the woman
>   who trusts God
>   to keep his promise to her!

Luke 1:39–45

MARY'S SONG

MARY RESPONDED with an outburst of thanksgiving:

> All that is within me praises the Lord,
>   and my spirit delights in God, my Savior;
> For he has seen fit to notice me,
>   his most humble servant, a nobody!
> For from now on, forever,
>   throughout all generations,
>   the world will regard me
>   as the woman God favored,
>   because Almighty God
>   has done great things for me.
> Holy is his name!

He is merciful
>   to generation after generation,
>   to those who reverence him.
How powerful and strong is his arm!
How he routs the proud and the haughty!
How he disposes strong rulers
>   and elevates the ordinary!
The hungry he has filled with good things,
>   but the rich go away with empty hands.
And now he has come to help his servant Israel.
His promise of mercy has not been forgotten,
>   the promises he made to our ancestors,
>   to Abraham and all his descendants,
>   forever and forever.

Mary stayed with Elizabeth about three months and then returned to her own home.

Luke 1:46–56

PROPHECY

**Behold, I will send my messenger
>   and he shall prepare a way before me.
Then the Lord whom you seek
>   shall suddenly come to his temple.
Even the messenger of the covenant,
>   for whom you desire.
Indeed, he is coming!**

So says the Lord of Hosts,
>   the Lord Almighty, Jehovah Sabaoth.

Recorded by the prophet Malachi, c. 425 B.C.
Malachi 3:1

PROPHECY

The people who walked in darkness
>   have seen a great light:
And those who dwell in the land of the shadow of death,
>   upon them a light has dawned.

Written by the prophet Isaiah, c. 700 B.C.
Isaiah 9:2

27

WHEN IT WAS TIME for Elizabeth to have her baby, she gave birth to a son. Her neighbors and relatives heard of the great goodness the Lord had shown her and rejoiced and celebrated with her.

When the baby was eight days old, they took him to the temple to have him circumcised. Everyone assumed that the child would be named Zacharias after his father. But Elizabeth said, "No, he must be named John."

"But none of your relatives is called John," they retorted. Then they turned to his father Zacharias, and, by making signs, they asked him what name he wanted. He gestured for a writing tablet and wrote, "His name is John." They were all astonished!

Immediately Zacharias's ability to speak returned, his voice was restored, and he began shouting praises to God!

Fear struck all of their neighbors as the news of all these incidents spread about the hill country of Judea. It made a deep impression on everyone who heard about it, and they asked themselves, "What kind of special person will he become?" For the hand of the Lord was plainly on him.

Filled with the Holy Spirit, his father Zacharias prophesied:

> Praise the Lord, the God of Israel!
> He has visited his people
>   and brought redemption.
> He has raised up a mighty Savior for us
>   in the house of his servant David.
> It is exactly as the prophets predicted,
>   that we should be saved
>   from our enemies,
>   and from the hand of all who hate us;
> To show us the mercy
>   promised to our fathers,
> And to remember his holy covenants,
>   the oath he swore to our father Abraham;
> To grant us that we,
>   being freed from the hand of our enemies,
>   might serve him without fear
>   in holiness and righteousness before him
>   all the days of our lives.
> And you, child, will be called
> "The prophet of the Most High"

For you will go before the Lord,
>   preparing the way for him, giving his people
>   the knowledge of salvation,
>   through the forgiveness of their sins,
>   because of the loving compassion of God.
Heaven's dawn is about to break
>   shining light on those in darkness,
>   those who are now
>   beneath the shadow of death,
>   guiding our feet in the path of peace.

The child grew and became spiritually strong. When he grew up, he left home and lived in the wilderness country until the time came to begin his public ministry in Israel.

Luke 1:57–80

I the Lord have called you in righteousness,
>   and will hold your hand,
>   and will keep you,
>   and give you a covenant of the people,
>   for a light to the Gentiles.

I bring near my righteousness;
>   it shall not be far off,
And my salvation shall not tarry:
And I will place salvation in Zion
>   for Israel my glory.

It is a light thing
>   that you should be my servant
>   to raise up the tribe of Jacob,
>   and to restore the preserved of Israel:
I will also give you a light to the Gentiles,
>   that you may be my salvation
>   unto the end of the earth.

Recorded by the prophet Isaiah, c. 700 B.C.
Isaiah 42:6; 46:13; 49:6

JESUS' BIRTH

circa 5 B.C.

IN THOSE DAYS, toward the end of Mary's pregnancy, the emperor Caesar Augustus decreed that a census be taken of the entire Roman Empire. This was the first census taken when Quirinius was governor of Syria. Everyone was required to register in his own city.

Since Joseph was a descendant of David, he went up from the city of Nazareth in Galilee, to Bethlehem, the city of David, in Judea. Mary, who was engaged to him and by now was close to full term, accompanied him, for she, too, was of the house of David and had to register.

While they were there, Mary went into labor and gave birth to her first-born son. She wrapped him in swaddling clothes and, because there had been no room for them in the inn, she gently laid him in a manger.

Luke 2:1–7

THE PROCLAMATION BY THE ANGELS

IN THE FIELDS outside of Bethlehem that night, some shepherds were tending their sheep. Suddenly an angel of the Lord appeared in their midst, and the glory of the Lord shone radiantly. The whole field lit up with his presence. The shepherds were petrified!

"Stop being afraid!" the angel said. "I have come to bring you good news which will bring great joy to all people of the world. The Messiah has come! Your Savior was born today in Bethlehem, the town of David! You will know you have found him when you discover a baby wrapped in swaddling clothes, lying in a manger."

Suddenly, an army of heavenly hosts appeared with the angel, filling the sky. They raised their voices in song:

> Glory to God in highest heaven!
> And on earth, peace to those
>   with whom God is pleased!

Then, as quickly as they appeared, the angels were gone back into heaven.

Luke 2:8–14

THE VISIT BY THE SHEPHERDS

THIS IS TOO GOOD to miss," the shepherds said to one another. "Let us go straight to Bethlehem now. Let us see for ourselves what the Lord has announced to us."

They raced into town as fast as they could and found their way to Mary and Joseph and, as they had been told, the baby, lying in a manger. Trembling with excitement at seeing the baby, the shepherds poured out the story the angel had told them about this child.

All the people listened, astonished. As for Mary, she treasured it all in her heart and kept thinking about it, but said nothing.

The shepherds eventually returned to their flocks, glorifying and praising God for all that they had heard and seen, just as had been told them.

Luke 2:15–20

PROPHECY

> If she cannot afford a lamb,
>   then she shall take two turtledoves
>   or two young pigeons,
>   the one for a burnt offering,
>   and the other for a sin offering;
> And the priest shall make atonement for her,
>   and she shall be clean.

From the law of Moses, c. 1440 B.C.
Leviticus 12:8

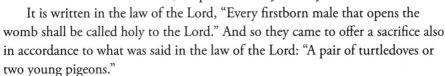

T HE BABY was circumcised when he was eight days old and named Jesus, the name given by the angel before he was conceived.

When the time came, according to the Mosaic law, for his mother's purification and his dedication to God, his parents took Jesus to Jerusalem.

33

It is written in the law of the Lord, "Every firstborn male that opens the womb shall be called holy to the Lord." And so they came to offer a sacrifice also in accordance to what was said in the law of the Lord: "A pair of turtledoves or two young pigeons."

Luke 2:21–24

THE TESTIMONY OF SIMEON

I N JERUSALEM was a man named Simeon. This man was deeply religious, dedicated to the service of God, filled with God's Holy Spirit, and living in the expectation of the imminent salvation of Israel. Each day Simeon expected that the Messiah would appear, because the Holy Spirit had promised him that he would see the Messiah before he died.

On this particular day, prompted by God, Simeon went into the temple. When Mary and Joseph brought Jesus to dedicate him according to the custom of the Law, Simeon took Jesus into his arms, blessed God, and prayed:

> Now Lord, let your servant depart in peace,
>   I am content to die.
> For you kept your word.
> My eyes have witnessed your salvation
>   which you have prepared
>   in the presence of all mankind,
> A light to reveal the unknown
>   to the Gentiles,
> A light to bring glory
>   to your people Israel.

Joseph and Mary marveled at what Simeon said about their son. Simeon then blessed them both, and turned to Mary his mother:

> Behold, this child is destined
>   for the fall and rise of many in Israel;
> And to establish a standard
>   that many will oppose,

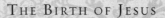

Because he will reveal
　　men's true motives.
A sword will also pierce
　　your own soul, Mary.

Luke 2:25–35

THE TESTIMONY OF ANNA

ALSO IN THE TEMPLE at the same time was a prophetess, Anna, the daughter of Phanuel, a descendant of Asher. She was very old, a widow of 84 years whose husband died only seven years after they were married.

The temple had become her home. She never left it, for she worshiped, fasted, and prayed at all hours of the day and night.

At the very moment Simeon was blessing the child, she came up and also gave thanks to God. Then she told all those who were looking for the redemption of Jerusalem that she had seen Jesus, the Messiah.

Then Joseph and Mary and Jesus returned to their home in Bethlehem.

Luke 2:36–38

PROPHECY

The kings of Tarshish and of the isles
　　shall bring presents;
The kings of Sheba and Seba
　　shall offer gifts. . . .
And he shall live,
　　and to him shall be given
　　the gold of Sheba:
Prayer also shall be made
　　for him continually;
　　and daily shall he be praised.

Written by King Solomon, c. 950 B.C.
Psalm 72:10–15

PROPHECY

The multitude of camels
　　shall cover you,
The dromedaries of Midian and Ephah;
　　all they from Sheba shall come:
They shall bring gold and incense;
　　and they shall show forth
　　the praises of the Lord.

Written by the prophet Isaiah, c. 700 B.C
Isaiah 60:6

S OMETIME LATER, still during the reign of Herod over Judea, Magi arrived in Jerusalem from the east. "Where is he who has been born King of the Jews?" they inquired. "We saw his star in the east, and have come to pay him homage."

Of course, when Herod the king heard about this, it concerned him. In fact, it created apprehension throughout the city. So Herod assembled all the ruling priests and scribes and questioned them where the Messiah was to be born.

"In Bethlehem," they told him, and quoted the prophecy:

> And you Bethlehem, in the land of Judah,
>> are by no means least
>> among the cities of Judah.
> For a ruler shall come from you
>> to govern my people Israel.

Then Herod summoned the Magi to a private meeting, and by questioning them, was able to determine when the star first appeared. Then he sent them to Bethlehem, saying, "Go and conduct a careful search for the child. When you have found him, report back to me and I'll come and join you and worship him with you."

Having heard the king, they left Jerusalem and followed the star on to Bethlehem until it stopped right above the house where the Christ child was now living.

As they watched the star, it stopped. They were ecstatic with joy. Entering the house, they saw the child with his mother Mary. Immediately they dropped to their knees and worshiped him. From their travel bags they took their treasures — gifts made of gold and containers filled with the fragrances of frankincense and myrrh.

When the Magi left Bethlehem for their home, they deliberately bypassed Jerusalem and returned by a different route, having been warned in a dream to avoid Herod.

Matthew 2:1–12

PROPHECY

> But you, Bethlehem Ephratah,
>> though you be little
>> among the thousands of Judah,
> Yet out of you shall he come forth unto me
>> that is to be ruler in Israel;
> Whose goings forth
>> have been from old,
>> from everlasting.

Written by the prophet Micah, c. 740 B.C.
Micah 5:2

I see him, but not now;
I behold him, but not near.
A Star shall come out of Jacob;
A Scepter shall rise out of Israel.

From the law of Moses, c. 1440 B.C.
Numbers 24:17

THE ESCAPE TO EGYPT

SHORTLY AFTER the Magi had departed, Joseph had a dream in which an angel of the Lord warned, "Rise up quickly! Take the child and his mother. Flee to Egypt, and remain there until I tell you. For Herod is preparing to search for the child to destroy him!"

Joseph got up and woke Mary. They hurriedly packed together some of their belongings and left for Egypt that night. They remained there until Herod died.

Once more, a prophecy was fulfilled, for Hosea had written, "I summoned my son out of Egypt."

Meanwhile, when Herod had not received a report from the Magi, he realized he had been tricked. In a furious rage he ordered his men to kill all the baby boys under the age of two in Bethlehem and all that vicinity. (He calculated the age at two based on what the Magi had told him.)

In this, a prediction of the prophet was fulfilled:

A voice is heard in Ramah,
    an anguished wail of mourning.
Rachael weeps for her children:
    bereft beyond all consolation
    because her children lie dead.

Matthew 2:13–18

When Israel was a child,
    then I loved him;
And called My son
    out of Egypt.

Written by the prophet Hosea, c. 725 B.C.
Hosea 11:1

Thus says the Lord:

> **A voice was heard in Ramah,**
> **lamentation,**
> **and bitter weeping;**
> **Rachael weeping for her children**
> **refused to be comforted for her children,**
> **because they were not.**

37

Written by the prophet Jeremiah, c. 600 B.C.
Jeremiah 31:15

THE BOYHOOD OF JESUS

HOME TO NAZARETH *circa 2 B.C.*

AFTER HEROD DIED, an angel of the Lord again appeared to Joseph in a dream. "It is time to go home now," the angel announced. "Take the child and his mother and go into the land of Israel. For those who attempted to murder the child are dead."

Joseph immediately took the child and his mother, left Egypt, and returned to the land of Israel.

As they neared the border, Joseph heard that Herod had been succeeded in Judea by his son Archelaus. This made Joseph afraid, and being warned in yet another dream, he skirted Judea, and settled instead in a town in Galilee called Nazareth. So the prophecies again were fulfilled when they said of the Messiah, "He shall be called a Nazarene."

It was in Nazareth that Jesus grew up. As he grew, he became spiritually strong, increasing in wisdom beyond his years. The grace of God was clearly on his young life.

Matthew 2:19–23; Luke 2:39–40

JESUS IN THE TEMPLE *circa A.D. 8 (or 9)*

THE CUSTOM of Jesus' parents was to go to Jerusalem each year for the Passover. When he was 12 years old, they took Jesus along.

When the festival was over, Mary and Joseph started back to Nazareth, assuming that Jesus was with other relatives or friends in the caravan. It was not until they had traveled all day, and the caravan had stopped for the night, that Mary and Joseph realized he was lost and began frantically searching for him.

When he was nowhere to be found, they returned to Jerusalem, searching for him everywhere along the road and in the city.

Three days later they finally found him. There he was, sitting among the teachers of the Law, listening to them, asking them questions, astonishing them all with his understanding and with his answers. Even his parents were amazed.

Then it was his mother's turn to ask questions: "Son, why have you treated your father and me like this? We have been anxiously looking everywhere for you! Did you not realize that we have been worried sick?"

Jesus responded to his parents: **"Why were you searching all over for me? Did you not know that I had to be right here in my Father's house?"**

But they did not fully understand his reply.

Luke 2:41–50

BACK IN NAZARETH

THEN HE RETURNED home to Nazareth and was an obedient son to them. His mother treasured all these early experiences.

As for Jesus, he grew older, taller, and wiser, popular with God and among his friends.

Luke 2:51–52

MESSIAH'S MINISTRY BEGINS:

GOING OUT INTO THE HARVEST

2

SECTION TWO

THE MESSENGER AND HIS MESSAGE   *circa A.D. 27*

IN THE 15TH YEAR of the rule of the emperor Tiberius Caesar, when Pontius Pilate was governor of Judea, and Herod was the tetrarch of Galilee, and his brother Philip tetrarch of Iturea and Trachonitus, and Lysanias tetrarch of Abiline — during the high priesthood of Annas and Caiaphas — the word of God came to John, son of Zechariah, in the desert wilderness.

Now in those days, John the baptizer went throughout the whole region around the Jordan, continually preaching in the desert wilderness, proclaiming a baptism of repentance for the forgiveness of sins, saying:

> Repent! Change the way you think and live!
> Turn from your sins and turn to God!
> For the kingdom of heaven is at hand!

For this is the one referred to by Isaiah, written in the book of the words of the prophet:

> Take notice! I will send my messenger ahead of you
>   who will prepare your way.
> A voice of one crying out in the desert,
> "Prepare the way of the Lord,
>   make straight paths for Him.
> Every valley shall be filled in,
>   and every mountain shall be leveled.
> And the winding paths shall be made straight,
>   and the rough roads made smooth.
> And all people shall see
>   the salvation of God."

People of the whole Jordan region and all the people from Jerusalem, and all Judea were going out to him. As they were acknowledging and confessing their sins, they were being baptized by him in the Jordan River.

Now John wore garments woven from camel's hair. And he wore a leather belt around his waist, and he fed on dried locusts and wild honey.

Matthew 3:1–6; Mark 1:1–6; Luke 3:1–6

PROPHECY

Behold, I will send my messenger
 and he shall prepare a way before me.
Then the Lord whom you seek
 shall suddenly come to his temple.
Even the messenger of the covenant
 for whom you desire,
Indeed, he is coming!

So says the Lord of Hosts,
the Lord Almighty, Jehovah Sabaoth.

Recorded by the prophet Malachi, year c. 425 B.C.
Malachi 3:1

PROPHECY

Comfort my people! Comfort them!
 says your God.

Speak tenderly to Jerusalem
And cry out to her
 that her hard service has ended,
 that her penalty has been paid,
 that from the hand of the Lord she has received
 double for all her sins.

A voice cries out:

"Prepare the way in the wilderness for the Lord.
Make a smooth highway in the desert for our God.
Let every valley be raised,
 and every mountain and hill leveled.
And let the rough ground become smooth,
 and the rugged terrain a level plain."

Then the glory of the Lord will be revealed,
 and all people will see it together,
 for the mouth of the Lord has spoken it.

Written by the prophet Isaiah, year c. 700 B.C.
Isaiah 40:1–5.

Questions from the Crowds

BUT WHEN JOHN SAW MANY of the Pharisees and Sadducees among the crowds that were coming to be baptized by him, he exclaimed to them, "You brood of vipers! Who warned you to flee from the coming wrath? Bear fruit consistent with repentance! Do not begin to presume that you can say to yourselves, 'We have Abraham as our ancestor,' for I tell you, God is able to raise up descendents to Abraham from these very stones! Even now the axe is already lying at the root of the trees. Every tree, therefore, that does not bear good fruit will be cut down and thrown into the fire."

"Then what shall we do?" the crowds were asking him.

"The man with two tunics should share with him who has none," John answered in reply to them. "And he who has food should do likewise."

Even tax collectors also came to be baptized. "Teacher," they asked, "what should we do?"

He answered them, "Collect no more than the amount you are prescribed to do."

Then some soldiers asked him, "And what should we do?"

"Do not extort money from anyone by force. Or do not falsely accuse," he responded to them. "Be satisfied with rations and your wages."

Now this was John's testimony when the Jews of Jerusalem sent priests and Levites to ask him, "Who are you?"

He acknowledged the truth and did not refuse to answer them. He readily acknowledged, "I am not the Messiah."

So they asked him, "What then? Are you Elijah?"

"I am not," he replied.

"Are you the prophet?"

He answered, "No."

Finally they said to him, "Who are you? Give us an answer that we can take back to those who sent us. What do you have to say about yourself?"

He said:

> I am the voice of one
> crying out in the wilderness,
> "Prepare the way for the Lord.
> Make his paths straight,"
> as Isaiah the prophet said.

Now some who had been sent were the Pharisees. They asked him, "Why then do you baptize if you are not the Messiah, nor Elijah, nor the prophet?"

45

John answered them, "I baptize in water. But there is one standing among you — unknown to you — who is coming after me, the thongs of whose sandals I am not worthy to untie."

This all occurred in Bethany on the east side of the Jordan, where John was baptizing.

Matthew 3:7–10; Luke 3:7–14; John 1:19–28

QUESTIONS FROM THE HEART

NOW WHILE THE PEOPLE WERE WAITING expectantly, and all wondering in their hearts whether John might possibly be the Messiah, John answered all of them by proclaiming and declaring:

"As for me, I baptize you with water for repentance. But one who is more mighty than I is coming after me, the thongs of whose sandals I am not worthy to stoop down and unfasten and remove. He will baptize you with the Holy Spirit, and with fire! His winnowing fork is in his hand, and he will thoroughly clear out his threshing floor, and will gather his wheat in the granary barn. But he will burn the chaff with unquenchable fire."

So with many other exhortations John proclaimed the good news to the people.

Matthew 3:11–12; Mark 1:7–8; Luke 3:15–18

THE BAPTISM OF JESUS

IT OCCURRED IN THOSE VERY DAYS that Jesus came from Nazareth of Galilee to the Jordan, to John, to be baptized by him in the Jordan.

But John tried to dissuade Him, saying, "It is I who needs to be baptized by you, and do you come to me!"

But Jesus replied to him, "Permit it at this time. For in this way it is proper for you to fulfill all righteousness." Then John consented.

Now it came about that when the people were being baptized, Jesus also was baptized. And immediately upon coming up out of the water, as Jesus was praying, John saw the heavens suddenly torn open, and the Holy Spirit in bodily form like a dove descending upon him. And a voice came out of heaven:

You are my Son, whom I love.
I am fully pleased with you.

When Jesus himself began his ministry, he was about 30 years of age.

Matthew 3:13–17; Mark 1:9–11; Luke 3:21–23

I will surely proclaim
    the decree of the Lord.

He said to me:

    You are my Son.
    Today I have begotten you.
    Ask of me,
    And I will surely give the nations
        as your inheritance,
    And the very ends of the earth
        as your possession.

47

Recorded by the Psalmist, year c. 1000 B.C.
Psalm 2:7–8

Behold, he is my servant
    whom I uphold;
My Chosen One,
    in whom my soul delights.
I have put my spirit upon him
    and he will bring forth justice to the nations.

He will not shout out nor raise his voice,
    nor make himself heard in the street.
A bruised reed he will not break,
    and a glimmering wick he will not extinguish.

He will faithfully bring forth justice.
He will not falter or be crushed
    until he establishes justice on earth,
    and the coastlines put their hope in his teachings.

Recorded by the prophet Isaiah, year c. 700 B.C.
Isaiah 42:1–4

The Ancestry of Jesus through Joseph

JESUS WAS PRESUMED to be the son of Joseph (so people thought),

    the son of Heli, the son of Matthat,
    the son of Levi, the son of Melki,
    the son of Jannai, the son of Joseph,
    the son of Mattathias, the son of Amos,
    the son of Nahum, the son of Esli,
    the son of Naggai, the son of Maath,

the son of Mattathias, the son of Semein,
the son of Josech, the son of Joda,
the son of Joanan, the son of Rhesa,
the son of Zerubbabel, the son of Shealtiel,
the son of Neri, the son of Melki,
the son of Addi, the son of Cosam,
the son of Elmadam, the son of Er,
the son of Joshua, the son of Eliezer,
the son of Jorim, the son of Matthat,
the son of Levi, the son of Simeon,
the son of Judah, the son of Joseph,
the son of Jonam, the son of Eliakim,
the son of Melea, the son of Menna,
the son of Mattatha, the son of Nathan,
the son of David, the son of Jesse,
the son of Obed, the son of Boaz,
the son of Salmon, the son of Nahshon,
the son of Amminadab, the son of Ram,
the son of Hezron, the son of Perez,
the son of Judah, the son of Jacob,
the son of Isaac, the son of Abraham,
the son of Terah, the son of Nahor,
the son of Serug, the son of Reu,
the son of Peleg, the son of Eber,
the son of Shelah, the son of Cainan,
the son of Arphaxad, the son of Shem,
the son of Noah, the son of Lamech,
the son of Methuselah, the son of Enoch,
the son of Jared, the son of Mahalaleel,
the son of Cainan, the son of Enosh,
the son of Seth, the son of Adam,
the son of God.

Luke 3:23–28

THE ANCESTRY OF JESUS THROUGH MARY

A RECORD OF THE GENEALOGY OF JESUS the Messiah, son of David, son of Abraham:

Abraham fathered Isaac,
Isaac fathered Jacob,

Jacob fathered Judah and his brothers,
Judah fathered Perez and Zerah,
    whose mother was Tamar,
Perez fathered Hezron,
Hezron fathered Ram,
Ram fathered Amminadab,
Amminadab fathered Nahshon,
Nahshon fathered Salmon,
Salmon fathered Boaz,
    whose mother was Rahab,
Boaz fathered Obed,
    whose mother was Ruth,
Obed fathered Jesse, and
Jesse fathered King David.

David fathered Solomon,
    whose mother had been Uriah's wife,
Solomon fathered Rehoboam,
Rehoboam fathered Abijah,
Abijah fathered Asa,
Asa fathered Jehoshaphat,
Jehoshaphat fathered Joram,
Joram fathered Uzziah,
Uzziah fathered Jotham,
Jotham fathered Ahaz,
Ahaz fathered Hezekiah,
Hezekiah fathered Manasseh,
Manasseh fathered Amon,
Amon fathered Josiah, and
Josiah fathered Jechoniah and his brothers.

Then the deportation to Babylon took place.

After the deportation to Babylon:

Jechoniah fathered Shealtiel,
Shealtiel fathered Zerubbabel,
Zerubbabel fathered Abiud,
Abiud fathered Eliakim,
Eliakim fathered Azor,
Azor fathered Zadok,
Zadok fathered Achim,
Achim fathered Eliud,

Eliud fathered Eleazar,
Eleazar fathered Matthan,
Matthan fathered Jacob, and
Jacob fathered Joseph, the husband of Mary.

Of her was born Jesus who is called Messiah.

Thus there were 14 generations in all from Abraham to David,
14 from David to the deportation to Babylon, and
14 from the deportation to the Messiah.

Matthew 1:1–17

THE TEMPTATION OF JESUS

JESUS, FULL OF THE HOLY SPIRIT, returned from the Jordan. And immediately the Spirit impelled him to go out into the desert wilderness, to be tempted by the devil.

And after he had fasted in the desert wilderness with the wild beasts, eating nothing for 40 days and 40 nights, being put to the test by Satan, he was famished. Then the devil, the tempter, came and said to him, "If you are the Son of God, order these stones — this stone here! — to become a loaf of bread!"

But Jesus answered him,

The Scriptures say:
"One does not live on bread alone,
But on every word that proceeds
out of the mouth of God."

Then the devil took him into the holy city Jerusalem, and had him stand on the pinnacle of the temple. "If you are the Son of God," he said, "then throw yourself down from here! For the Scriptures say:

He will give His angels charge over you
to protect you.

And again,

In their hands they will bear you up
so that you will not dash your foot against a stone.

Jesus responded to him,

The Scriptures also say:
"You shall not put the Lord your God to the test."

Again the devil took him to a very high mountain, and in an instant showed him all the kingdoms of the world, and their magnificence. And he said to him, "All this, and all their power and their splendor, I will give to you, if you will bow down and worship me. For it has been turned over to me, and I can give it to whomever I please. So if you worship me, it will be yours!"

Jesus answered him,

Away from me, Satan!
For the Scriptures say:
"Worship the Lord your God,
and serve Him only!"

Then when the devil had exhausted all his tempting, in every way possible, he left him until an opportune time. And the angels came and attended to him.

Matthew 4:1–11; Mark 1:12–13; Luke 4:1–13

PROPHECY

For he will give his angels charge over you
    to protect you wherever you go.
They will bear you up in their hands
    so that you will not dash your foot against a stone.

Written by the Psalmist, year c. 1500 to 950 B.C.
Psalm 91:11–12

JESUS, THE LAMB OF GOD

THE NEXT DAY, JOHN SAW JESUS coming toward him, and said, "Look! Here is the Lamb of God who takes away the sin of the world! This is he of whom I said, 'After me comes a man who ranks higher than me because he existed before I did.' I myself at first did not recognize him. However, the reason I came baptizing with water was that he might be revealed to Israel."

Then John testified further, saying, "I saw the Spirit descending from heaven as a dove, and permanently remain upon him. I would not have recognized him, except that the one who sent me to baptize in water said to me, **'He on whom you see the Spirit descend and remain is he who will baptize in the Holy Spirit.'** I have seen and now publicly testify that this is the Son of God!"

John 1:29–34

THE NEXT DAY, JOHN WAS AGAIN STANDING THERE with two of his disciples; and as he watched Jesus walking by exclaimed, "Look! Here is the Lamb of God!"

The two disciples heard him say this, and they followed Jesus.

Jesus turned around and saw them following him. **"What is it that you want?"** he asked them.

They said to him, "Rabbi" (which translated means *Teacher*), "where are you staying?"

"Come and you will see," he replied.

So they came and saw where he was staying, and remained with him the rest of that day; for it was about the tenth hour (about four in the afternoon).

One of the two who heard John and followed Jesus was Andrew, Simon Peter's brother. The first thing Andrew did was find his own brother Simon and tell him, "We have found the Messiah" (which translated means *Christ*, or *Anointed*). And he brought him to Jesus.

Jesus looked at him and said, **"You are Simon, son of John. You shall be called Cephas"** (which is translated *Peter*, or *Rock*).

The next day Jesus decided to go to Galilee. He found Philip and said to him, **"Follow me."** (Now Philip was from Bethsaida, the hometown of Andrew and Peter.)

Philip found Nathanael and told him, "We have found the one of whom Moses wrote in the Law, and about whom the prophets also wrote — Jesus, son of Joseph, from Nazareth."

"Can anything good come out of Nazareth?" Nathaniel asked.

"Come and see for yourself!" Philip told him.

When Jesus saw Nathaniel approaching him, he said of him, **"Here indeed is a genuine Israelite, in whom there is no deception."**

"How do you know me?" Nathaniel asked him.

Jesus replied by saying to him, **"Before Philip ever called you, when you were still under the fig tree, I saw you."**

Nathaniel answered him, "Rabbi, you are the Son of God! You are the King of Israel!"

Jesus responded and said to him, **"Do you believe because I said to you that I saw you under the fig tree? You shall see greater things than this!"** He then said to him, **"I guarantee you this truth: You shall see heaven opened, and the angels of God ascending and descending on the Son of Man."**

John 1:35–51

As I kept looking at the continuing night visions,
I saw there before me,
    coming with the clouds of heaven,
One like a Son of Man.

And He approached the venerable Ancient of Days
    and was presented before him.

53

And on him was conferred dominion,
    and glory, and sovereign power,
That all peoples, nations, and those of every language
    should serve and worship him.

His dominion is an everlasting dominion
    which will never pass away.
And his sovereignty is one
    which will never be destroyed.

Written by the prophet Daniel, year c. 550 B.C.
Daniel 7:13–14

Then Jacob had a dream.
And he saw a stairway
    which was resting on the earth
    with its top reaching to heaven.
And he saw the angels of God
    ascending and descending on it.
And he saw the Lord standing above it.

Written by the patriarch Moses, year c. 1450 B.C.
Genesis 28:12–13

6

THE FIRST MIRACLE, AT CANA

circa A.D. 27

O N THE THIRD DAY THERE WAS A WEDDING in Cana in Galilee, and the mother of Jesus was there. Jesus and his disciples were also invited to the wedding.

When the wine gave out, the mother of Jesus said to him, "They have no more wine."

Jesus said to her, **"Dear woman, why do you concern me? My time has not yet come."**

His mother said to the servants, "Do whatever he tells you."

Now standing there were six stone water jars, the kind used for the Jewish custom of purification or ceremonial washing, containing between two or three *firkins*, or 20 to 30 gallons each.

Jesus instructed them, **"Fill the jars with water."** So they filled them to the brim.

Then he told them, **"Now draw some out and take it to the banquet manager."**

They did so and the banquet manager tasted the water that had become wine. He did not know from where it had come (although the servants who had drawn the water knew). Then the banquet manager called the bridegroom aside, and said to him, "Everyone brings out the choice wine first, and when the guests have drunk freely, then an inferior wine. But you have saved the best until now."

This, the first of his miraculous signs, Jesus did in Cana in Galilee, and manifested his glory, and his disciples believed in him.

After this he went down to Capernaum, he and his mother, and his brothers, and his disciples; and they stayed there a few days.

John 2:1–12

The First Cleansing of the Temple

THE PASSOVER OF THE JEWS WAS APPROACHING, so Jesus went up to Jerusalem. In the temple courtyard he found those who were selling oxen and sheep and doves, and the moneychangers seated.

So he made a whip of cords, and drove them all, with the sheep and the oxen, out of the temple courtyard. He scattered the coins of the moneychangers, and overturned their tables. And to those who were selling doves he said, **"Get these out of here! Stop making my Father's house a marketplace!"**

His disciples remembered that it was written, "Zeal for your house will consume me."

At this the Jews responded by demanding of him, "What miraculous sign do you show us as authority for doing these things?"

"Destroy this temple, and in three days I will raise it up again," Jesus responded to them.

The Jews then retorted, "It took 46 years to build this temple, and you will reconstruct in three days?"

But he was speaking about the temple of his body.

Then after he was raised from the dead, His disciples then recalled that he had said this; and they believed the Scriptures and the word which Jesus had spoken.

John 2:13–22

Miraculous Signs at His First Passover

NOW WHEN HE WAS IN JERUSALEM at the Passover Festival, many believed in his name when they saw the miraculous signs he was doing.

But Jesus on his part was not entrusting himself to them, because he knew all men and because he did not need anyone to testify what people were like. For he himself knew human nature.

John 2:23–25

By Night

NOW THERE WAS A MAN OF THE PHARISEES named Nicodemus, a member of the Jews' ruling council. This man came to Jesus by night and said to him, "Rabbi, we know that you have certainly come from God as a teacher: for no one can perform these miraculous signs that you do unless God is with him."

Jesus replied and said to him,

> **In all truth I guarantee you:**
> **No one can see the kingdom of God**
> > **without being born again.**

"How can a man be born when he is old?" Nicodemus asked. "Surely he cannot enter a second time into his mother's womb and be born again, can he?"

Jesus answered,

> **In all truth I guarantee you:**
> **Unless one is born of water and the Spirit**
> > **he cannot enter the kingdom of God.**
>
> **What is born of flesh is flesh,**
> > **and what is born of the Spirit is spirit.**
> **Do not be surprised that I said to you,**
> **"You must be born again."**
>
> **The wind blows wherever it chooses.**
> **You hear the sound of it,**
> > **but you cannot tell from where it comes**
> > **or where it is going.**
> **So it is with everyone who is born of the Spirit.**

Nicodemus answered by asking him, "How can these things be?"

Jesus answered by asking him, **"You are a teacher of Israel and you do not understand these things?**

> **I guarantee you this truth:**
> **We speak of what we know**
> > **and testify to what we have seen,**
> > **and yet none of you accepts our testimony.**
>
> **If I have told you about earthly things**
> > **and you do not believe,**
> **How then will you believe**
> > **if I speak to you about heavenly things?**
>
> **No one has ascended into heaven**
> > **except he who has descended from heaven,**
> > **the Son of Man.**
>
> **And as Moses lifted up the serpent in the wilderness,**
> > **so the Son of Man must be lifted up,**
> > **that whoever believes may in him have eternal life.**

For God so loved the world
>that he gave his only begotten Son,
So that whoever believes in him
>should not perish
>but has eternal life.

For God sent the Son into the world
>not to judge and condemn the world,
>but that through him the world should be saved.

Whoever believes in him is not condemned;
Whoever does not believe has already been condemned,
>because he has not believed in the name
>of the only begotten Son of God.
And this is the verdict:
That the light has come into the world,
>but people loved the darkness rather than the light,
>because their actions were evil.

For everyone who does evil hates the light
>and does not come to the light
>for fear his deeds should be exposed.
But whoever practices the truth comes to the light
>so that it may be clearly seen
>that his deeds have been done through God.

John 3:1–21

The Groom's Best Man

AFTER THIS, JESUS AND HIS DISCIPLES went into the countryside of Judea, and there he was spending time with them, and baptizing. Now John was also baptizing at Aenon near Salim, because the water was abundant there. And people were continually coming and being baptized. (For John had not yet been put in prison.)

Now an argument arose between some of John's disciples and a certain Jew about ceremonial purification. So they came to John and reported to him, "Rabbi, the one who was with you on the other side of the Jordan — the one about whom you yourself testified — is now also baptizing, and everyone is coming to him."

John replied by saying, "One can receive nothing unless it has been given him from heaven. You yourselves bear me out as witnesses that I said, 'I am not the Messiah, but I have been sent ahead of him.' "

He who has the bride is the bridegroom;
Yet the friend of the bridegroom,
 who stands there and listens to him,
 rejoices greatly at the bridegroom's voice.

For this reason this joy of mine is now complete.
He must increase and become greater;
 but I must decrease and become less.

He who comes from above is above all;
He who is of the earth belongs to the earth
 and speaks as one from the earth.

He who comes from heaven is above all;
He testifies about what he has seen and heard,
 yet no one accepts his testimony.
Anyone who accepts his testimony
 has set his seal to certify that God is true.

For he whom God has sent speaks the words of God;
 for God gives the Spirit without measure.
The father loves the Son,
 and has placed all things in his hand.

Whoever believes in the Son has eternal life;
But whoever does not obey the Son shall not see life,
 but the wrath of God continues to remain on him.

John 3:22–36

7

THEN SAMARIA

JESUS DEPARTS JUDEA FOR SAMARIA   *circa A.D. 27*

NOW WHEN HEROD THE TETRARCH was rebuked by John because of Herodias, his brother's wife (with whom he was having an affair), and because of all the other evils which Herod had done, Herod also added this to them all: he locked John up in prison!

So when Jesus heard that John had been taken into custody, and then learned that the Pharisees had heard that he was making and baptizing more disciples than John (although it was not Jesus himself but his disciples who were baptizing), he left Judea and in the power of the Spirit returned again to Galilee.

Now he had to pass through Samaria.

Matthew 4:12; Mark 1:14; Luke 3:19–20, 4:14; John 4:1–4

THE SAMARITAN WOMAN AT THE WELL

SO JESUS CAME TO A TOWN OF SAMARIA called Sychar, near the parcel of ground that Jacob gave to his son Joseph. Jacob's Well was there and Jesus, being wearied from his journey, was sitting down by the well. It was about the sixth hour, around noon.

When a Samaritan woman came there to draw water Jesus said to her, **"Give me a drink."** (His disciples had gone into the town to buy food.)

The Samaritan woman then responded to him, "How is it that you, a Jew, ask for a drink from me, a woman of Samaria?" (For Jews have no dealings with Samaritans.)

Jesus answered her by saying, **"If you knew the gift of God and who it is who is saying to you, 'Give me a drink,' you would have asked him and he would have given you living water."**

"Sir," she said to him, "you have nothing with which to draw, and the well is deep. Where do you get that living water? Are you greater than our father Jacob who gave us this well and drank from it himself, as did his sons and his cattle as well?"

Jesus answered her by saying,

> **Everyone who drinks of this water**
>   **will be thirsty again.**
> **But whoever drinks of the water which I shall give him**
>   **will never thirst.**
> **Indeed, the water that I shall give**
>   **will become within him a spring of water**
>   **welling up to eternal life.**

"Please, sir," the woman said to him, "give me this water so that I may never be thirsty, nor have to keep coming all the way here to draw water."

"Go, call your husband and come back here," he told her.

"I have no husband," the woman answered in response.

"You are correct in saying, 'I have no husband,' " Jesus replied to her. **"For you have had five husbands, and the one whom you now have is not your husband. What you have said is true!"**

"Sir," the woman said to him, "I can see that you are a prophet. Our ancestors worshiped on this mountain, but you people claim that the place where men must worship is in Jerusalem."

Jesus responded to her,

> **Believe me woman, an hour is coming**
>   **when you will worship the Father**
>   **neither on this mountain nor in Jerusalem.**
> **You people worship that which you do not know.**
> **We worship that which we know,**
>   **for salvation is from the Jews.**
>
> **But an hour is coming and now is here**
>   **when the true worshipers will worship the Father**
>   **in spirit and truth.**
> **For the Father seeks such people**
>   **to be his worshipers.**

> **God is Spirit, and those who worship him**
> **must worship in spirit and truth.**

The woman said to him, "I know that Messiah who is called Christ is coming. When he does come he will explain everything to us."

Jesus responded to her, **"I am he, I who am speaking to you!"**

John 4:5–26

A SPIRITUAL HARVEST

JUST AT THAT MOMENT, HIS DISCIPLES RETURNED and were surprised He had been speaking with a woman. However no one asked, "What do you want from her?" or "Why are you talking with her?"

Then, leaving her water jar, the woman went back into the town and said to the men, "Come, see a man who told me everything I have ever done! Could not this be the Messiah?" They left the town and started on their way to him.

Meanwhile, the disciples were urging him, "Rabbi, eat something!"

But he said to them, **"I have food to eat of which you have no knowledge."**

So the disciples said to one another, "Surely no one brought him something to eat! Is that possible?"

Jesus explained to them:

> **My food is to do the will of him who sent me**
> **and to complete his work.**
> **Do you not have a saying,**
> **"Four months and then harvest"?**
> **Well I am saying to you:**
>
> **"Open your eyes and look at the fields;**
> **they are already ripe for harvest!**
> **The reaper is already receiving wages,**
> **and is gathering crop for eternal life;**
> **So that the sower and the reaper**
> **may celebrate together."**
>
> **For here the saying holds true:**
> **"One sows and another reaps."**
> **I sent you to reap**
> **that for which you have not worked.**
> **Others have done the work,**
> **and you have reaped the benefits of their work.**

John 4:27–38

MINISTERING IN SYCHAR

MANY OF THE SAMARITANS from that town believed in him because of what the woman said when she testified, "He told me everything that I have ever done!"

So when the Samaritans came to him, they urged him to stay with them and he stayed there two days. And many more believed in him because of what he said.

They said to the woman, "It is no longer just because of what you said that we believe, for we have heard for ourselves and know that this one is indeed the Savior of the world."

John 4:39–42

BACK HOME TO GALILEE

AFTER TWO DAYS HE DEPARTED from there to Galilee (for Jesus himself had testified that a prophet has no honor in his own country).

However when he came to Galilee, the Galileans welcomed him, since they had seen all the things he had done in Jerusalem at the festival, for they themselves had also gone to the festival.

Matthew 4:12; Mark 1:14; Luke 4:14; John 4:43–45

THE GREAT GALILEAN MINISTRY:

ACCEPTANCE AND REJECTION

3

SECTION THREE

THE GREAT GALILEAN MINISTRY BEGINS

circa A.D. 27–28

JESUS RETURNED TO GALILEE in the power of the Spirit, and news about him spread through the whole surrounding countryside. And he began teaching in their synagogues, and was praised by everyone.

Jesus was proclaiming the good news of the gospel of God, saying,

> **This is the time of fulfillment.**
> **The kingdom of God is at hand.**
> **Repent and believe the gospel!**
> **Change the way you think and live,**
>   **and believe the good news!**

Mark 1:14–15; Luke 4:14–15

HEALING THE CANA OFFICIAL'S SON

HE THEN RETURNED TO CANA in Galilee where he had made the water into wine. Now a royal official whose son lay ill at Capernaum was there. When he heard that Jesus had arrived from Judea into Galilee, he went to him and began begging him to come down and heal his son, for he was at the point of death.

"Unless you people see miraculous signs and wonders," Jesus therefore said to him, **"you will not believe."**

"Sir, come down before my child dies!" the royal official responded to him.

Jesus answered him, **"You may go: your son lives."**

The man believed the word that Jesus spoke to him and went on his way.

But even as he was going down on his way his slaves met him with the news, saying that his son was living. So he inquired of them as to the hour when his son began to recover. They replied to him, "Yesterday at the seventh hour the fever left him."

Then the father realized that it was at that hour when Jesus had said to him, **"Your son lives."**

So he himself believed, and his whole household.

This was now the second miraculous sign that Jesus did after he had come from Judea to Galilee.

John 4:46–54

Rejected at Nazareth

THEN HE CAME TO NAZARETH where he had been brought up and, as was his custom, he went into the synagogue on the Sabbath. And he stood up to read.

And the scroll of the prophet Isaiah was handed to him. He then opened the scroll, and found the place where it was written:

> **The Spirit of the Lord is upon me,**
> **because he has anointed me**
> **to preach the good news of the gospel to the poor.**
> **He has sent me to proclaim release to the captives**
> **and recovery of sight to the blind,**
> **to set free those who are oppressed,**
> **to proclaim the favorable year of the Lord.**

Then he rolled up the scroll, gave it back to the attendant, and sat down. And the eyes of all in the synagogue were focused on him.

He then began to say to them, **"Today this Scripture has been fulfilled in your hearing."**

And all were speaking well of him and marveling at the gracious words which were falling from his lips. "Is this not Joseph's son?" they were asking.

So he said to them, **"You will no doubt quote this proverb to me, 'Physician, heal yourself!' telling me 'Whatever we heard was done in Capernaum, do here in your home town as well.' I can guarantee you this truth,"** he continued, **"No prophet is accepted in his home town.**

"But in truth I say to you: There were many widows in Israel in the days of Elijah, when the sky was shut up for three years and six months, when a severe

famine spread over all the land. And yet Elijah was sent to none of them, except only to Zarephath in Sidon, to a woman there who was a widow. And there were many lepers in Israel in the time of the prophet Elisha, and none of them was cleansed, but only Naaman the Syrian."

When they heard these things, all in the synagogue were filled with rage, and they rose up and forced him out of the city. Then they led him to the brow of the hill on which their city had been built, in order to hurl him down the cliff. But passing through the middle of the crowd, he went his way.

Luke 4:16–30

The Spirit of the Lord God is upon me,
    because the Lord has anointed me
    to bring good news to the afflicted.
He has sent me to bind up the brokenhearted,
    to proclaim liberty to the captives
    and release from prison those who are bound,
    to proclaim the favorable year of the Lord
    and the day of vengeance of our God,
    to comfort all who mourn.

Written by the prophet Isaiah, year c. 700 B.C.
Isaiah 61:1–2

A NEW HOME IN CAPERNAUM

AND LEAVING NAZARETH, he went down and settled in Capernaum, a city which is on the Sea of Galilee, in the region of Zebulun and Naphtali, fulfilling what had been spoken through the prophet Isaiah:

Land of Zebulun — land of Naphtali —
    on the way to the Sea — beyond the Jordan —
    Galilee of the Gentiles.
The people who were sitting enveloped in darkness
    have seen a great light.
And to those who were sitting in the land of the shadow of death,
    upon them a light has dawned.

From that time Jesus began to proclaim and say,

Repent! Change the way you think and live!
For the kingdom of heaven is at hand.

Matthew 4:13–17; Luke 3:31

But there will be no more gloom
    for those who were in anguish.
In former times he humbled
    the land of Zebulun and the land of Naphtali.
But in later times he will glorify
    the way of the sea,
    the other side of the Jordan,
    Galilee of the Gentiles.
The people who walked in darkness
    have seen a great light.
And those who dwelt in the land of the shadow of death,
    upon them a light has dawned.

Written by the prophet Isaiah, year c. 700 B.C.
Isaiah 9:1–2

THE FIRST FOUR FISHERS OF MEN

ONE DAY AS HE WAS PASSING ALONG THE SEA OF GALILEE, which is also called the Lake of Gennesaret, he saw two brothers, Simon who was called Peter, and Simon's brother Andrew, who had been casting their net into the sea, for they were fishermen.

While he was standing there with the multitude of people who were crowding around him listening to the word of God, he saw two boats at the shore of the lake. But the fishermen had gone out of them and were washing their nets.

So he got into one of the boats, the one belonging to Simon, and asked him to push out a little from the shore. Then he sat down and began teaching the crowds of people from the boat.

When he had finished speaking, he said to Simon, **"Put out into the deep water and let down your nets for a catch."**

And in response Simon answered, "Master, we have worked hard all night and caught nothing! But if you say so, I will let down the nets."

Now when they had done this, they caught such an enormous quantity of fish that their nets were beginning to break. So they signaled to their partners in the other boat to come and help them. And they came and filled both boats so that they began to sink.

But when Simon saw this, he fell down at Jesus' feet, saying, "Go away from me, Lord, for I am a sinful man!" For astonishment had seized him and all that were with him because of the catch of fish that they had taken.

"**Do not be afraid,**" Jesus said to Simon and to those who were with him. "**Come, follow me, and I will make you fishers of men. From now on you will catch men.**" And immediately they brought their boats to shore, left their nets and everything, and followed him.

And going on from there, he saw two other brothers, James the son of Zebedee, and his brother John, who were partners with Simon. They too were in their boat, with their father Zebedee, repairing their nets. And without pausing, he called them. And immediately they left their boat, and their father Zebedee in the boat with the hired crew, and they followed him.

Matthew 4:18–22; Mark 1:16–20; Luke 5:1–11

HEALING IN THE SYNAGOGUE ON THE SABBATH

THEN THEY WENT TO CAPERNAUM, and on the next Sabbath he went into the synagogue and began to teach. They were astonished at his teaching, for unlike the scribes (the teachers of the religious Law), his message had authority.

And suddenly, in their synagogue, there was a man possessed by a demon, an unclean spirit, who shrieked at the top of his voice, "Oh no! What have you to do with us, Jesus of Nazareth? Have you come to destroy us? I know who you are — the Holy One of God!"

But Jesus rebuked him, saying, "**Be silent! Come out of him!**"

Then throwing him down into a convulsion in front of them, the unclean spirit with a loud shriek came out of him without injuring him.

And they were all so amazed so that they questioned among themselves, saying, "What is this new teaching? For with authority and power he even orders the unclean spirits and they obey him and come out!"

Then immediately his fame spread out everywhere into all the surrounding region of Galilee.

Mark 1:21–28; Luke 4:31–37

PETER'S MOTHER-IN-LAW IS HEALED

AS SOON AS THEY AROSE and had come out of the synagogue, Jesus immediately went with James and John to the home of Simon and Andrew.

Now Simon's mother-in-law was lying sick in bed, suffering with a high fever. When Jesus entered Simon Peter's home, immediately they spoke to him about her, and made a request of him on her behalf.

So he went to her, and bending over her, he rebuked the fever. Then taking her by the hand, he raised her up. The fever left her, and she immediately got up and began serving them.

Then when that evening had come, as the sun was setting and even after it had set, the people were bringing to him all who were sick and possessed with demons. And the whole city had congregated at the door. And laying his hands on each of the many who were ill with various diseases, he healed them all. This was to fulfill what was spoken through the prophet Isaiah:

> He himself bore our infirmities,
>> and carried away our diseases.

With a word, he also cast numerous demons out of many. Some of the demons came out screaming, "You are the Son of God!" But he rebuked them, and would not permit the demons to speak, because they knew he was the Messiah.

Matthew 8:14–17; Mark 1:29–34; Luke 4:38–41

THE GREAT GALILEAN MINISTRY GOES ON TOUR

AND EARLY IN THE MORNING, while it was still very dark, he arose and went out, and departed to a solitary place and was praying there.

Then Simon and his companions hunted for him, and when they found him said to him, "Everyone is looking for you!"

"Let us go somewhere else — to the nearby towns, so that I may preach there also," he replied to them. **"For that is why I came."**

The crowds were searching for him, and when they discovered him, they attempted to prevent him from leaving them.

"I must proclaim the good news of the kingdom of God to the other cities as well," he said to them, **"for I was sent for this purpose."**

So he went into their synagogues throughout all Galilee. He then continued teaching in the synagogues of Judea, and proclaiming the good news of the kingdom, and curing every kind of disease and every kind of sickness among the people, and casting out the demons.

So his fame spread throughout all Syria, and they brought to him all who were ill, those afflicted with various diseases and pains, demoniacs, epileptics, and paralytics, and he healed them. And great crowds followed him from Galilee and the Decapolis, and Jerusalem and Judea, and from beyond the Jordan.

Matthew 4:23–25; Mark 1:35–39; Luke 4:42–44

HEALING A LEPER

ON ONE OCCASION, while he was in one of the towns, suddenly a man covered with leprosy approached him. When the leper saw Jesus, he fell to the ground on his knees and bowed down before him, imploring him, saying, "Lord, if you are willing, you can make me clean!"

Then, moved with compassion, he stretched out his hand and touched him. **"I am willing,"** he said to him. **"Be cleansed!"** And instantly the leprosy left him, and he was made clean of his leprosy.

After sternly admonishing him, Jesus then immediately sent him away and ordered him, **"See that you say nothing to anyone; but go, show yourself to the priest, and offer for your cleansing the gift that Moses commanded, as certified evidence to them."**

Instead he went out and began to freely proclaim it and to spread the news about. As a result, Jesus could no longer enter a town openly, but had to stay out in secluded places.

Yet the news about him kept spreading even farther, so that huge crowds were still coming to him from everywhere. They were continually gathering to hear, and to be healed of their diseases. But he himself would withdraw to the wilderness, and pray.

Matthew 8:2–4; Mark 1:40–45; Luke 5:12–16

HEALING A PARALYTIC

THEN ON ONE OCCASION SEVERAL DAYS LATER, getting into a boat he crossed over and came to his own city. When he had returned to Capernaum it was rumored that he was at home. Then so many gathered together that there was no longer room, not even outside the entrance door. And he was speaking the word to them, and teaching them.

Sitting there were some Pharisees and teachers of the Law who had come from every village of Galilee and Judea, and from Jerusalem. And the power of the Lord was with him to perform healing.

Just then some men came to him, bringing a paralytic on a mat. The four that were carrying the paralytic attempted to take him into the house to lay him down in front of him. And not finding any way to bring the man in because of the crowd, they went up on the roof, to remove the roof above Jesus. And when they had dug an opening through the tiles, they lowered him on his mat on which he was lying into the center of the house, right in front of Jesus.

Then seeing their faith, Jesus said to the paralytic, **"My son and friend, take courage. Your sins are forgiven you!"**

Now there were some of the scribes (the teachers of the Law) and the Pharisees sitting there. They were then thinking to themselves, "Why does this man speak that way? Who does he think he is? He is blaspheming! Who can forgive sins but God alone?"

But Jesus instantly perceived in his spirit what they were thinking within themselves, and responded to them by asking, **"Why are you raising such evil questions in your hearts? Which is easier, to say to the paralytic 'Your sins are forgiven' or to say 'Stand up, and take up your mat and walk'?**

"But in order that you may know that the Son of Man has authority on earth to forgive sins," he then said to the paralytic, **"I say to you, stand up! Take up your mat and go home!"**

And immediately he got up in front of them, and took up the mat on which he had been lying, and went out to his home, glorifying God in full view of them all. So that when the crowd saw it they were all amazed, exclaiming, "We have never seen anything like this! We have seen incredible things today!"

And they were all seized with astonishment, and gripped with awe, and were praising and glorifying God who had given such authority to men.

Matthew 9:1–8; Mark 2:1–12; Luke 5:17–26

THE CONVERSION OF MATTHEW

ONCE AGAIN HE WENT OUT BESIDE THE SEA. And all the multitude of people were coming to him, and he continued teaching them.

And after that, as Jesus passed on by from there, he saw a tax collector named Levi, also called Matthew, the son of Alphaeus, sitting at the tax office. And he said, **"Follow me!"** and he got up, left everything behind, and followed him.

Then Levi held a great banquet reception for him in his house. And there was a large crowd of tax collectors and other notorious sinners who were reclining at the table, dining with Jesus and his disciples. For there were many such people who were following him.

When the teachers of the religious Law who were Pharisees saw that he was eating with disreputable sinners and tax collectors, they began grumbling at his disciples and asking, "Why is your teacher eating and drinking with tax collectors and other notorious sinners?"

But when Jesus heard this, he responded to them,

> **Those who are healthy have no need of a physician,**
> > **but those who are sick do.**
> **But go and learn what this means:**
> **"I desire compassion and not sacrifice."**
> **For I have not come to call the righteous,**
> > **but sinners to repentance.**

Matthew 9:9–13; Mark 2:13–17; Luke 5:27–32

PROPHECY

For I desire compassion
    rather than sacrifice,
And acknowledgement of God
    rather than burnt offerings.

Recorded by the prophet Hosea, year c. 725 B.C.
Hosea 6:6

FEASTING, NOT FASTING

NOW THE DISCIPLES OF JOHN and those of the Pharisees were fasting. Then some of John's disciples came and asked him, "Why is it that we as John's disciples frequently fast and offer prayers, and the disciples of the Pharisees are often doing the same, but your disciples do not fast? Your disciples go on eating and drinking."

Jesus then answered them,

> **While the bridegroom is present with them,**
> > **his attendants do not mourn, do they?**
> **While the bridegroom is with them,**
> > **you cannot make them fast, can you?**
> **As long as they have the bridegroom with them,**
> > **they cannot fast.**
> **But the days will come when the bridegroom**
> > **is taken away from them,**
> > **and then on that day they will fast.**

Then He also told them a parable:

No one tears a patch of unshrunk cloth
    from a new garment
    and sews it on an old garment.
Otherwise, he will have torn the new,
    and the patch from the new will not match the old.
Then the patch pulls away from it, the new from the old,
    and a worse tear is made.

No one puts new wine
    into old wineskins.
Otherwise the new wine will burst the skins,
    and the wine pours out, and the wineskins are ruined.
No, new wine must be poured into fresh wineskins,
    and so both are preserved.
And no one after drinking old wine wishes for new,
    for he says, "The old is better."

Matthew 9:14–17; Mark 2:18–22; Luke 5:33–39

THE SECOND PASSOVER

9

IN THE POOL ON A SABBATH

circa A.D. 28

AFTER THESE THINGS, JESUS WENT UP TO JERUSALEM for a festival, the Feast of the Jews (the Passover).

Now in Jerusalem by the Sheep Gate there was a pool called in Hebrew *Bethzatha* (or in Aramaic *Bethseda* or *Bethesda*), which has five porticoes or covered colonnades. In these lay numerous invalids — disabled, blind, lame, or paralyzed — waiting for the moving of the waters.

(For it was thought that an angel of the Lord went down into the pool from time to time, and whoever was the first one into the pool after the stirring of the water would be cured from whatever disease with which he was afflicted.)

One man who was there had been an invalid for 38 years. When Jesus saw him lying there, and realized that he had been there in that condition a long time, he asked him, **"Do you wish to become well?"**

"Sir," the invalid answered him, "I have no one to put me into the pool when the water is stirred up. And while I am making my way, another gets down in ahead of me."

Jesus replied to him, **"Get up! Pick up your mat and walk!"**

And instantly the man became well, and picked up his mat, and began to walk.

John 5:1–9

THE PERSECUTION BEGINS

NOW IT WAS A SABBATH on that day. Therefore, the Jews (the religious protectors of the Law) kept saying to him who had been healed, "It is a Sabbath, and it is not permissible for you to carry your mat."

But he answered them, "The man who made me well said to me, 'Pick up your mat and walk!' "

"Who is the man who said to you, 'Pick it up and walk'?" they asked him.

But the man who had been healed did not know who it was, for Jesus had disappeared into the crowd that was there in the place.

Later, Jesus found him in the temple and said to him, **"Look at yourself! You have become well! Do not sin anymore so that nothing worse happens to you."**

The man went away and informed the Jews that it was Jesus that had made him well.

Therefore, because Jesus was doing these things on a Sabbath, the Jews began persecuting him.

John 5:9–16

THE SON IS EQUAL TO THE FATHER

JESUS THEN SAID TO THEM, **"My father is still working until now, and I also am working."**

For this reason, the Jewish protectors of the religious Law were all the more determined to kill him, because he was not only breaking the Sabbath, but he was also even calling God his own Father, making himself equal with God.

Jesus then answered them by saying:

> I guarantee you this truth:
> The Son can do nothing of his own accord,
>   but only something he sees the Father doing.
> For whatever the Father does,
>   these same things the Son also does.
> For the Father loves the Son
>   and shows him everything that he himself is doing.
> And he will show him even greater works than these
>   so that you will be astonished.
> For just as the Father raises the dead and gives them life,
>   even so the Son also gives life to whomever he chooses.
> For the Father judges no one,
>   but has entrusted all judgment to the Son,
>   so that all may honor the Son
>   just as they honor the Father.
> Whoever does not honor the Son
>   does not honor the Father who sent him.

I guarantee you this truth:
Whoever hears my word, and believes him who sent me,
    has eternal life,
    and does not come into judgment,
    but has already passed out of death into life.

Believe me when I guarantee you this:
The time is coming — indeed has now come —
    when the dead shall hear the voice of the Son of God,
    and those who hear shall live!
For just as the Father has life in himself,
    so he granted the Son to also have life in himself;
And he has given him authority to execute judgment
    because he is the Son of Man.

Do not be astonished at this!
For the time is coming when all who are in their tombs
    shall hear his voice,
    and shall come out —
    those who have done good to a resurrection of life,
    those who have done evil to a resurrection of condemnation.

On my own authority I can do nothing.
As I hear, I judge;
    and my verdict is just,
    because I do not seek my own will,
    but the will of him who sent me.

If I testify on my own behalf,
    my testimony is not valid.
There is another who testifies on my behalf
    and I know that his testimony on my behalf is valid.

You have sent to John,
    and he has testified to the truth.
Not that I accept testimony which is from man,
    but I say this that you may be saved.
He was a burning and shining lamp,
    and for a while you were content to rejoice in his light.

But I have testimony which is greater than that of John:
For the works which the Father has assigned me to accomplish,
    the very works which I am doing,
    testify on my behalf that the Father has sent me.

And the Father who sent me,
>he himself has testified on my behalf.

You have never heard his voice at any time,
>nor have you seen his form;

Nor do you have his word abiding in you,
>because you do not believe him whom he has sent.

You diligently search the Scriptures
>because you think that by them you possess eternal life.

These are the Scriptures that testify about me!
>yet you refuse to come to me that you might possess life!

I do not accept honor from men;
>but I do know you —

I do know that you do not have the love of God in yourselves.

I have come in my Father's name and by his authority,
>and you do not accept me.

Yet if someone else comes in his own name
>and by his own authority, you will accept him.

How could you possibly believe
>when you accept honor from one another?

Yet you do not seek the honor
>that is from the one who alone is God!

Do not think that I will accuse you before the Father.

The one who accuses you is Moses,
>on whom you have set your hope!

For if you believed Moses,
>you would believe me,
>for he wrote of me.

But since you do not believe his writings,
>how will you believe my words?

John 5:17–47

AGAINST THE GRAIN ON A SABBATH

A T THAT TIME, AS JESUS WAS PASSING through the grainfields on a Sabbath, and as his disciples made their way along, it happened that they became hungry and began plucking some heads of grain, rubbing them in their hands, and eating them.

But when some of the Pharisees saw this they asked him, "Look at that! Why are your disciples doing what is not lawful to do on the Sabbath?"

But Jesus answered them by saying,

> **Have you never even read what David did**
> **when he was in need and became hungry,**
> **he and his companions who were with him?**
> **How in the days of Abiathar the high priest**
> **he entered the house of God,**
> **And taking the consecrated bread**
> **that was not lawful for him to eat,**
> **nor for those who were with him,**
> **but was only lawful for priests to eat,**
> **He ate it and also gave it to his companions,**
> **and they ate.**
>
> **Or have you not read in the Law**
> **that on the Sabbath**
> **The priests in the temple break the Sabbath,**
> **and yet are innocent?**
> **I tell you, something greater than the temple is here!**
> **But if you had known what this means —**

> "I desire mercy, not sacrifice" —
>> You would not have condemned the innocent.

Then he said to them,

> The Sabbath was made for man,
>> and not man for the Sabbath.
> Consequently the Son of Man is Lord
>> even of the Sabbath.

Matthew 12:1–8; Mark 2:23–28; Luke 6:1–5

DO GOOD ON THE SABBATH

MOVING ON FROM THERE, on another Sabbath he again entered a synagogue and was teaching. A man whose right hand was deformed happened to be there.

The scribes (the teachers of the religious Law) and the Pharisees were watching him closely, to see if he would heal on a Sabbath, in order that they might find reason to accuse him.

But he knew what they were thinking, so he said to the man with the deformed hand, **"Rise up, and come forward, and stand up here!"** So he got up, and came forward, and stood there.

Then to establish a reason to bring a charge against him, they asked him, "Is it lawful to heal on the Sabbath?"

Then he said to them, **"I ask you, is it lawful on the Sabbath to do good or to do harm, to save life or to kill and destroy it?"**

But they kept silent.

"Which one is there among you," he asked them, **"who would have one sheep, and it falls in a ditch on the Sabbath, will not take hold of it and lift it out? How much more valuable then is a man than a sheep! So then, is it lawful to do good on the Sabbath?"**

Then after angrily looking around at them all, and being grieved at their hard stubborn hearts, he said to the man, **"Stretch out your hand!"**

And he stretched it out, and his hand was completely restored, just as normal and sound as the other one.

But the Pharisees were furious with rage, and went out and discussed with one another what they might do, and then immediately plotted together with the Herodians against Jesus as to how they might destroy him.

Matthew 12:9–14; Mark 3:1–6; Luke 6:6–11

A WARE OF THE PLOT TO DESTROY HIM, Jesus, with his disciples, withdrew from there to the sea. A great multitude from Galilee followed him, and he healed all who were sick. Many more, when they heard all that he was doing, came from Judea, Jerusalem, Idumea, and from beyond the Jordan, and from the regions of Tyre and Sidon.

Because of the great multitude, he told his disciples to have a small boat standing ready for him, to prevent the people from crushing him. For he had cured so many, with the result that all those who had afflictions were pushing forward to touch him.

Whenever the unclean evil spirits saw him, they would fall down before him and would shriek, "You are the Son of God!" But he sternly warned them not to make him known. This was in fulfillment of what was spoken by Isaiah the prophet:

> **Behold! Here is my servant whom I have chosen,**
>> **my beloved in whom my soul is well pleased.**
> **I will place my Spirit upon him,**
>> **and he shall proclaim justice to the Gentiles.**
> **He will not quarrel, nor cry out,**
>> **nor will anyone hear his voice in the streets.**
> **A bruised reed he will not snap off,**
> **And a smoldering wick he will not snuff out,**
>> **until he leads justice on to victory.**
> **In his name the Gentiles will hope.**

Matthew 12:15–21; Mark 3:7–12

PROPHECY

> **Behold, he is my servant whom I uphold;**
>> **my Chosen One, in whom my soul delights.**
> **I have put my Spirit upon him**
>> **and he will bring forth justice to the nations.**
>
> **He will not shout out nor raise his voice,**
>> **nor make himself heard in the street.**
> **A bruised reed he will not break,**
>> **and a glimmering wick he will not extinguish.**
>
> **He will faithfully bring forth justice.**
> **He will not falter or be crushed**
>> **until he establishes justice on earth,**
>> **and the coastlines put their hope in his teachings.**

Recorded by the prophet Isaiah, year c. 700 B.C.
Isaiah 42:1–4

NOW IT WAS DURING THOSE DAYS THAT HE WENT OUT TO THE MOUNTAIN TO PRAY, and he spent the whole night in prayer to God. And when day came, he summoned those disciples whom he himself wanted, and they came to him.

He chose 12 of them, whom he also designated apostles — that they might accompany him, and to be sent out to preach. He also gave them authority over evil spirits — to drive them out and to heal every kind of disease and every kind of infirmity.

Now these are the names of the 12 apostles whom he appointed:

> the first, Simon, to whom he gave the name Peter;
> and Andrew, his brother;
> and James, the son of Zebedee;
> and John, the brother of James, whom he named Boanerges
>   (which means *Sons of Thunder*, or *Thunderbolts*);
> Philip;
> Bartholomew, also called Nathaniel;
> Matthew, the tax collector;
> Thomas;
> James, the son of Alphaeus;
> Thaddaeus, also called Lebbaeus as well as Judas, the son of James
>   (not Iscariot);
> Simon the Cananaean,
>   (the Zealot or Patriot);
> and Judas Iscariot from Kerioth,
>   who became a traitor and betrayed him.

Then he went home.

Matthew 10:1–4; Mark 3:13–19; Luke 6:12–16

11

THE SERMON ON THE MOUNT

THE BEATITUDES

circa A.D. 28

THEN HE DESCENDED WITH THEM, and stood on a level place. A great number of His disciples were there, and a great throng of people from all over Judea, from Jerusalem, and from the coastal region of Tyre and Sidon. They had all come to hear him, and to be healed of their diseases. Those troubled by unclean evil spirits were being cured, and every one of them in the huge multitude of people were trying to touch him, for power was coming from him and healing them all.

Now when he saw the multitude, he ascended the mountain and sat down. His disciples came to him. Then, focusing on his disciples, he opened his mouth and began to teach them. This is what he was saying:

> **Blessed are you who are spiritually impoverished,**
> **for yours is the kingdom of heaven.**
> **Blessed are you who mourn,**
> **for you shall be comforted.**
> **Blessed are you who weep now,**
> **for you shall laugh.**
> **Blessed are you who are humble,**
> **for you shall inherit the earth.**
> **Blessed are you who hunger now — and thirst for righteousness,**
> **for you shall be completely satisfied.**
> **Blessed are you who are merciful,**
> **for you shall receive mercy.**
> **Blessed are you who are pure in heart,**
> **for you shall see God.**

Blessed are you who are peacemakers,
for you shall be called children of God.
Blessed are you who suffer persecution for the sake of righteousness,
for yours is the kingdom of heaven.

Blessed are you when people hate you,
when they cast insults at you and ostracize you,
when they persecute you
and falsely utter all kinds of evil things against you,
and when they slander your name as evil on account of me,
the Son of Man.

Rejoice on that day, and be glad, and leap for joy,
because your reward in heaven is great,
for in the same way their forefathers persecuted the prophets
who were before you!

But woe to you who are rich,
for you are already receiving your comforts in full.
Woe to you who are well fed now,
for you shall go hungry.
Woe to you who are laughing now,
for you shall mourn and weep.
Woe to you when all men speak well of you,
for in the same way their forefathers treated the false prophets!

Matthew 5:1–12; Luke 6:17–26

THE LEAST AND THE GREAT IN THE KINGDOM

YOU ARE THE SALT OF THE EARTH!
But if the salt has lost its taste,
how can its saltiness be restored?
It is no longer good for anything,
except to be thrown out and trampled under foot.

You are the light of the world!
A city built on a hill
cannot be hidden.
Nor does anyone, after lighting a lamp,
put it under the bushel basket.
But it is set on a lampstand,
and it gives light to everyone in the house.

Let your light shine before others
>   in such a way that they may see your good works,
>   and praise your Father who is in heaven.

Do not think that I have come
>   to abolish the Law or the Prophets.
I have come not to abolish them,
>   but to fulfill them.

I guarantee you this truth:
Until heaven and earth disappear,
>   not the smallest letter
>   nor the least punctuation
>   shall disappear from the Law,
>   until all is achieved.

Whoever therefore disregards
>   one of the least of these commandments,
And teaches others to do the same,
>   shall be called least in the kingdom of heaven.
But whoever practices and teaches them
>   shall be called great in the kingdom of heaven.

For I guarantee you:
That unless your righteousness surpasses
>   that of the scribes and of the Pharisees,
You shall never enter the kingdom of heaven.

Matthew 5:13–20

SUPERIOR TO THE LAW

YOU HAVE HEARD that it was said
>   to your ancestors of ancient times:
>   "You shall not murder" and
>   "Whoever commits murder shall be liable to
>   judgment before the court."
But I guarantee you that everyone who harbors
>   anger against his brother
>   shall be liable to judgment before the court.
And whoever shall contemptuously say
>   "Raca! I spit on you!" to his brother
>   shall be answerable to the Sanhedrin supreme court.

And whoever shall say "You cursed fool!"
    shall be liable to the Gehenna of hellfire.

So if you are presenting your offering at the altar,
    and there remember that your brother has something against you,
    leave your offering there before the altar.
Go your way and first be reconciled to your brother;
    then return and present your offering.

Come to terms quickly with your accuser
    while you are with him on your way to court.
Or your accuser may hand you over to the judge,
    and the judge to the guard,
    and you will be thrown into prison.
I guarantee you this truth:
You will not get out
    until you have paid the last penny.

You have heard that it was said:
    "You shall not commit adultery."
But I guarantee you that everyone who looks
    at a woman to lust for her
    has already committed adultery with her in his heart.
If your right eye causes you to stumble and sin,
    gouge it out and throw it away from you;
For it is better for you that one of the members of your body perish
    than for your whole body to be thrown into Gehenna.
And if your right hand causes you to stumble and sin,
    cut it off and throw it away from you;
For it is better for you that one of the members of your body perish
    than for your whole body to be thrown into Gehenna.

It was also said:
    "Whoever divorces his wife, let him give her a certificate of divorce."
But I guarantee you that anyone who divorces his wife,
    except on the grounds of unchastity,
    causes her to commit adultery.
And whoever marries a divorced woman commits adultery.

Again you have heard that it was said
    to your ancestors of ancient times:
    "You shall not make false vows,
    but you shall fulfill the vows you have made to the Lord."

But I say this to you: Make no oath at all,
>neither by heaven, for it is the throne of God;
>nor by the earth, for it is the footstool of his feet;
>nor by Jerusalem, for it is the city of the Great King.
And do not swear by your head,
>for you cannot even make a single hair black or white.
But simply let your "yes" be "yes,"
>or your "no" be "no."
Anything more than this is of the evil one.

You have heard that it was said,
>>"An eye for an eye, and a tooth for a tooth."
But I say this to you: do not oppose him who is evil.
If anyone strikes you on the right cheek,
>turn and offer him the other also.
If anyone wants to sue you, and take your coat,
>let him have your shirt as well.
And if anyone forces you to go one mile,
>go with him two.
Give to everyone who keeps begging from you,
>and do not turn away from him who wants to borrow from you.
And if anyone takes what belongs to you,
>do not demand it back.
Treat others as you would have them treat you.

You have heard that it was said,
>"You shall love your neighbor and hate your enemy."
But I say this to you who are listening:
Love your enemies.
Do good to those who hate you.
Bless those who curse you.
And pray for those who abuse and persecute you,
>so that you may be children of your Father who is in heaven.
For he makes his sun rise on the evil and the good,
>and sends rain on the righteous and on the unrighteous.

For if you love those who love you, what credit is that to you?
Do not tax collectors do the same?
For even sinners love those who love them!
And if you do good to those who do good to you,
>what credit is that to you?
For even sinners do the same!

And if you lend to those from whom you expect repayment,
    what credit is that to you?
Even sinners lend to sinners,
    expecting to be repaid in full.
And if you greet your brothers only,
    what do you do more than others?
Do not even heathen Gentiles do that?

But love your enemies,
    do good to them,
    and lend expecting nothing in return.
Then your reward will be great,
    and you will be children of the Most High:
    for he himself is kind to the ungrateful and to the selfish.

Therefore you are to be perfect,
    as your Heavenly Father is perfect.
You are to be merciful,
    just as your Father is merciful.

Matthew 5:21–48; Luke 6:27–30, 32–36

REAL RIGHTEOUSNESS

BEWARE NOT TO PRACTICE your righteousness before men
    in order to be noticed by them.
Otherwise then you will have no reward
    from your Father who is in heaven.
So whenever you give charity to the poor,
    do not sound a trumpet fanfare before you!
This is what the hypocrites do in the synagogues and on the streets,
    to be honored by others.
I can guarantee you this truth:
    they have received their reward in full!
But when you give charity,
    do not let your left hand know what your right hand is doing,
    so that your charitable giving may be in secret.
Then your Father who sees in secret
    will reward you.

Also whenever you pray,
    do not be like the hypocrites!

For they love to stand in the synagogues
    and on the street corners to pray,
    to be seen by others.
I can guarantee you this truth:
    they have received their reward in full!
But when you pray,
    go into your own private room, and close the door.
Pray to your Father who is in the unseen secret place,
    and your Father who sees in secret will reward you.

And when you are praying,
    do not heap up meaningless repetitions
    as the heathen Gentiles do,
    for they suppose that they will be heard
    because of their many words.
Therefore do not be like them,
    for your Father knows what you need before you ask him.

Pray, then, like this:

Our Father in heaven:
May your name be held holy.
May your kingdom come.
May your will be done,
    on earth as it is in heaven.
Give us this day our daily bread.
And forgive us our debts,
    as we have forgiven our debtors.
And do not put us to the test,
    but deliver us from the evil one.

For if you forgive others for their transgressions,
    your Heavenly Father will also forgive you.
But if you do not forgive others,
    then your Father will not forgive your transgressions.

And whenever you are fasting,
    do not put on a dismal face as the hypocrites do,
For they disfigure their faces
    in order to be obvious to others to be fasting.
I guarantee you this truth:
    they have their reward in full!

But you, whenever you are fasting,
Perfume your head, and wash your face,
    so that you may be obvious to be fasting —
Not by others,
    but by your Father who sees in secret.
And your Father who sees in secret
    will reward you.

Matthew 6:1–18

DEVOTION TO GOD

DO NOT STORE UP FOR yourselves treasures on earth,
    where moths and rust destroy,
    and where thieves break in and steal.
But store up for yourselves treasures in heaven,
    where neither moths nor rust destroy,
    and where thieves do not break in and steal.
For where your treasure is,
    there your heart will be as well.

The eye is the lamp of the body.
So if your eye is unclouded,
    your whole body will be full of light.
But if your eye is bad,
    your whole body will be full of darkness.
If then the light that is in you is darkness,
    how great is the darkness!

No one can serve two masters!
For either he will hate the one
    and love the other,
Or be devoted to the one,
    and despise the other.
You cannot serve both God and wealth.

For this reason I tell you:
Stop worrying about your life,
    what you will eat or what you will drink;
Or about your body,
    what you will wear.
Is not life more than food,
    and the body more than clothes?

Look at the birds of the air!
They neither sow nor reap nor store away in barns,
    and yet your Heavenly Father feeds them.
Are you not worth much more than they?
And who of you by worrying
    can add a single moment to your lifespan?

And why do you worry about clothes?
Notice how the lilies of the field grow:
    they neither toil nor spin.
Yet I assure you that even Solomon in all his magnificence
    was never attired like one of them.
But if that is how God clothes the grass of the field,
    which is alive today and tomorrow is thrown into the furnace,
Will he not much more certainly clothe you?
    O you of little faith!

So do not worry, asking,
    "What shall we eat?" or
    "What shall we drink?" or
    "What shall we wear?"
For the heathen Gentiles are always pursuing all of these things.
And your Heavenly Father certainly knows
    that you need all of these things.
But seek first his kingdom and his righteousness,
    and all of these things shall be subsequently provided to you.
So do not worry about tomorrow,
    for tomorrow will bring its own worries.
Each day has enough troubles of its own.

Matthew 6:19–34

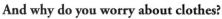

THE BLIND LEADING THE BLIND

DO NOT JUDGE others,
    and you will not be judged.
And do not condemn,
    and you will not be condemned.
Forgive and you will be forgiven.
Give and it will be given to you.
A good measure, pressed down, shaken together, and running over
    will be poured into your lap.

For in the same way you judge,
  you will be judged.
And by the standard of measure you use,
  it will be measured to you in return.

He also told them a parable:

Can a blind person guide a blind person?
Will they not both fall into a pit?
A student is not above his teacher,
  but everyone who is fully trained
  will be like his teacher.

Why do you see the speck
  that is in your brother's eye,
But do not notice the log
  that is in your own eye?
Or how can you say to your brother:
  "Brother, let me remove the speck
  that is in your eye,"
When you yourself fail to see the log
  that is in your own eye?

You hypocrite! First take the log
  out of your own eye!
And then you will see clearly
  to remove the speck that is in your brother's eye.

Matthew 7:1–5; Luke 6:37–42

PEARLS, PIGS, AND PRAYER

DO NOT GIVE WHAT IS SACRED to dogs.
Do not throw your pearls to pigs,
  or they may trample them under their feet,
  and turn and tear you to pieces.

Ask, and it shall be given to you.
Seek, and you shall find.
Knock, and the door shall be opened to you.

For everyone who keeps asking receives.
And the one who keeps seeking finds.
And to the one who keeps knocking, the door will be opened.

Or is there a man among you,
    if his son should ask for a loaf of bread,
    would give him a stone?
Or if he should ask for a fish,
    he would not give him a snake, would he?

If you then, evil as you are,
    know how to give good gifts to your children,
How much more shall your Father who is in heaven
    give good gifts to those who ask him!

So then, in everything,
"Do to others what you would have them do to you,"
    for this is the essence of the Law and the Prophets.

Matthew 7:6–12

PERSONAL RIGHTEOUSNESS

ENTER THROUGH THE NARROW GATE!
For the gate is wide and the road is easy
    that leads to destruction,
    and those who enter through it are many.
For the gate is narrow and the road is constricted
    that leads to life,
    and those who find it are few.

Beware of the false prophets!
They come to you in sheep's clothing,
    but inwardly are devouring wolves.
You will recognize them by their fruits,
    for each tree is known by its own fruit.
Grapes are not gathered from thorn bushes,
    nor figs from thistles or brambles, are they?
In the same way every good tree bears good fruit,
    but the bad tree bears bad fruit.
For no good tree bears bad fruit,
    nor does a bad tree bear good fruit.
Every tree that does not bear good fruit is cut down
    and thrown into the fire.
So you will know them by their fruits.
The good man out of the good treasure stored in his heart
    produces what is good;

And the evil person out of the evil storehouse
    produces what is evil.
For from what overflows from his heart
    his mouth speaks.

Why do you call me, "Lord, Lord"
    and do not do what I tell you?
Not everyone who says to me, "Lord, Lord"
    will enter the kingdom of heaven,
But only the one who does the will of my Father
    who is in heaven.
Many will say to me on that day:
"Lord, Lord, did we not prophesy in your name,
    and did we not drive out demons in your name,
    and did we not work many miracles in your name?"
Then I will solemnly and publicly declare to them:
"I have never known you!
Depart from me, you evildoers!"

I will show you what he is like
    who comes to me,
    and listens to these words of mine,
    and acts upon them.
He is like a wise man building a house
    who dug down deep and laid a foundation upon rock.
When the rain descended,
    and the floods rose,
    and the winds blew,
The swollen torrents burst against that house
    but could not shake it!
The house did not collapse
    because it had been soundly built
    and solidly founded upon the rock.

But the one who hears these words of mine,
    and does not act upon them,
He is like a foolish man
    who built his house upon sand without any foundation.
And the rain descended,
    and the floods came,
    and the winds blew,

And the torrents burst against that house,
   and it immediately collapsed!
It fell with a great crash,
   and the destruction of the house was complete.

Matthew 7:13–27; Luke 6:43–49

97

AMAZING AUTHORITY

W HEN JESUS HAD FINISHED these words, the multitudes were amazed at his teaching. For he was teaching them as one having authority, and not as their scribes, their teachers of the Law.

Then, when he descended from the mountainside, huge crowds followed him.

Matthew 7:28–8:1

TWELVE

A CENTURION'S FAITH

circa A.D. 28

AFTER JESUS HAD COMPLETED HIS DISCOURSE in the hearing of the people, he went to Capernaum. And when he had entered Capernaum, a centurion (who when he heard about Jesus) sent some elders of the Jews to him. A slave of the centurion, whom he highly valued, was sick and close to dying. The elders were sent to Jesus to ask him to come and save the life of his slave.

And when they reached Jesus, they earnestly pleaded with him, saying, "He is worthy to have you grant this for him, for he loves our nation and is the one who built our synagogue for us."

So Jesus went with them. But when he was not far from the house, the centurion came to him appealing for help. "Lord," he said, "my slave is lying at home, paralyzed and suffering terrible pain."

Then Jesus said to him, "**I will come and heal him**."

But the centurion replied, "Lord, do not trouble yourself further, for I am not worthy for you to enter under my roof! That is why I did not even presume myself worthy to come to you. But just say the word, and my slave will be healed. For I am also a man under authority, with soldiers under me: I say to one 'Go' and he goes, and to another 'Come' and he comes, and to my slave 'Do this' and he does it."

Now when Jesus heard this, he was amazed at him. Then turning to the crowd that was following him, he said,

> **I guarantee you this:**
> **In no one in Israel have I found such great faith!**
>
> **I guarantee you that**
> **Many shall come from east and west**
> **and shall recline at the table with Abraham,**

and Isaac, and Jacob,
and shall dine at the feast in the kingdom of heaven.
But the heirs to the kingdom will be cast out into outer darkness,
where there will be weeping and grinding of teeth.

Then to the centurion Jesus said, **"Go your way. Let it be done for you just as you believed."**

And when those who had been sent returned to the house, they found the slave had recovered at that very moment, and was in good health.

Matthew 8:5–13; Luke 7:1–10

A WIDOW'S ONLY SON

SOON AFTERWARD, JESUS WENT TO A TOWN called Nain. His disciples and a huge crowd accompanied him. As he approached the gate of the town, a dead man was being carried out in a funeral procession. He was his mother's only son, and she was a widow. With her was a sizeable crowd from the town.

When the Lord saw her, he felt compassion for her and said to her, **"Do not weep."**

Then he stepped forward and touched the funeral bier. At this the pallbearers stood still. Then he said, **"Young man, I say to you, Arise!"**

Then the dead man sat up and began to speak, and Jesus gave him back to his mother.

Fear engulfed all of them. Then they began glorifying God. "A great prophet has arisen among us!" they exclaimed, and "God has visited his people!"

And this account concerning Jesus spread out all over Judea and the entire surrounding region.

Luke 7:11–17

A BAPTIST'S DOUBTS

THE DISCIPLES OF JOHN REPORTED ALL THESE THINGS to him. Now when John, who was in prison, heard what the Messiah was doing, he summoned two of his disciples and sent them to the Lord to ask him, "Are you the Expected One, or are we to expect someone other?"

When the men came to him, they said, "John the baptizer sent us to ask, 'Are you the Expected One, or are we to expect someone else?' "

At that very hour, Jesus had just cured many of their diseases, afflictions, and evil spirits; and he had bestowed sight to many who were blind. So Jesus replied and said to them:

Go back and report to John
>> what you have seen and heard.
The blind receive sight.
The lame walk.
Lepers are cleansed.
The deaf hear.
The dead are raised up.
And the poor have the gospel proclaimed to them.
And blessed is he who is not offended by me.

As John's disciples were departing, Jesus began to speak to the crowds about John:

What did you go out into the wilderness to see?
>> Tall grass swayed by the wind?
What then do you go out to see?
>> A man dressed in soft robes?
No, those who wear soft robes and live in luxury
>> are in kings' palaces!

What then did you go out to see?
>> A prophet?
Yes, I assure you,
>> and one who is more than a prophet!
This is the one about whom it is written:

>> "Pay attention!
>> I am sending my messenger before your face,
>> Who will prepare your way before you."

I guarantee you this truth:
Among those born of women
>> there has appeared no one greater than John, the baptizer.
Yet he who is least significant in the kingdom of heaven,
>> yes in the kingdom of God,
>> is greater than he.

From the days of John the baptizer until now,
>> the kingdom of heaven has suffered violence,
>> and the violent have been forcefully seizing it.
All of the Prophets and the Law
>> prophesied until the time of John.

> And if you are willing to accept it,
> > John is Elijah who is to come.
> Let the person who has ears listen!

And when all the people, including the tax collectors, heard this, they acknowledged the justice of God, having been baptized with the baptism of John. But the Pharisees and the experts in the Mosaic law, not having been baptized by John, rejected God's purpose for themselves.

> But to what shall I compare the people of this generation?
> > And what are they like?
> They are like children playing in the marketplace,
> > and calling out to one another, saying:
>
> > "We played the wedding flute for you,
> > > and you did not dance.
> > We sang a funeral dirge,
> > > and you did not mourn."
>
> For John the baptizer has come
> > neither eating bread nor drinking wine,
> > and they say, "He has a demon in him!"
> The Son of Man came eating and drinking,
> > and they say, "Look at him!
> > a glutton and a drunkard!
> > a friend of tax collectors and notorious sinners!"
> Yet wisdom is vindicated by all who are her children,
> > and by her actions and results.

Matthew 11:2–19; Luke 7:18–35

PROPHECY

> Behold, I will send my messenger,
> > and he shall prepare the way before me.
> Then the Lord whom you seek
> > shall suddenly come to his temple,
> Even the messenger of the covenant,
> > for whom you desire,
> Indeed, he is coming!

So says the Lord of Hosts, The Lord Almighty,
Jehovah Sabaoth.

Recorded by the Prophet Malachi, year c. 425 B.C.
Malachi 3:1

And the Lord said:

**On that day the deaf shall hear
    the words of a book,
And out of their gloom and darkness
    the eyes of the blind shall see.
The humble shall again find joy in the Lord,
    and the poorest of people shall
    exult in the Holy One of Israel.**

**Then the eyes of the blind shall be opened,
    and the ears of the deaf unplugged.
Then shall the lame leap like a deer,
    and the mute tongue sing for joy.
For waters shall gush in the wilderness,
    and streams in the desert.**

**The Spirit of the Lord God is upon me,
    because the Lord has anointed me
    to bring good news to the afflicted.
He has sent me
    to bind up the brokenhearted,
    to proclaim liberty to the captives,
    and release from prison those who are bound.**

Recorded by the prophet Isaiah, year c. 700 B.C.
Isaiah 29:18–19; 35:5–6; 61:1

103

For this is how the Lord spoke to me,
    with His strong hand upon me,
And He warned me not to walk in the way of this people, saying:

**But the Lord of Sabaoth, the Lord of Hosts,
    him you should regard as holy.
Let him be what you fear,
    and let him be what terrifies you.
And he shall become a sanctuary,
    and a stone of offense
    and a rock of stumbling
    to both houses of Israel,
    and a trap and a snare
    to the inhabitants of Jerusalem.
And many shall stumble over it.
    They shall fall and be broken.
    They shall be trapped and caught.**

Recorded by the prophet Isaiah, year c. 700 B.C.
Isaiah 8:11, 13–15

THE CITIES REPROACHED

THEN JESUS BEGAN TO REPROACH THE CITIES in which most of his miracles had been done, because they did not repent.

> Woe to you, Chorazin!
> Woe to you, Bethsaida!
> For if the mighty miracles which had been done in you
>   had been done in Tyre and Sidon,
> They would have repented long ago
>   in sackcloth and ashes.
> But I guarantee you: on the Day of Judgment
>   it will be more tolerable for Tyre and Sidon
>   than for you.
>
> And as for you, Capernaum,
>   will you be exalted to heaven?
> No, you will descend to hades!
> For if the mighty miracles which have been done in you,
>   had been done in Sodom,
>   it would have remained to this day.
> But I guarantee you: on the Day of Judgment
>   it will be more tolerable for the land of Sodom
>   than for you.

Matthew 11:20–24

THE SON'S INVITATION

AT THAT TIME, JESUS CONTINUED and declared:

> I praise you, Father, Lord of heaven and earth,
>   because you have hidden these things
>   from the clever and the educated,
>   and have revealed them to the simplest children.
> Yes, Father, for such was your gracious will and good pleasure.
>
> All things have been entrusted to me by my Father.
> And no one fully knows the Son, except the Father.
> Nor does anyone fully know the Father, except the Son,
>   and anyone to whom the Son chooses to reveal him.

Come to me,
>   all who are weary and overburdened,
>   and I will give you rest.
Take my yoke upon you and learn from me,
>   for I am gentle and humble in heart,
>   and you will find rest for your souls.
For my yoke is easy,
>   and my burden is light.

Matthew 11:25–30

This is what the Lord says:

**Stand at the crossroads, and look.
Ask for the ancient paths,
>   where the good way is,
And walk in it,
>   and you will find rest for your souls.**

But they said:
"We will not walk in it."

Recorded by the prophet Jeremiah, year c. 600 B.C.
Jeremiah 6:16

THE MESSIAH ANOINTED

NOW ONE OF THE PHARISEES INVITED JESUS to dine with him. So he went to the Pharisee's house, and took his place, reclining at the table.

Suddenly a woman of the city, who was a sinner, having learned that he was eating at the table in the Pharisee's house, brought an alabaster jar of perfume ointment. Standing behind him at his feet, weeping, she began to bathe his feet with her tears. Then she kept wiping his feet with the hair of her head, and affectionately kissing them, and anointing them with the perfume ointment.

But when the Pharisee who had invited him saw this, he said to himself, "If this man were really a prophet, he would know who and what kind of a woman is touching him — that she is a sinner!"

Then Jesus spoke up and said to him, **"Simon, I have something to say to you."**

"Teacher," he responded, "tell me!"

"A certain creditor had two debtors. One owed five hundred *denarii* (the *denarius* being equivalent to a day's wages or about one hundred dollars), **and the**

other fifty. When neither could pay, he freely cancelled the debt of both of them. Now which of them will love him more?"

"I suppose the one whom he forgave more," Simon replied.

Then Jesus responded to him, **"You have judged correctly."**

Then turning toward the woman he said to Simon, **"Do you see this woman? When I entered your house, you gave me no water for my feet. But she has wet my feet with her tears and wiped them with her hair. You gave me no kiss of greeting. But since the time I entered she has not ceased kissing my feet. You did not anoint my head with oil. But she has anointed my feet with perfumed ointment. For this reason I say to you, her sins, which are many, have been forgiven. That is why she has loved much. But someone who is forgiven little, loves little."**

Then he said to her, **"Your sins have been forgiven!"**

The other guests who were reclining at the table with him began to say among themselves, "Who is this who even forgives sins?"

But Jesus said to the woman, **"Your faith has saved you! Go in peace!"**

Luke 7:36–50

CHAPTER

13

FIRST PUBLIC REJECTION

THIRTEEN

The Second Great Galilean Tour _____ *circa A.D. 28*

S OON AFTER THIS, JESUS BEGAN TRAVELING from one city and village
to another, proclaiming and sharing the good news of the kingdom of God.

Accompanying him were the Twelve, as well as some women who had been
cured of evil spirits and various illnesses — Mary who was called Mary of Magdala, out of whom seven demons had gone, and Joanna the wife of Herod's steward
Chuza, and Susanna, and many others who provided for them out of their own
personal resources.

Luke 8:1–3

Jesus and Beelzebub

T HEN MULTITUDES GATHERED AGAIN, coming together from one
town after another, to such an extent that it was impossible for them even
to eat a meal. And when his own family heard about this, they went out to take
custody of him, because they kept saying, "He has gone out of his mind!"

Then the crowd brought him a demon-possessed man who was blind and
mute. And Jesus cured him by driving out the mute demon. When the demon
had gone out, the man who had been mute could both talk and see! And all the
multitudes were amazed and began to say, "This man cannot be the Son of David,
can he?"

But when the Pharisees and the scribes, the teachers of the Law, who had
come down from Jerusalem heard this, they kept repeating, "He is possessed by
Beelzebub!" and "It is only by the power of Beelzebub, the prince of demons, that
this man drives out demons!" And others, to test him, kept demanding from him
a spectacular sign from heaven.

- 107 -

But knowing what they were thinking, Jesus summoned them to himself and began speaking to them in parables.

How can Satan drive out Satan?
And if a kingdom is divided against itself,
    that kingdom cannot stand.
It will collapse and be laid waste.
And if a city or household is divided against itself,
    that city or household will fall and not be able to stand.
And if Satan drives out Satan
    and has raised an insurrection against himself and is divided,
    how can his kingdom stand?
He cannot stand, but his end has come!

For you say that I drive out demons by Beelzebub.
So if I drive out demons by Beelzebub,
    by whom do your own sons drive them out?
Therefore, they will be your judges!
But if I drive out demons by the finger of God, by the Spirit of God,
    then the kingdom of God has come upon you!

In fact, when a strong man, fully armed, guards his own home,
    his possessions are secure.
No one can enter a strong man's house and plunder his property
    unless he first binds the strong man.
When someone stronger that he attacks and overpowers him,
    he takes away his armor on which he relied.
Then indeed he can plunder his house and distribute his plunder.

Whoever is not with me is against me.
And whoever does not gather with me scatters.

Believe me therefore when I assure you:
Every sin shall be forgiven the sons of men,
    and whatever blasphemous words they utter.
But whoever blasphemes against the Spirit shall never be forgiven,
    but is guilty of an eternal sin.
And whoever shall speak any abusive word against the Son of Man
    shall be forgiven.
But whoever shall speak abusively against the Holy Spirit
    shall not be forgiven him,
    either in this age or in the age to come.

He said this because they persisted in saying, "He has an evil spirit."

> Either make the tree good,
>> and its fruit will be good.
> Or make the tree and its fruit bad.
> For the tree is recognized by its fruit.

> You brood of vipers!
> How can you, being evil, speak anything that is good?
>> for out of the overflow of the heart the mouth speaks.
> The good man out of the good treasure stored up in him
>> brings forth what is good.
> And the evil man out of his evil treasure
>> brings forth what is evil.

> And I guarantee you that on the judgment day:
> People will have to give account
>> for every careless word they have spoken.
> For by your words you shall be acquitted,
>> and by your words you shall be condemned.

Matthew 12:22–37; Mark 3:20–30; Luke 11:14–23

THE SIGN OF JONAH

A S THE CROWDS WERE INCREASING, then some of the scribes (the teachers of the religious Law) and the Pharisees responded to him, saying, "Teacher, we need to see a miraculous spectacular sign from you."

But he began to respond to them by saying,

> This generation is a wicked generation!
> An evil and unfaithful generation craves for a spectacular sign.
> But no sign shall be given to it
>> except the sign of Jonah the prophet.
> For just as Jonah was three days and three nights
>> in the belly of the sea monster,
> So the Son of Man shall be three days and three nights
>> in the heart of the earth.
> For just as Jonah became a sign to the Ninevites,
>> so the Son of Man shall be to this generation.

> At the Judgment, the men from Nineveh shall rise up
>> with this generation.

And they shall condemn it
    because they repented at the preaching of Jonah.
And, take notice! Something greater than Jonah is here!

At the Judgment, the Queen of the South shall rise up
    with the people of this generation.
And she shall condemn them
    because she came from the ends of the earth
    to hear the wisdom of Solomon.
But, take notice! Something greater than Solomon is here!

No one, after lighting a lamp, puts it away in a cellar,
    nor under a bushel basket,
But on a lampstand
    so that those who enter may see the light.

Your eye is the lamp of your body.
When your eye is good,
    your whole body is full of light.
But when it is bad,
    your body is also full of darkness.
So be certain that the light in you is not darkness.
If then your whole body is full of light
    with no part of it in dark shadow,
It will be as fully illuminated
    as when the lamp illumines you with its rays.

Matthew 12:38–42; Luke 11:29–36

Woe to You, Pharisees!

NOW WHEN HE HAD FINISHED SPEAKING, a Pharisee invited him to have dinner with him. So he went in and reclined at the table. But when the Pharisee noticed that Jesus had not first ceremonially washed before the meal, he was surprised.

Then the Lord said to him,

You Pharisees!
Now you clean the outside of the cup and of the platter,
    but inside of you, you are full of extortion and wickedness!
You senseless fools!

Did not the one who made the outside
    make the inside also?
Instead, give as charity that which is within,
    and then you will see.
All things will be clean for you.

Woe to you Pharisees!
For you tithe mint, and spice, and every little herb,
    and yet you disregard justice and the love of God.
But these are the things you ought to have done,
    without neglecting the others!

Woe to you Pharisees!
For you love the front seats of honor in the synagogues,
    and public recognition in the marketplaces.

Woe to you!
For you are like unmarked graves,
    and people walk over them without realizing the corruption!

Then one of the scholars of the Law responded to him, saying, "Teacher, when you say all this, you insult us as well!"

But he responded:

Woe to you experts in the Law as well!
For you weigh people down with burdens hard to bear,
    while you yourselves will not even touch the burdens
    with one of your fingers!

Woe to you!
For you build the memorial tombs of the prophets,
    and it was your own forefathers who killed them!
Consequently you bear witness that you approve
    of the deeds of your fathers.
Because it was they who killed them,
    and it is you who build their memorial tombs!

Also for this reason, the wisdom of God said:
"I will send prophets and apostles to them,
    some of whom they will kill,
    and some they will persecute,"
So that the blood of all the prophets
    shed since the foundation of the world
    shall be charged against this generation —

From the blood of Abel to the blood of Zechariah
    who was killed between the altar and the sanctuary!
Yes! I guarantee you!
All of it shall be charged against this generation!

Woe to you experts in the Law!
For you have taken away the key to knowledge;
    you did not enter yourselves,
    and you prevented those who were wanting to enter.

Then when he left there, the scribes (those experts in the Law) and the Pharisees began to be vehemently hostile, and to furiously oppose him, and to closely cross examine him on innumerable subjects, plotting against him to ensnare him in something he might say.

Luke 11:37–54

THE DANGER OF A SPIRITUAL VACUUM

NOW WHEN THE UNCLEAN spirit goes out of someone,
    it roams through arid places seeking a resting place.
But not finding any, it then says,
    "I will return to my house from which I came."
When it arrives it finds it unoccupied,
    swept clean, and put in order.

Then it goes and brings back with it
    seven other spirits more evil than itself,
    and they all move in and live there.
And the last condition of the person
    becomes worse than the first.

    That is the way it will also be with this evil generation.

Now it occurred that while he was saying these things, one of the women in the crowd raised her voice and said to him, "Blessed is the womb that bore you, and the breasts that nursed you!"

But he said, **"Even more blessed are those who hear the word of God and observe it!"**

Matthew 12:43–45; Luke 11:24–28

THE TRUE FAMILY OF JESUS

WHILE HE WAS STILL SPEAKING TO THE MULTITUDES, his mother and brothers arrived, but remained standing outside, wanting to speak to him. They were unable to get near him because of the crowd. Then they sent a message to him that they were calling for him.

A crowd was sitting around him. Someone said to him, "Give me your attention! Your mother and your brothers are outside looking for you, wanting to see and speak to you."

In response to the one who told him this, he asked, **"Who is my mother, and who are my brothers?"**

Then looking about at those who were seated in a circle around him, and stretching his hand toward his disciples, he said,

> **Pay attention to this: Here are my mother and my brothers!**
> **For whoever hears the word of God**
> **and does the will of God — of my Father who is in heaven**
> **is my brother, and my sister, and my mother!**

> *Matthew 12:46–50; Mark 3:31–35; Luke 8:19–21*

14

SECRETS OF THE KINGDOM

THE SETTING BY THE SEA

circa A.D. 28

O N THAT SAME DAY JESUS WENT OUT OF THE HOUSE, and was sitting by the sea.

When he began to teach by the sea, such immense crowds congregated around him that he got into a boat. Then he sat down in it out in the sea, while the whole multitude was on the shore at the water's edge.

There he began teaching them many things in parables, using stories as illustrations, and in his teachings said the following to them.

Matthew 13:1–3; Mark 4:1–2

THE SOIL

H E BEGAN WITH THIS PARABLE by saying,

Give me your attention!

Imagine that a sower went out to sow his seed.
And as he was scattering the seed around,
 some seeds fell on the footpath beside the road,
 and they were trampled under foot.
And the birds flying around swooped down
 and devoured them.

Other of the seeds fell on rocky ground
 where they did not have much soil.
So they sprouted up quickly
 because they had no depth of soil.

But when the sun had risen,
    they were scorched.
And because they had not taken root and lacked moisture,
    they withered away.

Other seeds fell among thorn plants,
    and the thorn plants sprung up and choked them out.
Then the seeds yielded no grain.

Still other seeds fell onto the rich soil
    and yielded grain.
They continued to grow, producing a crop,
    and multiplying thirty, sixty, and a hundredfold.

As he had finished saying these things, he exclaimed,

Let anyone with ears to hear listen and comprehend!

As soon as he was alone, his followers, along with the Twelve, gathered around him and began asking him about the parables, and what this parable meant. Then this is what he answered in response to their question, "Why do you speak to them in parables?"

The knowledge of the mysteries of the kingdom of God
    has been entrusted to you,
    but it has not been given to those who are outside.
To them everything remains in parables.

Whoever has, more will be given,
    and they will have an abundance.
But whoever has nothing,
    even what they have will be taken away.

This is why I speak to them in parables, so that

They may be ever looking and seeing
    but never perceiving,
And ever hearing and listening
    but never comprehending,
That they may never return again
    and it never be forgiven them.

Indeed, in them the prophecy of Isaiah
    is being fulfilled when it says:

You will indeed keep listening,
    but you will never understand.
And you will indeed keep looking,
    but you will never perceive.
For this people's heart has grown callous,
    and their ears can barely hear,
    and their eyes have closed,
Lest they should see with their eyes,
    and hear with their ears,
    and understand with their hearts,
    and return to me,
And I would heal them.

But blessed are your eyes because they see,
    and your ears because they hear.

For I guarantee you this truth:
Many prophets and the righteous desired to see what you see
    and did not see it;
And to hear what you hear
    and did not hear it.

Then Jesus challenged them,

Do you not understand this parable?
    How then will you understand any of the parables?
Pay attention, then, to the meaning of the parable of the sower.

The seed is the word of God.
The sower sows the word.

And those who are on the footpath beside the road
    where the word is sown
    are those who have heard.
But when they hear the word of the kingdom
    and do not assimilate it,
Satan immediately comes and snatches away the word
    which is sown in them.
The devil, the evil one, snatches away the word from their heart
    so that they may not believe and be saved.
This is the seed sown on the footpath beside the road.

And in a similar way, those on the rocky ground
    on whom seed was sown

Are those who when they hear the word,
    instantly and enthusiastically receive it with joy.
But since they have no deep root in themselves,
    they believe and endure only temporarily.
Then in the time of testing,
    when suffering or persecution arises because of the word,
    they immediately wilt and fall away.

Still others, who like seed sown among the thorn plants,
    hear the word.
Then as they go on their way,
    the worries of the world,
    the lure of wealth,
    the ambition for other acquisitions,
    and the pleasures of this life
Enter in and choke the word,
    and their fruit never matures,
    and they yield nothing.

But those on whom seed was sown on the rich soil,
    hear the word, and accept, comprehend
    and embrace it in an honest and good heart.
Then by persevering they indeed bear fruit—
    in one instance thirty,
    in another sixty,
    and even a hundred times what was sown.

Then he continued saying to them,

Now, no one after lighting a lamp
    brings it in and covers it up
    by putting it under a bucket
    or by hiding it under a bed.
Instead, is it not brought in to be placed on a lampstand,
    so that those who enter may see the light?

For nothing is concealed
    that will not be revealed,
Nor is anything secret
    that will not be made known and come to light.

Let anyone with ears to hear listen and comprehend!

He continued saying to them,

Pay attention then to how you listen.
The measure you give will be the measure you receive,
and still more will be added to you.
For whoever has,
more will be given.
But whoever has nothing,
even what he thinks he has will be taken away from him.

Matthew 13:3–23; Mark 4:3–25; Luke 8:4–18

PROPHECY

Then I heard the voice of the Lord saying,

Whom shall I send, and who will go for us?

Then I said,

"Here am I. Send me!"

And he said,

Go, and tell this people:

"Keep listening, but do not perceive;
Keep looking, but do not understand."

Render the heart of this people calloused,
make their ears dull,
and their eyes dim.
Otherwise they might see with their eyes,
and hear with their ears,
and understand with their hearts,
And return and be healed.

Recorded by the prophet Isaiah, year c. 700 B.C.
Isaiah 6:8–10

THE SEEDS

THE KINGDOM OF GOD is like this,

He then continued saying.

It is as if a man scatters his seed on the soil.
Night and day he sleeps and gets up,
and the seeds sprout and grow, though he knows not how.

The soil produces crops on its own —
    first the blade,
    then the head,
    then the mature grain in the head.
But when the grain is ripe and ready,
    he immediately goes in with the sickle,
    because the harvest time has come.

Mark 4:26–29

PROPHECY

The Lord has spoken:

    Put in the sickle,
        for the harvest is ripe.
    Go in, tread the grapes,
        for the wine press is full;
        the vats overflow,
        for their wickedness is great.
    Multitudes on multitudes,
        in the valley of decision!
    For the Day of the Lord is near
        in the valley of decision.

Recorded by the prophet Joel, year c. 825 B.C.
Joel 3:13–14

THE WEEDS

H E PRESENTED ANOTHER PARABLE to them, saying:

The kingdom of heaven may be compared
    to a man who sowed good seed in his field.
But while his own men were sleeping,
    his enemy came and also sowed darnel among the wheat,
    and slipped away.
But when the wheat sprang up and formed kernels,
    then the darnel became evident as well.

Then the landowner's slaves came and said to him,
"Did you not sow good seed in your field?
    How then does it have darnel weeds?"

"An enemy has done this!"
    he then replied to them.

So the slaves asked him,
"Do you want us to go, then,
    and pull them up?"

But he replied,
"No! for while you are pulling up the wild darnel weeds,
    you might uproot the wheat along with them.
Let them both grow together until the harvest.
Then at harvest time I will say to the reapers:
Gather the darnel weeds first,
    and bind them in bundles to be burned.
But gather the wheat into my barn."

Matthew 13:24–30

THE MUSTARD SEED

THEN HE CONTINUED and presented another parable to them.

What is the kingdom of God like?
With what shall we picture the kingdom of God,
    or what parable shall we use to illustrate or compare it?

The kingdom of heaven is like a mustard seed
    which a man took and sowed in his own garden.
When sown upon the soil,
    it is the smallest of all other seeds on earth.
Yet once it is sown,
    it grows up
And when full-grown
    becomes the largest of all the garden shrubs.
It becomes a tree
    and extends such large branches
    that the birds of the air can come and nest in its shade.

Matthew 13:31–32; Mark 4:30–32; Luke 13:18–19

THEN HE TOLD THEM ANOTHER PARABLE. Again he asked,

To what shall I compare the kingdom of God?

The kingdom of heaven is like yeast,
which a woman took and mixed into three measures of flour
until it was all leavened.

Jesus spoke all these things to the crowds in parables. And with many such parables he spoke the word to them, as much as they were able to comprehend. Indeed, he did not speak to them without a parable. This was to fulfill what had been spoken through the prophet:

I will open my mouth in parables.
I will explain things that have been concealed
    since the foundation of the world.

Then privately, to his own disciples, he explained everything.

Matthew 13:33–35; Mark 4:33–34; Luke 13:20–21

PROPHECY

Listen, O my people, to my instruction;
Turn your ears to the words of my mouth.

I will open my mouth in a parable;
I will explain concealed sayings from long ago.

Written by the psalmist Asaph, year c. 750 B.C.
Psalm 78:1–2

FIFTEEN

THE WEEDS EXPLAINED

circa A.D. 28

THEN HE LEFT THE CROWDS and went into the house. And his disciples approached him, saying, "Explain to us the parable about the darnel in the field."

Then he responded and said:

> The one who sows the good seed
>   is the Son of Man.
> The field
>   is the world,
> And as for the good seed,
>   these are the children of the kingdom.
> And the darnel weeds
>   are the children of the evil one,
> And the enemy who sowed them
>   is the devil.
> The harvest
>   is the end of the age.
> And the reapers
>   are angels.
>
> Just as the darnel weeds
>   are separated out and burned in fire,
> So shall it be at the end of the age.
> The Son of Man
>   will dispatch his angels,

And they will gather out of his kingdom
>
>> all who cause others to sin
>> and all who commit evil.
>
> Then they will hurl them into the blazing furnace
>
>> where in that place there will be wailing
>> and grinding of teeth.

Then the righteous will shine brightly
>
>> like the sun in the kingdom of their father.
>
> Let the person who has ears listen!

Matthew 13:36–43

THE HIDDEN TREASURE AND PRICELESS PEARL

THE KINGDOM OF HEAVEN
>
>> is like a treasure hidden buried in a field
>> which a man discovered and reburied.
>
> Then in his joy he goes and sells all that he has,
>
>> and buys that field.
>
> Again the kingdom of heaven
>
>> is like a merchant in search of fine pearls.
>
> On finding one priceless pearl,
>
>> he went and sold everything he had,
>> and bought it.

Matthew 13:44–46

THE DRAGNET AND THE STOREROOM

AGAIN, THE KINGDOM OF HEAVEN
>
>> is like a dragnet cast into the sea
>> which caught every kind of fish.
>
> When it was filled,
>
>> the men hauled it ashore.
>
> Then they sat down
>
>> and sorted the good fish into containers,
>> but threw the worthless away.

So it will be at the end of the age.
>
> The angels will come out
>
>> and separate the wicked from among the righteous

And throw them into the blazing furnace
where in that place there will be wailing
and grinding of teeth.

Have you understood all these things?

"Yes!" they replied to Him.
Then He said to them:

Therefore every scribe,
who as a teacher of the religious Law
becomes a disciple of the kingdom of heaven.
He is like the owner of a household
who brings out of his storeroom both new and old treasures.

When Jesus had finished these parables, he departed from that place.

Matthew 13:47–53

16

CALMING THE STORM

circa A.D. 28

NOW ON THAT DAY, when evening had come, and when Jesus saw a crowd still around him, it came about that he and his disciples got into a boat. Then he gave orders to cross over to the other side. **"Let us go across to the other side of the lake,"** he said to them.

So leaving the crowds behind, they launched out and took him along with them, just as he was, in the boat. And other disciples in other boats were with him and followed him.

Then as they were sailing along, he fell asleep. But without warning, a furious gale-force windstorm arose and descended upon the lake. And the waves kept breaking into the boat, so much so that the boat was almost being swamped by the waves, and they were in great danger.

But he himself was in the stern, still sleeping on the cushion.

So the disciples went to him and woke him, shouting to him, "Master! Master! Save us, Lord! We are perishing! Do you not care that we are drowning?"

So he arose, and rebuked the wind, and said to the raging waves, **"Quiet! Be still!"**

Then the wind suddenly stopped! It became completely calm!

Then he said to them, **"Why are you so afraid, you of such little faith? Why is it that you still have no faith?"**

And they were overcome with great fear and awe, and kept asking one another in amazement, "Who then is this man that he even commands the wind and the waves, and they obey him?"

Matthew 8:18, 23–27; Mark 4:35–41; Luke 8:22–25

CURING THE DEMONIAC

THEN THEY SAILED ACROSS THE LAKE to the other side, to the region of the Gerasenes, near the district of Gadara, which is opposite Galilee.

As they arrived and he had climbed out of the boat onto the land, immediately a man from the town who was demon possessed rushed out of the burial tombs and went to meet him. For a long time he had not worn any clothes, and did not live in a house, but lived in the cemetery tombs. And no one was able to restrain him anymore, not even with a chain. For he had often been bound with shackles and chains. But the chains had been wrenched apart by him, and the shackles smashed in pieces, and no one had enough strength to subdue him. Night and day, among the tombs and in the mountains, he was constantly shrieking, and gashing himself with stones. He was so dangerously violent that no one could pass by that roadway.

And seeing Jesus from a distance, he suddenly ran up and fell down at his feet and bowed down before him, shrieking at the top of his voice. "What have you to do with me, Jesus, Son of the most high God?" he screamed. "I beg you and implore you by God, do not torment me! Have you come here to torment me before the appointed time?"

For Jesus had been commanding the unclean spirit to come out of the man, saying to him, **"Come out of the man, you evil spirit!"** For many times it had seized him, and though he was bound with chains and shackles and kept under guard, yet he would burst his chains and be driven by the demon into the desert wilderness.

"What is your name?" Jesus then asked him.

"My name is Legion," he replied, "for there are many of us." Many demons had entered him (a legion being six thousand). And he began desperately and repeatedly pleading him not to send them out of the region nor order them to depart into the abyss, the bottomless pit.

Now there on the hillside, some distance from them, a large herd of many pigs was feeding. The demons pleaded with him to permit them to enter them, saying, "If you are going to cast us out, send us among the herd of swine so that we may enter them." And he gave them permission. **"Go!"** he said to them.

Then coming out of the man, the evil spirits (or demons) entered the pigs. The herd, about two thousand, suddenly charged down the steep bank into the sea, and drowned in the water.

When the swine herdsmen saw what had happened, they fled and reported it in the city and out in the countryside. They reported everything, including what had happened to the demoniac.

Then the entire city came to see for themselves what it was that had occurred, and to meet Jesus.

When they came and saw Jesus, and observed the man who had been demon-possessed, from whom the evil spirits had gone out, sitting there at the feet of Jesus, clothed and in his right mind, the very man who had had the "Legion," they became frightened.

Then those who had witnessed it described how the demoniac had been healed — and what had happened to the swine. Then all the people of the country of the Gerasenes and the surrounding district began to implore him to leave their region, because they were gripped with great terror.

As he was getting into the boat, the man who had been demon-possessed, from whom the demons had gone out, kept begging him that he might accompany him.

But Jesus did not permit him. Instead he sent him away, saying, **"Go back home. Return to your own people and describe to them what great things the Lord God has done for you, and how he had mercy on you."** Then Jesus started back.

So the demoniac departed and began to proclaim throughout the entire Decapolis what great things Jesus had done for him. And everyone was amazed.

Matthew 8:28–34; Mark 5:1–20; Luke 8:26–39

HEALING A WOMAN AND RAISING A DAUGHTER

THEN WHEN JESUS HAD CROSSED AGAIN IN THE BOAT and returned to the opposite side, a great multitude gathered about him, and welcomed him back, for they had all been waiting for him. And he stayed by the seashore.

Just then, while he was speaking to them, one of the synagogue officials named Jairus came forward. And upon seeing Jesus, he fell at his feet. Bowing down before him, he desperately pleaded with him, "My little daughter is at the point of death! Please come to my house, and lay Your hands on her, so that she may be made well and live!" For he had an only daughter, about 12 years old, and she was dying.

So Jesus rose and went off with him, and so did his disciples. As Jesus was accompanying him, a great multitude followed and pressed in against him from every side.

Suddenly a woman who had had a chronic, continuing period for 12 years came up behind him. She had endured much under the care of many physicians, and had spent all that she had and was not helped at all. Rather she had gotten worse. She could not be helped by anyone.

She had heard the reports about Jesus, so she came up from behind through the crowd and touched the fringe of his cloak. For she kept thinking to herself, *If I just touch his garment, I shall be made well.*

Instantly her hemorrhaging stopped. The discharge of blood immediately ceased. And she felt in her body that she was healed of her suffering.

Immediately aware in himself that the power had gone out from him, Jesus swung around in the crowd and asked, **"Who is the one who touched My garments?"**

While all of them were denying it, Peter and his disciples responded: "Master, you see the crowds surrounding and pushing in on you from all sides! How can you ask, 'Who touched me?' "

But Jesus replied, **"Someone did touch me! For I was aware that power had gone out from me."**

Still he kept looking around to see who had done it.

But the woman, knowing what had happened to her, and realizing that she could not escape undetected, came and fell down before him. Trembling with fear, she told him the whole truth, declaring in the presence of all the people the reason why she had touched him, and how she had been immediately healed.

Then he turned to her, and looking at her said to her, **"Daughter, take courage. Your faith has made you well! Go in peace, and be continually healed of your suffering!"**

And from that hour the woman's health was completely restored.

While he was still speaking, someone from the house of the synagogue official arrived, saying, "Your daughter has died! Why trouble the teacher any further?"

Overhearing but ignoring what was being said, Jesus said to the synagogue official, **"Do not be afraid! Just keep believing and she will be made well!"**

Then he permitted no one to accompany him, except Peter and James, and John the brother of James, and the girl's father and mother. When they arrived at the house of the synagogue official, he observed a commotion — people loudly weeping and wailing, and mourning for her.

Then when he had entered the official's house, and saw the funeral musicians playing their flutes and the noisy commotion of the mourners, he said to them, **"Why make such a commotion and weep? Depart! The child has not died, but is asleep!"**

But they scoffed at him, knowing that she had died. So he put the crowd all outside, and took the child's father and mother and those who were with him, and went into the room where the child was. Then taking the child by the hand, he said to her, **"*Talitha koum!*"** which translated means, **"Little girl, I say to you arise!"**

Immediately her spirit returned and the girl got up and began walking around (for she was 12 years old). At this, her parents were utterly overcome with amazement! They were all completely astounded!

Then he told her parents that something should be given to her to eat. And he gave them all strict orders that no one should know about what had happened. And the news of this spread out through that entire district.

Matthew 9:18–26; Mark 5:21–43; Luke 8:40–56 [131]

HEALING THE BLIND AND THE MUTE

THEN AS JESUS WENT ON FROM THERE, two blind men followed him, loudly shouting, "Have pity and mercy on us, Son of David!"

And after he had entered the house, the blind men came up to him, and Jesus said to them, **"Do you believe that I am able to do this?"**

"Yes, Lord!" they replied to him.

Then he touched their eyes, saying, **"According to your faith, be it done to you!"**

And their eyes were opened — their sight was restored. Then Jesus sternly warned them, saying, **"See that no one knows about this!"**

But they went out and spread the news about him throughout that whole region.

As they were leaving, a demoniac who was mute was brought to him. Then as soon as the demon had been cast out, the one who had been mute spoke!

And the crowds marveled, exclaiming in amazement, "Never has anything like this been seen in Israel!"

But the Pharisees were saying, "By the ruling prince of the demons he casts out the demons."

Matthew 9:27–34

LAST VISIT TO NAZARETH

THEN HE DEPARTED FROM THERE with his disciples accompanying him, arriving in his hometown. And when the Sabbath had come, he began teaching them in their synagogue. And many who were listening were utterly astonished

"Where did this man acquire these things?" they were asking. "And what is this wisdom given to him? And such miraculous powers — these remarkable miracles performed by his hands! Is this not the carpenter — the carpenter's son? Is he not the son of she who is named Mary? Is he not the brother of James and

Joseph and Simon and Judas? And his sisters — are they not all here among us? Where then did this man get all these things?" So they took offense at him, unable to accept him.

Then Jesus said to them, **"A prophet is not without honor except in his home town and among his own relatives and his own house."**

So he could not do any miracles there because of their unbelief, except that he laid his hands upon a few sick people and healed them. And he was amazed at their unbelief.

Matthew 13:54–58; Mark 6:1–6

SEVENTEEN

SHORTAGE OF WORKERS

circa A.D. 28

THEN JESUS WENT ABOUT AMONG ALL THE CITIES AND THE VILLAGES, teaching in their synagogues, and proclaiming the good news of the kingdom, and curing every kind of disease and every kind of disability.

When he saw the vast crowds, he was deeply moved with compassion for them, because they were distressed and helpless, like sheep without a shepherd.

Then he said to his disciples, **"The harvest is abundant, but the laborers are few. Therefore, ask the Lord of the harvest to send out laborers into his harvest field."**

Matthew 9:35–38; Mark 6:6

COMMISSIONING THE TWELVE

THEN SUMMONING HIS TWELVE DISCIPLES TOGETHER TO HIM, Jesus began to send them out in pairs — two by two — giving them power and authority over all demons — to cast them out, and to cure diseases and every kind of infirmity. And he sent them out to proclaim the kingdom of God, and to perform healing.

Jesus sent these Twelve out after instructing them, saying, **"Go nowhere among the Gentiles, and do not enter any city of the Samaritans. But go rather to the lost sheep of the house of Israel. And preach as you go, saying, 'The kingdom of heaven is at hand!'**

"Heal the sick. Raise the dead. Cleanse lepers. Drive out demons.

"You received without paying. Give without charging.

"Take nothing for the journey, other than a staff as a walking stick. Take no bag, and no food. Take no gold nor silver nor copper in your money belts.

"Take the sandals you wear, but do not take additional sandals or a second tunic. For the worker is worth his support."

And he continued to say to them, **"Into whatever city or village you enter, search for who is worthy in it, and abide there. Whenever you enter a house, stay there until you leave town, and depart from there.**

"And as you enter the house, give it your greeting and wish it peace. If the house is deserving, let your greeting of peace come upon it. But if it is not deserving, let your greeting of peace return to you.

"If anyone or any place will not welcome you, or refuses to listen to your words, as you leave that house or town, shake the dust off the soles of your feet as a testimony against them. I guarantee you this truth: it will be more tolerable for the land of Sodom and Gomorrah in the Day of Judgment, than for that town.

"Pay close attention! I am sending you out like sheep into the midst of wolves. So be shrewd as serpents and innocent as doves.

"Be on your guard against them! For they will hand you over to the courts, and scourge you in their synagogues. Because of me, you will also be dragged before governors and kings as testimony to them and to the Gentiles.

"But when they arrest you and hand you over, do not worry about how you are to speak or what you are to say. For at that very moment what you are to say will be given to you. For it will not be you speaking, but the Spirit of your Father who will be speaking through you.

"Brother will betray brother to death, and a father his child. And children will rise up against parents and cause them to be put to death. You yourselves will be universally hated and persecuted because you bear my name. But the one who endures to the end will be saved.

"When they persecute you in one town, flee to the next. For I solemnly tell you the truth: You will not have finished going through the towns of Israel before the Son of Man comes.

"A disciple or student is not above his teacher, nor a slave or servant above his master. It is enough for the disciple to become like his teacher, and the slave like his master. If they have called the head of the house Beelzebub (that is, *Prince of Demons*), **how much more will they malign the members of his household!**

"So have no fear of them! For there is nothing concealed that will not be revealed, and nothing secret that will not become known. What I say to you in the dark, speak in the light; and what you hear whispered in your ear, proclaim from the housetops. And do not fear those who kill the body but are unable to kill the soul. But instead fear him who is able to destroy both body and soul in Gehenna (that is, the *Pit*, or *Hell*).

"Are not two sparrows sold for an *assarion* (that is, a penny)**? And yet not one of them will fall to the ground apart from your Father knowing. But even**

the very hairs of your head are all numbered. So do not be afraid! You are of more value than many sparrows.

"Everyone therefore who acknowledges me before others, I also will acknowledge before my Father in heaven. But whoever disowns me before others, I will also disown before my Father in heaven.

"Do not assume that I have come to bring peace upon the earth. I did not come to bring peace, but a sword!

> For I came to set a man against his father,
>   and a daughter against her mother,
>   and a daughter-in-law against her mother-in-law.
> And a person's enemies
>   will be the members of his own household.

"Whoever loves father or mother more than me is not worthy of me. And whoever loves son or daughter more than me is not worthy of me. And whoever does not take up his cross and follow after me is not worthy of me. Whoever finds his life shall lose it, and whoever loses his life for my sake shall find it.

"Whoever welcomes and receives you receives me. And whoever welcomes and receives me receives the one who sent me.

"Whoever receives a prophet because he is a prophet shall receive a prophet's reward. And whoever receives a righteous person because he is a righteous person shall receive a righteous person's reward. And whoever gives even a cup of cold water to one of these little ones because he is a disciple — I guarantee you this truth — will certainly not lose his reward."

Matthew 10:1–42; Mark 6:7–11; Luke 9:1–5

PROPHECY

Put no trust in a neighbor.
Have no confidence in a friend.
Even from her who lies in your embrace
    guard the words of your mouth.

For son treats the father with contempt,
    daughter rises up against her mother,
    daughter-in-law against her mother-in-law.
A man's enemies are the members of his own household.

But as for me,
    I will watch expectantly for the Lord.
    I will wait for the God of my salvation,
For my God will hear me.

Written by the prophet Micah, year c. 740 B.C.
Micah 7:5–7

THE DISCIPLES DEPUTIZED

NOW WHEN JESUS HAD FINISHED instructing his twelve disciples, he departed from there with them, to teach and to preach in their towns.

Then the Twelve began going out among the towns and villages, preaching the good news of the gospel, and proclaiming that all should repent and change the way they think and live.

They cast out many demons and anointed many sick people with oil, healing them everywhere they went.

Matthew 11:1; Mark 6:12–13; Luke 9:6

JESUS MISTAKEN FOR JOHN

NOW AT THAT TIME, KING HEROD THE TETRARCH heard reports about Jesus and all that was happening, for his name had become well known. Herod was deeply perplexed, for it was being rumored by some that John had risen from the dead.

Some, including Herod, were saying, "John the baptizer has risen from the dead, and that is why these miraculous powers are at work in him!"

But others were saying, "He is Elijah. Elijah has appeared."

Still others were saying, "He is a prophet, like one of the ancient prophets of long ago, arisen and come back to life."

So when Herod heard all of this, he kept saying to his servants, "This is John the baptizer! But I myself had John beheaded! So who is this man about whom I hear such things? Has John risen from the dead, and that is why miraculous powers are at work in him? He has not risen, has he?"

And he kept trying to see him.

Matthew 14:1–2; Mark 6:14–16; Luke 9:7–9

JOHN THE BAPTIZER BEHEADED

FOR IT WAS HEROD HIMSELF WHO HAD SENT MEN and had John arrested, and bound, and put in prison on account of Herodias, the wife of his brother Philip, because he had married her. For John had kept telling him, "It is not lawful for you to have your brother's wife!" And although Herod wanted to put him to death, he feared the people, because they regarded him as a prophet.

Herodias also harbored a grudge against him, and wanted to put him to death. But she could not do so because Herod feared John. Knowing that he was a righteous and holy man, Herod kept him under guard. When he heard him, he was extremely perplexed, yet he liked to listen to him.

But a strategic opportunity came when Herod, for his birthday celebration, gave a banquet for his courtiers and his commanding officers, and for the prominent leaders of Galilee. When the daughter of Herodias herself came in and danced for them, she pleased Herod and his dinner guests so much that he promised on an oath to grant her whatever she might ask.

The king said to the girl, "Ask me for whatever you desire, and I will grant it to you." And he solemnly swore under oath to her, "Whatever you ask of me, I will grant it to you, even up to half of my kingdom!"

Then she went out and asked her mother, "For what shall I ask?"

She replied, "The head of John the baptizer!"

Immediately she rushed back before the king and, having been prompted by her mother, made her request, saying, "I want you to give me here right now, on a platter, the head of John the baptizer!"

And although the king was deeply distressed, because of his oaths and because of his dinner guests he did not want to break his word by refusing her, so commanded it to be given.

Immediately the king sent an executioner with orders to bring John's head.

So he went and beheaded John in prison, and brought his head on a platter, and presented it to the girl. And the girl took it, and carried it to her mother.

Then, when his disciples heard about it, they came and took away his torso and buried it in a tomb. And they went and reported to Jesus.

Matthew 14:3–12; Mark 6:17–29

TRAINING THE TWELVE:

Lessons on Discipleship

4

Section Four

18

LESSONS ON THE BREAD OF LIFE

THE CAPERNAUM RETREAT

circa A.D. 28

NOW WHEN JESUS HEARD THIS, Jesus privately withdrew from there in a boat to a remote place on the other side of the Sea of Galilee (that is, the Sea of Tiberias).

The apostles had returned and gathered together with Jesus, and reported to him everything that they had done and taught. But because there were so many people that were constantly coming and going that they did not even have time to eat, he said to them, **"Come away by yourselves to a deserted place, and rest awhile."**

So taking them with him, he privately withdrew toward a town called Bethsaida. But when the crowds learned about it, they followed him.

Then they went away in a boat to a desolate place by themselves.

But many saw them departing, and recognized them. So hearing of this, the huge crowds followed him on foot, because they were seeing the miraculous signs which he was performing on those that were sick. The multitudes ran there together from all the towns, and arrived there ahead of them.

When he went ashore and saw the vast multitude, he felt compassion for them, for they were like sheep without a shepherd. So he welcomed them.

Then Jesus went up on the mountain, and there he sat with his disciples and began to teach them many things about the kingdom of God. And he cured their sick who had need of healing.

Now the Passover, the Festival of the Jews, was approaching.

Matthew 14:13–14; Mark 6:30–34; Luke 9:10–11; John 6:1–4

AS THE DAY BEGAN TO DECLINE and evening approached, when it was already quite late in the day, his disciples, the Twelve, came up to him and began saying, "This is a remote place here where we are, and it is already quite late. Send the crowds away so that they can go into the surrounding farms and villages, and find lodging and buy themselves something to eat."

But he responded and said to them, **"They do not need to go away. You give them something to eat!"**

When Jesus looked up and saw the vast crowd that had come to him, he said to Philip, **"Where are we to buy bread for these people to eat?"** He said this to test him, for he himself knew what he was going to do.

Philip answered him, "Two hundred *denarii* (a *denarius* being equivalent to a day's wage or one hundred dollars) worth of bread is not sufficient for them, even for every one to receive a little!"

Then they said to him, "Are we to go and spend two hundred *denarii* or twenty thousand dollars on bread and give it to them to eat?"

And he asked them, **"How many loaves do you have? Go and see!"**

When they found out, one of the disciples, Andrew, Simon Peter's brother, said to him, "There is a boy here who has five barley loaves and two fish. But what are they among so many people?"

Then they said to him, "We have no more than five loaves and two fish, unless perhaps we go and buy food for all this multitude!" (For there were about five thousand men there.)

"Bring them here to me!" he then responded.

"Have the people recline in groups of about 50 each," Jesus then directed his disciples.

Now there was a great amount of grass in that place. So the disciples did so, and had them all recline on the green grass in rows of hundreds and groups of fifties, in number about five thousand men alone.

Jesus then took the five loaves and the two fish and looking up toward heaven he gave thanks and blessed the food. Then he broke the loaves apart and kept giving them to the disciples to set before the multitudes who were seated. Likewise he also divided up the two fish and distributed them among them all as much as they all wanted. And they all ate, and were fully satisfied.

Then when they were all filled, he said to his disciples, **"Gather up the leftover pieces. Let nothing be wasted."**

So the broken pieces from the five barley loaves which were left over by those who had not eaten were all gathered up — 12 full baskets! And they also gathered up the fish.

There were about five thousand men who ate the loaves, not counting women and children.

When therefore the people saw the miraculous sign which he had performed, they said, "This most surely is the Prophet who is to come into the world!"

Matthew 14:15–21; Mark 6:35–44; Luke 9:12–17; John 6:5–14

PROPHECY

The Lord your God will raise up for you
    a prophet like me from among you,
    from among your own brothers.
You must listen to him!
Then the Lord said to me:

They are right in what they have spoken.
I will raise up for them a prophet like you
    from among their own brothers.
And I will put my words in his mouth;
    and he shall speak to them everything that I command him.

Written by the patriarch Moses, year c. 1500 B.C.
Deuteronomy 18:15, 17–18

The Crowds Dispersed

REALIZING THAT THEY WERE intending to come and take him by force to make him king, Jesus therefore withdrew again to the mountain, alone by himself.

So he quickly directed his disciples to get into the boat, and go on ahead of him across to the other side toward Bethsaida, while he himself was sending the vast crowd home. Then, after he had dispersed the multitude, and having said goodbye to them, he departed to the mountain by himself to pray. So when evening came, He was there alone.

Matthew 14:22–23; Mark 6:45–46; John 6:15

Jesus Walks on Water

NOW WHEN EVENING CAME, his disciples went down to the sea. Then after getting into the boat, they started to cross the sea to Capernaum. By now it had become dark, and Jesus had not yet rejoined them.

Then the sea began to churn and become rough, because a strong gale wind was blowing. Now by this time the boat was in the middle of the sea, already many *stadia* away from the land (a *stadia* being about two hundred yards), battered by the waves — for the wind was against them.

Jesus was alone on land, watching them straining at the oars against an adverse wind. Then when they had rowed about 25 or 30 *stadia* (about three and a half to four miles), at about the fourth watch of the night (the fourth watch being between three and six in the morning), he came to them. He was walking on the sea! It appeared that he was about to pass by them.

But when the disciples saw Jesus walking on the sea, and approaching the boat, they shrieked in fear, "It is a ghost!" For they had all seen him and were terrified.

But immediately Jesus spoke to them, and said, **"Have courage! I am here! Stop being afraid!"**

"Lord! If it is you," Peter shouted in response, "command me to come to you on the water!"

"Come!" he said.

Then Peter got out of the boat and started walking on the water toward Jesus. But when he noticed how strong the gale wind was, he panicked. Then, as he started to sink, he cried out, shouting, "Lord! Save me!"

Immediately Jesus stretched out his hand and caught hold of him. **"O you of little faith!"** he said to him. **"Why did you doubt?"**

The other disciples were now eager to take him into the boat. Then when they climbed into the boat with them, immediately the wind ceased. They were all utterly astounded, for they had not gained any insight about the significance of the loaves, because their hearts were callous.

Then those who were in the boat worshiped him, exclaiming, "Truly you are the Son of God!"

Immediately the boat reached the shore toward which they were heading.

Matthew 14:24–33; Mark 6:47–52; John 6:16–21

TRIUMPH AT GENNESARET

W HEN THEY HAD CROSSED OVER, they came to land at Gennesaret, and moored to the shore.

Then as soon as they got out of the boat, the men of that place immediately recognized him. Then the people scurried about the surrounding countryside, and sent word throughout the entire region, and began to carry the sick to him on mats, to whatever place they heard he was.

And wherever he went — into villages, or towns, or rural areas — they were laying the sick in the streets, and begging him to let them touch even the fringe of his cloak. And as many as touched it were completely cured.

Matthew 14:34–36; Mark 6:53–56

HE NEXT DAY THE CROWD THAT HAD STAYED BACK on the
other side of the sea realized that there had been only one small boat there,
and that Jesus had not gotten into it with his disciples, but that his disciples had
gone away alone.

Then several other small boats from Tiberias landed near the place where the
people had eaten the bread after the Lord had given thanks. So when the crowds
saw that neither Jesus nor his disciples were there, they themselves got into these
boats and went to Capernaum, looking for Jesus.

And when they found him on the other side of the sea, they asked him,
"Rabbi, when did you come here?"

Jesus replied to them and said:

> **I can most solemnly guarantee you this truth:**
>
> **You seek me**
> > **not because you saw miraculous signs,**
> > **but because you ate the loaves and were filled.**
>
> **Do not work for the food that perishes,**
> > **but for the food which endures to eternal life**
> > **which the Son of Man shall give to you.**
>
> **For it is on him that the Father, God himself, has set his seal.**

Then they asked him, "What must we do that we may work the works of
God?"

Jesus replied and said to them:

> **This is the work of God:**
> > **that you believe in the one whom he has sent!**

So they said to him, "Then what miraculous sign do you give us so that we
may see it and believe you? What supernatural work do you do? Our forefathers
ate the manna in the desert wilderness. As it is written, 'He gave them bread out of
heaven to eat.'"

Then Jesus said to them:

> **I can most solemnly guarantee you this truth:**
>
> **It was not Moses who has given you the bread out of heaven;**
> > **but it is my Father who gives you**
> > **the true bread out of heaven.**

**For the true bread of God is that which comes down out of heaven
and gives life to the world.**

"Sir," they then responded to him, "give us this bread forever!"
Jesus then declared to them:

**I am the bread of life!
Whoever comes to me shall never hunger.
And whoever believes in me shall never thirst.**

**But as I told you,
although you have seen me,
still you do not believe.**

**All whom the Father gives me
shall come to me
And whoever comes to me
I will most certainly never reject.**

**For I have come down from heaven,
not to do my own will,
but the will of him who sent me.**

**And this is the will of him who sent me:
That of all whom he has given me,
I should lose none,
but raise them up to eternal life on the last day.**

**For this is the will of my Father:
That all who behold the Son and believe in him
should have eternal life.
And I myself will raise them up on the last day.**

Then the leaders of the Jews began grumbling about him, because he said, **"I
am the bread that came down from heaven."** For they were saying, "Is not this
Jesus, the son of Joseph, whose father and mother we know? How can he now say,
'I have come down from heaven'?"

Stop grumbling among yourselves!

Jesus answered them in response.

**No one can come to me unless the Father
who sent me draws him —
and I will raise him up on the last day!**

It is written in the Prophets:
    "And they shall all be taught by God."

Everyone who has listened to the Father,
    and learned from him,
      comes to me.
Not that anyone has seen the Father,
    except the one who is from God.
Only he has seen the Father!

I most solemnly guarantee you this truth:
    Whoever believes has eternal life!

I am the bread of life!

Your forefathers ate the manna in the wilderness,
    yet they died.
This here is the bread which comes down from heaven,
    so that anyone may eat of it and never die.

I am the living bread
    that came down from heaven!
Anyone who eats this bread
    shall live forever.
What is more, this bread is my own flesh,
    which I shall give for the life of the world.

The Jewish leaders then began arguing angrily among themselves, saying, "How can this man give us his own flesh to eat?"

Jesus therefore responded to them:

I can most solemnly guarantee you this truth:

Unless you eat the flesh of the Son of Man,
    and drink his blood,
    you have no life within you!
Whoever eats my flesh and drinks my blood has eternal life,
    and I shall raise him up on the last day!

For my flesh is true food, and my blood is true drink.
Whoever eats my flesh and drinks my blood abides in me,
    and I in him.

Just as the living Father sent me,
    and I live because of the Father,

So whoever feeds on me
    shall also live because of me.

This is the bread which came down from heaven,
    unlike that manna which your forefathers ate, and died.
But whoever eats this bread
    shall live forever!

He said these things while he was teaching in the synagogue in Capernaum.

John 6:22–59

DISCIPLES DEFECT

MANY OF HIS DISCIPLES ON HEARING HIM then exclaimed, "What he is teaching is intolerable to accept! Who wants to listen to him anymore?"

But Jesus, aware that his disciples were complaining like this, asked them,

Does this offend you?
Then what if you should see the Son of Man
    ascending to where he was before?

It is the Spirit who gives life;
    the flesh contributes nothing!
The words that I have spoken to you
    are spirit and are life.
Yet there are some among you
    who still do not believe!

For Jesus knew from the beginning who were the ones that did not believe, and who it was who would betray him. So he continued, saying,

For this is the reason I have told you
    that no one can come to me
    unless it has been granted him by the Father.

As a consequence of this, many of his disciples turned back and no longer walked with him.

Jesus then asked the Twelve, **"You do not want to leave me as well, do you?"**

Simon Peter answered him, "Lord, to whom shall we go? You alone have the words of eternal life! We have come to believe and now know that you are the Holy One of God!"

Jesus responded to them, **"Did I myself not choose you, the Twelve? Yet one of you is a devil!"**

He was referring to Judas, the son of Simon Iscariot. For he, one of the Twelve, was going to betray him.

John 6:60–71

CHAPTER

NINETEEN

19

LESSONS ON LEAVEN

CEREMONIAL DEFILEMENT

circa A.D. 28–29

FTER THIS, JESUS TRAVELED ABOUT GALILEE, for he did not want to travel in Judea because the Jewish leaders there were looking for an opportunity to kill him.

Then some Pharisees and some of the scribes (the teachers of the religious Law) came from Jerusalem to interview Jesus. When they gathered together around him they observed that some of his disciples were eating their bread with defiled (that is ceremonially unwashed) hands.

(For the Pharisees, and in fact all the Jews, do not eat unless they ceremonially wash their hands, thus observing the traditions of the elders. When they come home from the marketplace, they do not eat unless they purify themselves. And there are also many other traditions that they have been taught to observe, such as the purification washing of cups, pitchers, copper utensils, and dining couches.)

So the Pharisees and the scribes questioned him. "Why do your disciples not walk according to the traditions of the elders?" they inquired. "For they break the tradition of the elders and do not ceremonially wash their hands before they eat, but eat their bread with defiled hands."

In response he replied to them,

> You hypocrites!
> Isaiah was correct when he prophesied about you,
>   when he said, as it is written:
>
> These people honor me with their lips,
>   but their hearts are far away from me.
> But in vain do they worship me,
>   teaching as doctrine their own man-made rules.

You abandon the commandments of God
   to cling to the traditions of men.

Then he continued saying to them,

You conveniently set aside the commandments of God
   in order to preserve your own traditions!
So why do you yourselves break the commandments of God
   for the sake of your own traditions?

For example, Moses spoke this from God:

   "Honor your father and your mother" and
   "Whoever reviles father or mother,
      let him be put to death."

But you say:

   Whoever shall say to father or mother,
   "Whatever support you may have received from me is *corban*"
   (that is to say, consecrated as a gift given to God),
   Then he is not obligated to honor his father nor his mother.

and you no longer permit him to do anything for father or mother!

Thus you have invalidated the word of God
   for the sake of protecting your own tradition
   which you have handed down.

And you observe many other similar practices such as that!

Matthew 15:1–9; Mark 7:1–13; John 7:1

Internal Defilement

THEN AFTER HE CALLED THE multitude to him again, he began saying to them,

Listen to me, every one of you, and understand!

There is nothing by going into the mouth from outside
   that defiles a person.
Rather, the things which come out of the mouth,
   that defiles a person.

Then the disciples came to him, and asked, "Do you realize that when the Pharisees heard what you said, they were offended?"

But he replied by saying,

> **Every plant that my Heavenly Father did not plant**
> **will be uprooted — pulled up by the roots!**
> **Leave them alone—**
> **they are the blind guides of the blind!**
> **And if a blind person leads a blind person,**
> **both will fall into a ditch.**

When he had left the multitude and had entered the house, his disciples questioned him about this parable. Then Peter asked him, "Explain the parable to us."

So then he asked, **"Are even you still lacking in understanding? Do you not comprehend that everything that goes into the mouth from outside cannot defile, because it does not go into the heart but passes into the stomach, and is eliminated into the toilet?"** (Thus he declared all foods ceremonially clean.)

Then he continued saying, **"But the things that come out of the mouth of the person come from the heart, and these defile the person. For it is out of the heart that come evil intentions, murder, adultery, all other sexual immorality, stealing, lying, malicious slander, greed, wickedness, deceit, lewdness, profanity, envy, arrogance, foolish recklessness. All these evil things come from within and defile the person. But to eat with unwashed hands does not defile the person."**

Matthew 15:10–20; Mark 7:14–23

Rewarding a Syrian Mother's Faith

THEN FROM THERE HE AROSE and departed, and withdrew to the region of Tyre and Sidon. There he entered a house. He wanted no one to know he was there. Yet he could not escape notice.

Instead, right away, after hearing about him, a woman from that area whose little daughter was possessed by an evil spirit immediately came and flung herself at his feet. Now the woman was a Gentile, a Canaanite, born in Phoenicia, in Syria. And she kept begging him to drive the demon out of her little daughter. She continued urgently crying out, "Have mercy on me, O Lord. Son of David! My daughter is possessed and cruelly tormented by a demon!"

But he did not answer her a word.

Then his disciples came to him and kept urging him, imploring, "Send her away, for she keeps following us and screaming out at us!"

But he replied in response, **"I was sent only to the lost sheep of the house of Israel."**

But she came and knelt before him, pleading, "Lord, help me!"

"Let the children be fed first," he began saying to her, **"for it is not right to take the children's bread and throw it to the dogs."**

But she responded by saying to him, "That is true, Lord, but even the dogs eat the children's crumbs that fall under the master's table."

Then Jesus responded and said to her, **"O woman, your faith is great! Let it be done for you as you wish! Because of this response, you may go your way. The demon has gone out of your daughter!"**

And her daughter was instantly healed — at that very moment! Then she returned home, found the little child lying on the bed, and the demon gone.

Matthew 15:21–28; Mark 7:24–30

Healing the Impaired

SOON AFTER THIS JESUS departed from there, from the region of Tyre, and went through Sidon towards the Sea of Galilee, in the region of the Decapolis, the ten cities. He passed along by the Sea of Galilee, then ascended into the mountain where he sat down.

And vast multitudes came to him, bringing with them those who were lame, disabled, blind, mute, and many others. They simply placed them at his feet, and he healed them, so that the crowd was amazed when they saw the mute speaking, the disabled restored, the lame walking, and the blind seeing. And they glorified the God of Israel.

Then they brought to him one who was deaf and had difficulty speaking, and they implored him to place his hands upon him.

He took him aside privately by himself, away from the crowd. Then he thrust his fingers in the man's ears, and after spitting on his own fingers, touched the man's tongue with his own saliva. Then looking up to heaven, he sighed deeply and said to the man, *"Ephphata!"* which means, **"Be opened!"**

Immediately the man's ears were opened, and the speech impediment of his tongue was released, and he began speaking distinctly.

Then he admonished them not to tell anyone. But the more he insisted, the more zealously they proclaimed it. They were utterly astonished, absolutely amazed beyond comprehension. "He has done everything excellently!" they kept repeating. "He even makes the deaf to hear and the mute to speak!"

Matthew 15:29–31; Mark 7:31–37

DURING THAT SAME TIME, when there was again a great multitude that had nothing to eat, Jesus summoned his disciples to him and said to them, **"I have great concern for all these people, because they have remained with me now for three days, and have nothing remaining to eat. And I do not want to send them away to their home hungry, for they may collapse on the way. For some of them have come from a distance."**

The disciples responded to him, "Where in this isolated, desolate place would we or anyone obtain so many loaves of bread to satisfy such a great multitude?"

"How many loaves do you have?" Jesus then asked them.

"Seven," they replied, "and a few small fish."

Then he directed the multitude to sit on the ground, and taking the seven loaves he gave thanks and broke them. Then he started handing them to his disciples to serve them, and they in turn kept serving them to the multitude.

Then he also took the few small fish, and after he had blessed them, he directed these to be distributed as well.

So all of them ate as much as they wanted, and they were all satisfied. Afterward, they collected seven large baskets full of the broken pieces that were left over.

Those that had eaten were four thousand men, besides women and children.

After this, he dismissed the multitude and sent them on their way to their homes.

Matthew 15:32–38; Mark 8:1–9

DEMAND FOR MIRACULOUS PROOF DENIED

AFTER DISMISSING THE MULTITUDE, he immediately got into the boat with his disciples, and went to the district of Dalmanutha, or Magadan (also known as Magdala).

Then the Pharisees and Sadducees came up to him and began to argue with him to test him, demanding him to show them a spectacular sign from heaven.

But sighing deeply in his Spirit, he responded by saying to them,

> **When it is evening, you say,**
> > **"It will be fair weather, for the sky is red."**
> **And in the morning,**
> > **"It will be stormy today, for the sky is red and angry."**

> Do you know how to interpret the appearance of the sky,
>> but you cannot interpret the obvious signs of the times?
>
> Why does this generation want a sign?
>> An evil and adulterous generation asks for a sign!
> I can guarantee you this truth:
> No sign will be given to this generation
>> — except the sign of Jonah!

Then he left them and went away.

Matthew 15:39–16:4; Mark 8:10–12

ADMONITION AGAINST HYPOCRISY

HE GOT BACK INTO THE BOAT AGAIN and crossed to the other side. When the disciples reached the other side, they had forgotten to bring any bread, and had no more than one loaf with them in the boat.

In the meantime, as the multitude began gathering together by the many thousands so that they were trampling on one another, Jesus began addressing his own disciples first. Cautioning them, he began by saying to them, **"Be on the alert! Guard against the yeast of the Pharisees and Sadducees, and the yeast of Herod and the Herodians!"** (That is, guard against their hypocrisy — their sheer phoniness!)

Then they began to deliberate among themselves, concluding, "It is because we did not bring any bread!"

But Jesus, aware of their debate, asked, **"Why are you deliberating among yourselves about having no bread? You little faiths! Do you not yet perceive or comprehend? Are your hearts so hardened? Having eyes, do you not see? And having ears, do you not hear? And do you not remember, when I broke the five loaves for the five thousand, how many small hand baskets of left over broken pieces you collected?"**

They answered him, "Twelve."

"Or when I broke the seven loaves for the four thousand, how many large provision baskets of left over broken pieces did you gather?"

And they responded, "Seven."

Then he kept repeating to them, **"Do you not yet understand! Do you still not comprehend! How do you fail to understand that I was not speaking to you about bread? But what I said was, 'Be on constant guard against the yeast of the Pharisees and Sadducees!'**

"But there is nothing concealed that will not be revealed, nor secretly hidden that will not be publicly exposed. Accordingly, whatever you have said in

the dark shall be heard in the daylight, and what you have whispered in the private rooms shall be broadcast from the housetops."

Then they grasped that he had not told them to beware of the yeast of bread, but of the teaching of the Pharisees and Sadducees.

Matthew 16:5–12; Mark 8:13–21; Luke 12:1–3

PROPHECY

And he said,

>Go, and tell this people:
>
>"Keep listening, but do not perceive;
>Keep looking, but do not understand."
>
>Render the hearts of this people calloused,
>>and their ears dull,
>>and their eyes dim.
>Otherwise they might see with their eyes,
>>and hear with their ears,
>>and understand with their hearts,
>And return and be healed.

Recorded by the prophet Isaiah, year c. 700 B.C.
Isaiah 6:9–10

PROPHECY

Declare this in the house of Jacob
and proclaim it in Judah, saying,

>"Hear this, you foolish and senseless people,
>>who have eyes, but do not see;
>>and have ears, but do not hear."
>"Do you not fear me?" demands the Lord.
>"Do you not tremble in my presence?"

Recorded by the prophet Jeremiah, year c. 600 B.C.
Jeremiah 5:20–22

PROPHECY

Then the word of the Lord came to me, saying,

>Son of man, you live in the midst of a rebellious house,
>>who have eyes to see but do not see,
>>who have ears to hear but do not hear;
>For they are a rebellious house.

Recorded by the prophet Ezekiel, year c. 575 B.C.
Ezekiel 12:1–2

LESSONS ON LEAVEN

Admonition to Fear God Only

I GUARANTEE YOU, MY FRIENDS," Jesus continued addressing his own disciples, **"do not be afraid of those who kill the body, and after that have nothing more that they can do. But I will warn you whom to fear. Fear the only one who after he has killed the body has authority to cast into hell. Gehenna! Yes, I admonish you, fear him! He is the only one to fear!**

"Are not five sparrows sold for two *assaria*? (An *assaria* is equivalent to a penny or a cent.) **And yet not one of them is forgotten before God. Indeed, even the very hairs of your head are all counted. Do not be afraid. You are of more value than a whole flock of sparrows.**

"I personally guarantee you, everyone who openly acknowledges me here before others, the Son of Man will also acknowledge before the angels of God. But anyone who publicly denies me before others shall be denied before the angels of God! And everyone who speaks a word against the Son of Man shall be forgiven. But the person who slanders against the Holy Spirit, it shall not be forgiven him.

"Now when they bring you on trial before the synagogues, and the rulers, and the authorities, do not be anxious about how or when you are to defend yourselves, or what you are to say in your defense. For the Holy Spirit will instruct you, at that very hour, what you ought to say."

Luke 12:4–12

Admonition against Materialism

J UST THEN SOMEONE IN THE CROWD spoke to him, "Teacher, tell my brother to divide the family inheritance with me!"

But he replied to him, **"Friend, who appointed me a judge or arbiter between you?"**

Then he spoke to them all:

> **Beware, and be on your defense**
> **against every form of greed.**
> **For one's life does not consist**
> **in the abundance of his possessions!**

Then he told them all a parable. This is what he said:

> **The land of a certain rich man produced abundantly.**
> **And he began reasoning within himself,**

"What should I do?
    For I have no place to store my crops!"
Then he thought,
"This is what I will do:
I will tear down my barns and build bigger ones.
And there I will store my grain and my surplus goods.
And I will say to my soul:
    'Soul, you have ample goods laid up for many years to come.
    Take it easy. Relax. Eat, drink, and enjoy yourself!' "

But God said to him:
    "You fool!
    This very night your soul is being demanded of you!
    So now who will own what you have accumulated for yourself?"

So it is with anyone who piles up possessions for himself,
    and is not rich toward God.

Luke 12:13–21

HEALING THE BLIND AT BETHSAIDA

T HEN THEY WENT TO BETHSAIDA. And some people brought a blind man to him, and begged him to touch him. Then taking the blind man by the hand, he led him outside the village. After putting his saliva on the man's eyes and laying his hands upon him, he asked him, **"Do you see anything?"**

Then the man looked up and replied, "I can see people. But they look like trees walking around!"

Then he laid his hand upon the man's eyes once again. Then the man focused intently, and his sight was fully restored, and he could see everything clearly.

Then he sent him away to his home, telling him, **"Do not even enter the village!"**

Mark 8:22–26

PETER'S PROCLAMATION: JESUS IS THE MESSIAH

circa A.D. 29

NOW JESUS ALONG WITH HIS DISCIPLES continued on, and came into the villages in the district of Caesarea Philippi.

Once on the way, while he was praying in private with only his disciples with him, he questioned them, asking, **"Who do people say that the Son of Man is? Who do the multitudes say that I am?"**

So they replied, "Some say John, the baptizer. Others, Elijah. But still others, Jeremiah, or one of the other prophets — that one of the ancient prophets has come back to life."

"But what about you?" he pressed them. **"Who do you yourselves say I am?"**

Then Simon Peter replied, "You are the Messiah of God — the Christ — the Son of the living God!"

"Blessed are you, Simon Bar-Jonah!" Jesus responded. Then he continued saying to him, **"For flesh and blood has not revealed this to you, but my Father who is in heaven. And I also tell you that you are now *Petros* — Peter the rock! And upon this *petra* — this huge rock — I will build my church. And the gates of hades shall not overpower it!**

"I will give you the keys of the kingdom of heaven. So whatever you shall lock on earth shall have been locked in heaven. And whatever you shall free on earth shall have been freed in heaven."

Then he sternly warned and instructed the disciples that they should tell no one that he was Christ — the Messiah.

Matthew 16:13–20; Mark 8:27–30; Luke 9:18–20

Jesus' First Prediction:
Rejection, Crucifixion, and Resurrection

FROM THAT TIME ONWARD, Jesus began to inform his disciples, saying that **"The Son of Man must go to Jerusalem and undergo great suffering of many forms at the hands of the elders, and the ruling priests, and the scribes** (the teachers of the religious Law). **He must be rejected by them, and be killed, and after three days be raised up again and brought back to life."**

He was clearly explaining all of this openly to them all. Then Peter took him aside, and privately began to rebuke him. "Never, Lord! God forbid it!" Peter said. "This must never happen to you!"

But turning around and seeing his disciples, Jesus sternly rebuked Peter. **"Get behind me, Satan!"** Jesus said to him. **"You are a stumbling block — an obstacle to me! For you are not focusing your mind on God's perspective, but on man's."**

Then Jesus summoned the multitude along with his disciples, and addressed them all:

> **If anyone wishes to follow after me,**
>   **let him deny himself,**
>   **and take up his cross,**
>   **and carry it daily,**
>   **and then follow me.**
> **For whoever wants to save his life**
>   **will lose it.**
> **But whoever loses his life for my sake and for the gospel,**
>   **he is the one who will find his life**
>   **and save it.**
> **For what does it profit a man**
>   **to gain the whole world**
>   **and in the process lose his life — his very soul?**
> **Or what will a man offer in exchange to buy back his soul?**

Matthew 16:21–26; Mark 8:31–37; Luke 9:21–25

Jesus' Promise: The Coming Kingdom of the Son of Man

THEN HE CONTINUED SAYING TO THEM:

> For whoever is ashamed of me and my words
>> in this unfaithful adulterous and sinful generation,
> Of him the Son of Man will also be ashamed
>> when he comes in his own majestic glory,
>> and in the glory of his Father and the holy angels.
>
> For the Son of Man is going to come with his angels,
>> in the majestic glory of his Father,
> And then he will repay everyone
>> according to what he has done.
>
> But I solemnly guarantee you this truth:
> There are some of you who are standing here
>> who shall not taste death
>> before they see the Son of Man coming in his kingdom.
> For they shall see the kingdom of God
>> come with great power!

Matthew 16:27–28; Mark 8:38–9:1; Luke 9:26–27

Jesus' Transfiguration: The Chosen One, the Beloved Son of God

AFTER THESE TEACHINGS, about six or eight days later, Jesus took Peter and James, and his brother John with him, and led them up to a high mountain by themselves to be alone, to pray. And there he was transfigured in front of them!

While he was praying, the appearance of his face became changed. His face shone as bright as the sun, and his garments became radiant, and gleaming, and dazzling — extremely white as a flash of lightning — as no bleach on earth could whiten them!

Just then, suddenly they saw two men — Moses and Elijah, who appeared before them in glorious splendor, were talking with Jesus! They were speaking of his departure, which he was about to accomplish at Jerusalem.

Now Peter and his companions had been overcome with a deep sleep. But when they became fully awake, they saw his glory and the two men who were standing with him.

Then it occurred, that just as these men were departing from him, Peter reacted by blurting to Jesus, "Master, it is wonderful for us to be here! Lord, if you wish, we will erect three tabernacle shelters here — one for you, one for Moses, and one for Elijah." (He did not realize what he was saying, for he did not know how to respond. They had all become so very frightened!)

Then, while he was still babbling, suddenly a radiant cloud formed and began to envelope them. And they were terrified as they entered the cloud.

Then a voice came from out of the cloud, saying,

> **This is my Son**
>> **whom I love, my Chosen One.**
>> **with him I am very pleased!**
> **Always listen to him!**

Then when the disciples heard this, they were terrified, and fell flat on their faces! But Jesus came over and touched them, and began saying, **"Rise up! And do not be afraid!"**

When they then immediately looked up, they saw no one with them anymore, except Jesus himself, alone. For when the voice had spoken, Jesus was found alone.

Matthew 17:1–8; Mark 9:2–8; Luke 9:28–36

> **Behold, he is my servant,**
>> **whom I uphold;**
> **My Chosen One,**
>> **in whom my soul delights,**
>> **with whom I am very pleased.**
> **I have put my Spirit upon him.**

Recorded by the prophet Isaiah, year c. 700 B.C.
Isaiah 42:1

JESUS' DESCENT: THE RETURN OF ELIJAH AND THE SUFFERING OF MESSIAH

THEN, AS THEY WERE DESCENDING FROM THE MOUNTAIN, Jesus gave them strict orders, admonishing them, **"Tell no one about the vision that you have seen until the Son of Man has risen from the dead!"**

So they carefully kept the matter to themselves, and related to no one in those days any of the things which they had seen, debating among themselves however what "risen from the dead" might mean.

Then his disciples asked him, "Why then do the scribes, the teachers of the religious Law, say that first Elijah must come?"

And he replied to them by telling them, **"Elijah indeed must come first, and restore everything in order again. Yet why is it written of the Son of Man, that he must suffer many grievous things, and be treated with contempt and be rejected? But I guarantee you that Elijah has in reality already come, and they did not recognize him. On the contrary, they did to him whatever they wanted, just as it is written of him. So also the Son of Man is certainly about to suffer at their hands."**

Then the disciples comprehended that He was speaking to them about John, the baptizer.

Matthew 17:9–13; Mark 9:9–13; Luke 9:36

163

PROPHECY

Behold, I will send you Elijah the prophet
before the great and terrifying Day of the Lord comes.
And he will restore the hearts of the fathers to their children,
and the hearts of the children to their fathers,
Lest I come and smite the land with a curse of utter destruction.

Recorded by the prophet Malachi, year c. 400 B.C.
Malachi 4:5–6

PROPHECY

He was despised and rejected by others,
a man of sorrows and acquainted with suffering.
Like one from whom men avert their gaze,
we despised him
and we gave him no esteem.

Written by the prophet Isaiah, year c. 700 B.C.
Isaiah 53:3

HEALING THE DEMONIC BOY: UNBELIEF REBUKED

circa A.D. 29

N OW IT OCCURRED ON THE NEXT DAY, when they had descended from the mountain, they came to the other disciples. There they saw a huge crowd around the other disciples, and scribes (those teachers of the religious Law) disputing with them. They approached the crowd.

Then immediately, as soon as the entire crowd saw him, they were overcome with awe, and began running up to greet him and meet him.

"What are you disputing with them?" he asked them.

Just then a man from the crowd approached him, and falling on his knees before him, cried out in response. The man answered him, saying, "Master, I beg you to look at my son, for he is my only child, and I have brought him to you. Please take pity on him, for he is an epileptic, and suffers seizures severely.

"My son is possessed with a spirit which makes him mute. Often when without warning it possesses him, he suddenly shrieks, and it throws him into a convulsion. And whenever it seizes him, it dashes him down to the ground, and he foams at the mouth and grinds his teeth, and becomes rigid. Often he falls into the fire, and as often into the water. It is destroying him, and will scarcely leave him.

"And I brought him to your disciples, and begged your disciples to cast it out, and cure him. But they could not."

Then Jesus answered him by replying,

> **You unbelieving and thoroughly perverted generation!**
> **How much longer must I be with you?**
> **How much longer must I endure you?**
> **Bring your son here to me!**

So they brought the boy to him. And even while the boy was approaching, when the demon spirit saw Jesus, it immediately threw the boy to the ground into a convulsion. Falling to the ground, the boy began writhing around, and foaming at the mouth.

"How long has this been happening to him?" Jesus then asked the father.

"From childhood," he replied. "It has often thrown him into the fire and into the water, intending to destroy him. But if you are able do anything, have pity on us and help us!"

"If *you* are able?" Jesus responded to him. **"All things are possible to him who believes!"**

Immediately the boy's father cried out, "I do believe! Help my unbelief!"

As the boy was approaching, Jesus, on seeing a crowd rapidly gathering, rebuked the unclean demon spirit. **"You deaf and mute spirit,"** he said, **"I command you: Come out of him and never enter him again!"**

And after shrieking, and hurling the boy to the ground into violent convulsions, the demon spirit came out. Then the boy became so much like a corpse that most exclaimed, "He is dead!"

But Jesus took him by the hand, and began raising him. And he got up, and was able to stand! Instantly, from that moment, the boy was cured!

Jesus, having healed the boy, gave him back to his father. And they were all astounded at the great majesty of God!

After they had gone indoors, into the house, his disciples privately approached Jesus and began asking him, "Why could we not cast it out?"

Then he responded to them, **"Because of the littleness of your faith! For this truth I guarantee you: If you have faith the size of a mustard seed, you shall say to this mountain, 'Move from here to there' and it shall move! And nothing will be impossible to you!**

"But this kind cannot be driven out by anything but prayer!"

Matthew 17:14–21; Mark 9:14–29; Luke 9:37–43

JESUS' SECOND PREDICTION: DEATH AND RESURRECTION

WHILE EVERYONE WAS MARVELING at all that he was doing, they left from there and traveled through Galilee. But he was unwilling for anyone to know about it, because he was instructing his own disciples.

As they were traveling together in Galilee, Jesus told his disciples, **"Let these words sink into your ears: For the Son of Man is about to be betrayed and** delivered into the hands of men. And they will kill him. And three days after he has been killed, he will rise again. He will be raised alive on the third day!"

Then they were deeply grieved. But they did not totally comprehend what he was saying, its full significance being concealed from them so that they could not grasp it. But they were afraid to ask him about it.

Matthew 17:22–23; Mark 9:30–32; Luke 9:43–45

JESUS' CONTRIBUTION: PAYMENT OF THE TEMPLE TAX

WHEN THEY ARRIVED IN CAPERNAUM, the collectors of the *double-drachmas* (temple tax, the equivalent of two *denarii* or about two hundred dollars), came to Peter and asked, "Does your teacher not pay the *double-drachmas?*"

"Certainly he does!" he replied.

Then when he entered the house, Jesus was first to speak. **"What do you think, Simon?"** he asked. **"From whom do the kings of the earth collect tariffs or tribute tax — from their own sons, or from others?"**

When Peter responded "from others," Jesus said to him, **"Consequently, the sons are exempt!**

"However, so that we may not give offense to them, go to the Sea and cast a fishhook. Take the first fish that comes up, and when you open its mouth, you will find a *stater* (worth four *drachmas*). **Take that and give it to them, for me — and for you!"**

Matthew 17:24–27

THE DISCIPLES' CONTENTION: THE GREATEST IN THE KINGDOM

THEN THEY CAME TO CAPERNAUM, and a dispute arose among them as to which one of them was the greatest.

When Jesus was in the house, he began questioning them, **"What were you arguing about on the way?"** For Jesus perceived what they were thinking in their hearts.

But they remained silent.

Later on the same occasion, the disciples approached Jesus and asked, "Who, then, is the greatest in the kingdom of heaven?"

Then sitting down, he called the Twelve and said to them, **"If anyone wants to be first, he must be last of all, and servant of all."**

Then he called a small child over to himself, whom he took and stood by his side among them. Then wrapping the child in his arms, he said to them, **"I guarantee you this truth: Unless you repent and change, and become like little children, you will never enter the kingdom of heaven!**

"Whoever therefore will become humble — like this child — is the greatest in the kingdom of heaven. And whoever embraces and accepts one such child in my name embraces and accepts me; and whoever embraces and receives me does not embrace and receive me only, but the one who sent me.

"For whoever is least among you, that is the one who is the greatest!"

Matthew 18:1–5; Mark 9:33–37; Luke 9:46–48

JESUS' ADMONITION: ANYONE NOT AGAINST US IS FOR US

MASTER, WE SAW SOMEONE DRIVING out demons, using your name," John responded, interrupting him, "and we attempted to prevent him, because he does not follow along with us. He is not one of us!"

But Jesus replied by saying, **"Do not prevent him. For no one who performs a miraculous work in my name can in the next instant speak evil of me. For whoever is not against us is for us. He is one of us!**

"Whoever gives you a cup of water to drink because of your reputation as followers of Messiah, the Christ, I can guarantee you shall certainly never lose his reward.

"But whoever causes one of these little ones — who believe in me — to stumble and sin, it would be better for him that, with a great millstone hung around his neck, he be thrown into the depth of the sea and drowned!

"Woe to the world because of its stumbling blocks! For it is inevitable that occasions of stumbling come: But woe to that person through whom the stumbling block comes!

"And if your hand causes you to stumble, cut it off and throw it away from you! For it is better for you to enter life maimed than, having two hands, to enter into the unquenchable fire of hell!

"And if your foot causes you to stumble, cut it off and throw it away from you! For it is better for you to enter life crippled than, having two feet, to be hurled into the eternal fire of hell!

"And if your eye causes you to stumble, gouge it out and throw it away from you! It is better for you to enter the kingdom of God with one eye than, having two eyes, to be cast into the hell fire of Gehenna where

> their worm does not die,
> and the fire is not quenched.

"For everyone will be salted with fire. Salt is beneficial, but if the salt has lost its saltiness with what will you make it salty again? Have salt within yourselves, and preserve peace with one another.

"Take care that you do not despise a single one of these little ones. For I say to you that in heaven their angels are continually in the presence and looking upon the face of my Father, who is in heaven.

"What do you think? If a man owns a hundred sheep, and one of them wanders away, does he not leave the ninety-nine on the mountains and go and search for the one that is straying? And if it turns out that he finds it, I guarantee you this truth: He rejoices over it more than over the ninety-nine that never strayed!

"So in just the same way, it is not the will of your Father in heaven that a single one of these little ones should be lost."

Matthew 18:6–14; Mark 9:38–50; Luke 9:49–50

PROPHECY

For just as the new heavens and the new earth,
    which I will make,
    shall endure before me,
declares the Lord,

So your descendents and your name
    shall endure.
From new moon to new moon
    and from sabbath to sabbath,
All mankind will come to worship before me,
says the Lord.

Then they shall go out and look on the corpses of those
    who have rebelled against me.
For their worm shall not die,
And their fire shall not be quenched;
    and they shall be abhorrent to all mankind.

Recorded by the prophet Isaiah, year c. 700 B.C.
Isaiah 66:22–24

Dealing with Sin against You: There I am in Your Midst

IF YOUR BROTHER SINS AGAINST YOU, go and show him his fault when the two of you are alone, in private. If he listens to you, you have won back your brother.

"But if he does not listen, take one or two others along with you, so that 'by the evidence of two or three witnesses every fact may be verified.'

"If he refuses to listen to them, tell it to the church community. And if he refuses to listen even to the church, let him be to you as a heathen Gentile and a tax collector.

"I guarantee you this: Whatever you prohibit on earth must be already prohibited in heaven; and whatever you permit on earth must be already permitted in heaven.

"Again I guarantee you: That if two of you on earth agree about anything that they may ask in prayer, it shall be accepted for them by my Father who is in heaven. Because where two or three have gathered together in my name, there I am in the midst of them."

Matthew 18:15–20

PROPHECY

A single witness shall not suffice to convict a person
   on account of any crime or any offense
   which he may have committed.
Only on the evidence of two or three witnesses
   shall a charge be sustained.

Written by the patriarch Moses, year c. 1500 B.C.
Deuteronomy 19:15

Forgiveness: The Parable of the Contemptible Slave

THEN PETER APPROACHED HIM AND ASKED, "Lord, how often could my brother sin against me and I must forgive him? Up to seven times?"

"I do not tell you up to seven times," Jesus responded, "but up to seventy times seven!

"For this reason the kingdom of heaven may be compared to a certain king who wished to settle accounts with his bondservants and his slaves. And when he had begun the accounting, a person was brought to him who owed him ten thousand *talents* (a *talent* being equivalent to 20 years' wages), **or about ten million dollars!** But because he could not repay, his master commanded him to be sold, along with his wife and his children and everything that he possessed, and repayment of the debt be made.

"At this, the bondservant fell on his knees before him, imploring, 'Have patience with me, and I will repay you everything!' And the master of that slave felt compassion, and released him, and forgave the debt.

"But when that same slave went out, he found one of his fellow slaves who owed him a hundred *denarii* (a *denarius* being equivalent to one day's wage), **or about ten thousand dollars.** He seized him by the throat and began to choke him. 'Pay back what you owe me!' he demanded.

"At this, his fellow slave fell down on his knees and pleaded with him, 'Have patience with me and I will repay you!' But he refused. On the contrary, he went out and had the man thrown into prison until he could repay the debt that he owed.

"So when his fellow slaves saw what had happened, they were deeply distressed, and went and reported to their master everything that had happened. The master then summoned him. 'You contemptible wicked slave!' he said to him. 'I forgave you that entire huge debt of yours because you pleaded with me. Should you not have had mercy on your fellow slave, just as I had mercy on you?'

"Then his master, moved with anger, handed him over to the jailers — the 'torturers' — until he would pay the entire debt that he owed him. So shall my Heavenly Father also do to every one of you, if each of you does not forgive your brother from your heart."

Matthew 18:21-35

LESSONS ON COMMITMENT

TWENTY-TWO

LISTEN FOR THE LORD'S TIMING: REJECTING BROTHERLY ADVICE

circa A.D. 29

OW THE FEAST OF THE JEWS, the Festival of Booths (also known as the Feast of Tabernacles), was drawing near. So his brothers said to him, "You ought to leave here and go into Judea, so that your disciples there may also see the marvelous works that you are doing. For no one does anything in secret when he wants to be publicly known. Since you are doing these things, show yourself openly to the world!" For even his own brothers were not believing him.

In response Jesus said to them, **"My time has not yet come, but your time is always right. The world cannot hate you, but it hates me because I testify against it that its works are evil.**

"You go up to the festival yourselves. I am not publicly going up to the festival right now, because my time has not yet fully come." After saying these things to them, he remained in Galilee.

John 7:2–9

LOOK FOR THE LORD'S DIRECTION: REJECTION IN SAMARIA

OW HOWEVER, SINCE THE DAYS WERE APPROACHING for him to be taken up in his ascension, after his brothers had gone up to the festival, then he also left, resolutely setting his face to go to Jerusalem. But he went, not publicly, but as it were privately.

And he sent messengers on ahead of him. As they went on their way, they entered a village of the Samaritans to make preparations for him. But the people did not welcome him, because he was journeying with his face set toward Jerusalem.

Then when his disciples James and John saw this, they said, "Lord, do you want us to command fire to come down fom heaven and consume them?"

But he turned and rebuked them. **"Do you not know of what kind of Spirit you are?"** he challenged them. **"For the Son of Man has not come to destroy people's lives, but to save them!"**

Then they journeyed on to another village.

Luke 9:51–56; John 7:10

COUNT THE COST OF COMPLETE COMMITMENT: TRUE TOTAL DISCIPLESHIP

AS THEY WERE GOING ALONG the road, someone — a scribe — came up to him and said to him, "Teacher, I will follow you wherever you go!"

"The foxes have dens, and the birds of the sky have nests," Jesus then replied to him, **"but the Son of Man has nowhere to lay his head."**

And to another he said, **"Follow me!"** But that disciple responded, "Lord, first let me go and care for until death and then bury my father." But Jesus said to him, **"Let the dead bury their own dead. But as for you, go and proclaim everywhere the kingdom of God."**

Still another offered, "I will follow you, Lord. But first let me go back and say goodbye to my family at home." But Jesus responded to him, **"No one, once he puts his hand to the plow and then keeps looking back at what he has left behind, is fit for the kingdom of God."**

Matthew 8:19–22; Luke 9:57–62

MESSIAH'S FINAL MISSIONS:

THE JUDEAN AND PEREAN MINISTRIES

5

SECTION FIVE

TWENTY-THREE

THE FEAST OF TABERNACLES: JESUS TEACHES AT THE TEMPLE

circa A.D. 29

NOW AT THE FESTIVAL, the Jews — the religious leaders — were looking for him. "Where is he?" they were inquiring.

Among the crowds there was considerable controversy. "He is a wonderful man," some were whispering. Others countered, "No, on the contrary, he is deceiving the people." Yet no one would dare to speak openly about him for fear of the Jewish leaders.

Now when the festival was already half over, Jesus went up into the temple courtyard and began to teach. The Jewish leaders were astonished. "How does this man have such learning," they therefore questioned, "when he has never studied?"

Then in response, Jesus answered them:

> **My teaching is not my own,**
> > **but it is from him who sent me.**
> **If anyone purposes to do God's will,**
> > **he will know if the teaching is from God,**
> > **or whether I am speaking from my own authority.**
> **Anyone who speaks from his own authority**
> > **seeks his own glory.**
> **But whoever seeks the glory of the one who sent him,**
> > **he is a man of truth,**
> > **and there is no dishonesty in him.**
> **Did Moses not give you the Law?**
> > **and yet not one of you is keeping the Law!**
> **Otherwise, why are you seeking for an opportunity to kill me?**

"You are possessed by a demon!" the crowd responded. "Who is seeking to kill you?"

Jesus answered them by replying:

> I performed one work,
>> and you are all astonished because of it.
> Well then, Moses has given you circumcision —
>> though it did not originate from Moses,
>> but from the previous patriarchs —
>> and on a sabbath you circumcise a man.
>
> If a man receives circumcision on a sabbath
>> in order that the law of Moses may not be broken,
> Why are you angry with me
>> because I healed a man's entire body on a sabbath?
> Do not judge according to outward superficial appearances,
>> but judge with discerning judgment.

Then at that point some of the people of Jerusalem began asking among themselves, "Is this not the man they are seeking to kill? Just look! Here he is, speaking publicly, and they are saying nothing to him! Could it be possible that the authorities have really concluded that this is the Messiah? Yet we know where this man originates. But when the Messiah appears, no one will know where he originates."

Then Jesus, still teaching in the temple courtyard, cried out, saying,

> You both know me,
>> and you also know where I originate,
>> do you?
> Yet I have not come of my own accord,
>> but the one who is true sent me,
>> and him you do not know!
> I know him,
>> because I am from him,
>> and it was he who sent me.

Then, at this, they began attempting to seize and arrest him. But no one laid a hand on him, because his time had not yet come. Still, many in the crowd believed in him, and kept saying, "When the Messiah shall come, he will not perform more miraculous signs than this man has, will he?"

The Pharisees heard the crowd whispering such things about him. Then the ruling priests and the Pharisees sent temple guards to seize and arrest him.

Jesus therefore responded,

> **I am with you for a little while longer,**
>> **then I am returning to him who sent me.**
>
> **You will look for me,**
>> **but you will not find me.**
>
> **And where I am,**
>> **you cannot come!**

Then the ruling Jews said to one another, "Where does this man intend to go that we will not find him? Surely he does not intend to go to the Dispersion among the Greeks, and teach the Greeks, does he? What does this statement that he made mean, 'You will look for me but you will not find me, and where I am you cannot come'?"

Now on the last day, the greatest day of the festival, as Jesus was standing there in the temple courtyard, he cried out in a loud voice:

> **If any man is thirsty,**
>> **let him come to me and drink!**
>
> **He who believes in me, as the Scriptures said,**
> **"From within his innermost being**
>> **shall flow rivers of living water."**

(But by this he was speaking of the Spirit, whom those who believed in him were later to receive. For at that time, the Spirit was not yet given, because Jesus was not yet glorified.)

As a result, when they heard those words, some in the crowd were saying, "Surely this man is the prophet!" Others were saying, "He is the Messiah!" Still others were questioning, "Surely the Messiah does not come from Galilee, does he? Has not the Scripture said that the Messiah descends from the offspring of David, and comes from Bethlehem, the village where David lived?"

So there arose a division in the crowd because of him. And some of them wanted to arrest him, but no one laid a hand on him.

The temple guards then returned to the ruling priests and Pharisees, who demanded of them, "Why did you not bring him in?"

"Never did a man speak the way this man does!" the guards declared.

"Surely, you have not also been deceived, have you?" the Pharisees therefore retorted. "Has any one of the authorities or the Pharisees believed in him? No! But this rabble crowd, which does not know the Law, they are damned anyway!"

Nicodemus, who had previously gone to him, and was one of them, challenged them, "Our Law does not pass judgment on a man unless it first gives him a hearing and determines what he is doing, does it not?"

They retorted, and said to him, "Surely you are not also from Galilee, are you? Search, and you will see that no prophet arises out of Galilee!"

John 7:11–52

PROPHECY

These are the words Moses spoke to all Israel
    across the Jordan in the wilderness.
Moses proclaimed to the people of Israel
    according to all that the Lord Jehovah
    had commanded him to give them:

        The Lord your God will raise up for you
            a prophet like me from among you,
            from among your own brothers.
        You must listen to him!

Then the Lord said to me,

    They are right in what they have spoken.
    I will raise up for them a prophet like you
        from among their own brothers.
    And I will put my words in his mouth,
        and he shall tell them everything that I command him.

Written by the patriarch Moses, year c. 1500 B.C.
Deuteronomy 1:1, 3; 18:15, 17–18

PROPHECY

You have said,

    I have made a covenant with my Chosen One.
    I have sworn an oath to David my servant:

    I will establish your descendants as kings forever,
        and construct your throne for all generations.

Recorded by the psalmist Ethan the Ezrahite, year c. 1000 B.C.
Psalm 89:3–4

PROPHECY

But you, Bethlehem Ephratah,
    though you be little among the thousands of Judah,
Yet out of you shall he come forth unto me
    that is to be ruler in Israel;
Whose goings forth have been from old,
    from everlasting.

Recorded by the prophet Micah, year c. 730 B.C.
Micah 5:2

FORGIVENESS OF AN ADULTRESS:
CAST THE FIRST STONE

THEN EVERYONE RETURNED to his own home. But Jesus went to the Mount of Olives.

Early in the morning, at dawn, he returned to the temple courtyard, where all the people began coming to him. So he sat down and began to teach them.

Then the teachers of the Law and the Pharisees brought a woman caught in adultery. They then made her stand in the middle of them, and said to him, "Teacher, this woman has been caught committing adultery, in the very act! Now in the Law, Moses commanded us to stone such women. What do you say?" They were questioning him to entrap him, in order that they might have grounds for accusing him, to bring some charge against him.

But Jesus bent down, and with his finger wrote in the dirt.

When they persisted in questioning him, he straightened up, and said to them, **"Let any one among you who is without sin be first to throw a stone at her."** And again he bent down and wrote in the dirt.

And at hearing this they began to depart, one by one, beginning with the oldest, until only Jesus was left alone with the woman who was still standing before him in the middle of the courtyard. Then straightening up, Jesus asked her, **"Woman, where are they? Has no one condemned you?"**

"No, no one, Lord," she replied.

"Neither do I condemn you!" Jesus then declared. **"Go your way. From now on sin no more."**

[Most of the earliest Greek manuscripts do not include this account.]

John 7:53–8:11

THE LIGHT OF THE WORLD:
CONFLICT WITH THE PHARISEES

THEN JESUS ONCE AGAIN ADDRESSED the crowd. He proclaimed:

> **I am the Light of the World!**
> **Whoever follows me**
> > **will never walk in darkness,**
> > **but will have the light of life.**

At this, the Pharisees challenged him, "You are testifying on your own behalf — your testimony is not valid!"

Jesus responded and said to them:

> **Even though I testify on my own behalf,**
> **my testimony is valid**
> **Because I know from where I came,**
> **and I know where I am going.**
> **However, you do not know**
> **from where I came,**
> **nor where I am going.**
> **You judge by human standards:**
> **I am not passing judgment on anyone.**
> **Yet even when I do judge,**
> **my judgment is valid.**
> **For it is not I alone who judge,**
> **but it is I—and the Father who sent me!**
> **Even in your own Law it is written**
> **that the testimony of two witnesses is valid.**
> **I am one who testifies on my own behalf;**
> **and the Father who sent me testifies about me.**

So then they asked him, "Where is your Father?" Jesus replied:

> **You know neither me,**
> **nor my Father.**
> **If you knew me,**
> **you would know my Father also.**

He spoke these words while teaching in the treasury of the temple. Yet no one seized him, because his hour had not yet come.

John 8:12–20

THE PROPHECY TEST: RELATION TO THE FATHER GOD

ONCE AGAIN HE SAID to them,

> **I am going away,**
> **and you will look for Me,**
> **and you will die in your sin.**
> **Where I am going,**
> **you cannot come!**

At this, the Jews — the leaders — began asking among themselves, "Surely he will not kill himself, will he? Is that why he says, 'Where I am going, you cannot come'?"

Then he continued addressing them,

> You are from below:
> I am from above.
> You are of this world:
> I am not of this world.
> That is why I told you
> that you will die in your sins.
> For unless you believe that I am,
> you will assuredly die in your sins.

"Then just who are you?" they demanded of him.
Jesus responded,

> Precisely what have I been telling you
> from the very beginning!
> About you I have much to say,
> and much to judge.
> But the one who sent me is true,
> and only the things which I heard from him
> will I declare to the world.

They did not comprehend that he had been speaking to them about the Father. So Jesus added,

> When you have lifted up the Son of Man,
> then you will realize who I am,
> And that I do nothing on my own authority,
> but speak only what the Father has instructed me.
> Yes, the one who sent me is ever with me:
> He has not left me alone,
> for I always do what is pleasing to him.

As he spoke these things, many came to believe in him.

John 8:21–30

Then Jesus said to those Jews who had believed in him,

If you continue to abide in my word,
  you are truly my disciples.
Then you will know the truth,
  and the truth will set you free.

"We are descendants of Abraham," they responded to him, "and have never been enslaved to anyone! What do you mean when you say, 'You will be set free'?" Jesus replied to them,

I can guarantee this truth:
Everyone who commits sin
  is the slave of sin.
Now the slave does not have a permanent place in the household,
  but the son remains in the family forever.
So if the son liberates you and sets you free,
  you shall be absolutely, unquestionably free!
I know that you are descendants of Abraham,
  yet you look for an opportunity to kill me
  because there is no place in you for my word.
I declare that which I have seen in the Father's presence;
  as for you, you also do that which you have heard
  from your father!

"Abraham is our father!" they retorted to him.
Jesus replied to them,

If you were truly the children of Abraham,
  then you would be doing that which Abraham did.
But as it is, you are determined to kill me,
  a man who has told you the truth,
  which I heard directly from God.
These are not the things that Abraham would have done:
  you are indeed doing those things your *real* father does.

"We are not illegitimate children born out of immorality!" they responded to him. "We have one real father, God himself!"

Jesus then told them,

> If God were your *real* father, you would love me,
>> for I have originated from God,
>> and have come here from him.
> I did not even come on my own authority,
>> but he sent me.

> Why do you not understand what I am saying?
>> Because you are unable to accept what I say!
> You are from your real father, the devil!
>> and you choose to gratify your father's desires!
> He was a murderer from the beginning,
>> and does not stand in the truth,
>> because there is no truth in him!
> When he lies, he speaks from his own natural character,
>> for he is a liar and the father of lies.
> Yet it is because I speak the truth
>> that you do not believe me!

> Which one of you can convict me of sin?
> Since I speak the truth,
>> why do you not believe me?
> Whoever is of God
>> comprehends the words of God.
> The reason why you do not comprehend
>> is because you are not of God!

The leaders of the Jews responded and said to him, "Are we not right in saying that you are a Samaritan and have a demon?"

Jesus answered:

> I do not have a demon!
>> but I honor my Father,
>> and you dishonor me!
> I do not seek honor and glory for myself.
> There is one who seeks my glory, however,
>> and he is the one who is the judge of it.
> I most solemnly guarantee you this truth:
> Anyone who keeps my word
>> will never experience death — ever!

At this the Jews — the leaders — exclaimed to him, "Now we know that you have a demon! Abraham died, and so did the prophets! Yet you say, 'Anyone who keeps my word will never taste death.' Are you greater than our father Abraham, who died? Or the prophets, who also died? Who do you make yourself out to be?"

Jesus responded,

> **If I glorify myself,**
> > **my glory means nothing.**
> **It is my Father who glorifies me —**
> > **he of whom you say, "He is our God."**
> **You do not know him, however,**
> > **but I do know him.**
> **And if I were to say, "I do not know him,"**
> > **I would be a liar, as you are!**
> **But I do know him,**
> > **and I keep his word.**
>
> **Your father Abraham rejoiced**
> > **that he would see my day.**
> **He saw it and was glad!**

"You are not yet 50 years old!" the Jews then said to him, "and have you seen Abraham?"

Jesus replied,

> **I most solemnly guarantee you:**
> **Before Abraham was,**
> **I am!**

At this they picked up stones to throw at him. But Jesus concealed himself, and went out of the temple complex.

John 8:31–59

THE MAN BORN BLIND: HEALING AND CONSEQUENCES

AS HE PASSED ALONG, he observed a man blind from birth. And his disciples asked him, "Rabbi, who sinned, this man or his parents, that he was born blind?"

Jesus responded, **"It is not that either this man or his parents sinned. But this happened so that the works of God might be evidenced in him.**

As long as it is day,
    we must work the works of him who sent me.
Night is coming
    when no man can work.
As long as I am in the world,
    I am the light of the world.

When he had said this, he spit on the ground, and made clay with the saliva. Then he smeared the clay on the man's eyes, saying to him, **"Go! Wash in the pool of Siloam."** (Siloam means *Sent*.) And so he went and washed and when he returned he could see!

Now his neighbors and those who had previously seen him as a beggar began asking, "Is this not the one who used to sit and beg?" Some were responding, "This is he!" Still others were saying, "No! But it is someone who looks like him."

He kept insisting, "I am the one!"

So then they were asking him, "How then were your eyes opened?"

He responded, "The man called Jesus made clay and smeared it on my eyes. Then he told me, 'Go to Siloam, and wash.' So I went and washed, and I received my sight!"

"Where is he?" they then asked him.

"I do not know," he replied.

They then brought him who was previously blind to the Pharisees.

Now it was a Sabbath on the day when Jesus made the clay and opened his eyes. So the Pharisees also began grilling him how he had received his sight. And to them he again said, "He applied clay to my eyes, and I washed, and now I see!"

Some of the Pharisees then said, "This man is not from God, because he does not observe the Sabbath!" But others asked, "How can a man who is a sinner perform such miraculous signs?" And there was a division among them.

So finally they again asked the blind man, "What do you say about him? Since it was your eyes he opened!"

"He is a prophet!" he replied.

However, until they summoned the parents of the very one who had received his sight, the Jews (the leaders) still did not believe him — that he had been blind and had received his sight. "Is this your son?" they then questioned them. "Is this the one who you contend was born blind? Then how does he now see?" they demanded.

"We know that this is our son, and that he was born blind," his parents answered. "But how it is that he now sees, we do not know. Nor do we know who opened his eyes! Ask him! He is of age. He will speak for himself."

His parents said this because they were afraid of the Jewish authorities. For the leaders of the Jews had already agreed that anyone who acknowledged him to be Messiah would be excommunicated from the synagogue. That is why his parents said, "He is of age. Ask him!"

So for a second time they summoned the man who had been blind. "Give glory to God!" they then said to him. "We know that this man is a sinner."

"Whether he is a sinner, I do not know," he then replied. "One thing I do know — that although I was blind, now I see!"

"What did he actually do to you?" they then questioned him. "How did he open your eyes?"

"I have already told you, and you did not listen," he answered them. "Why do you want to hear it again? You do not want to become his disciples, too, do you?"

At this they yelled abuses at him. "You are his disciple! But we are disciples of Moses!" they jeered. "We do know that God has spoken to Moses. But as for this man, we do not even know where he comes from!"

The man responded by answering them, "Why, this is such an amazing thing! Is it not? He opened my eyes, yet you do not know where he comes from! We do know that God does not listen to sinners. But he does listen to anyone who is God-fearing, who is a worshiper of God and obeys his will. Never since the beginning of time has it been heard that anyone opened the eyes of a man born blind. Never! If this man were not from God, he would be able to do nothing like this!"

"You were born in total depravity, utterly in sin!" they countered by retorting to him, "and you are teaching us?" And they forcefully ejected him from the synagogue.

When Jesus heard that they had expelled him, he found him and asked him, **"Do you believe in the Son of Man?"**

"And who is he, sir?" the man responded. "Tell me so that I may believe in him!"

"You have now seen him!" Jesus answered him. **"In fact, he is the one speaking with you!"**

Then he said, "Lord, I believe!" And he worshiped him.

"For judgment I have come into this world," Jesus then continued, **"so that those who do not see may see, and so that those who do see may become blind."**

Some of the Pharisees who were near him overheard these things, and said to him, "So we are also blind, are we?"

"If you were really blind," Jesus responded to them, **"you would have no sin. But since you say, 'We see,' your sin remains!"**

John 9:1–41

I MOST SOLEMNLY GUARANTEE YOU THIS TRUTH:
Anyone who does not enter the sheepfold through the gate,
  but climbs in by some other way,
  is a thief and a robber!
But the one who enters through the gate
  is the shepherd of the sheep.
The gatekeeper opens the gate for him.

And the sheep respond to his voice.
Then he calls his own sheep by name,
  and leads them out.
When he has brought all his own out,
  he goes ahead of them,
And the sheep follow him
  because they recognize his voice.
They will never follow a stranger
  but will run away from him,
  because they do not recognize the voices of strangers.

Jesus spoke to them in this parable, but they did not comprehend what he was saying to them. So Jesus once again addressed them:

I most solemnly assure you:
I am the gate for the sheep!
All who came before me are thieves and robbers,
  but the sheep did not listen to them.
I am the gate!
Whoever enters through me will be safe,
  and will come in and go out and find pasture.
The thief comes only to steal
  and kill and destroy.
I have come that they may have life,
  and may have it abundantly.

I am the good shepherd!
The good shepherd lays down his life
  for the sheep.

The hired hand is not the shepherd,
    nor does he own the sheep.
So when he sees the wolf coming,
    he abandons the sheep and runs away.
Then the wolf attacks some,
    and scatters the rest.
This is because he works only to be paid,
    and does not care about the sheep.

I am the good shepherd!
And I know my own,
    and my own know me—
Just as the Father knows me,
    and I know the Father—
And I lay down my life
    for the sheep.

I also have other sheep
    that are not of this fold.
I must bring them out as well,
    and they too will recognize my voice.
So there shall be one flock,
    with one shepherd.

For this reason the Father loves me:
    because I lay down my own life
    in order to take it up again!
No one is taking it from me:
    on the contrary I lay it down voluntarily.
I have authority and power to lay it down,
    and have authority and power to take it up again.
This authority
    I have received from my Father.

Because of these words, the Jews — the authorities — were again divided. Many of them were saying, "He has a demon and is insane. Why listen to him?"

Others were arguing, "These are not the words of one who has a demon. A demon cannot open the eyes of the blind, can it?"

John 10:1–21

This is what the Lord God says to them:

> Behold I, even I myself, will judge
>> between the fat sheep and the lean sheep.
>
> Because you shove with side and with shoulder,
>> and butt all the weak sheep with your horns,
>> until you have driven them out in every direction.
>
> Therefore, I will rescue my flock,
>> so that they will no longer be prey.
>
> And I will judge between one sheep and another sheep.
>
> Then I will set one shepherd over them,
>> my servant David.
>> and he shall pasture them.
>
> He shall pasture them himself,
>> and be their shepherd.
>
> And I, the Lord, will be their God,
>> and my servant David shall be prince among them.
>
> I, the Lord, have spoken!

Recorded by the prophet Ezekiel, year c. 575 B.C.
Ezekiel 34:20–24

COMMISSIONING THE SEVENTY

circa A.D. 29

N OW AFTER THIS, THE LORD APPOINTED 70 OTHERS and sent them in pairs on ahead of him to every town and place where he himself planned to go.

Then he began telling them:

> The harvest is abundant, but the laborers are few. Implore the Lord of the harvest, therefore, to send out laborers into his harvest field. Now go on your way! and be careful! I am sending you out as lambs in the midst of wolves. Carry no wallet, no provisions bag, no extra shoes. And do not get delayed by greeting anyone along the way.
>
> Into whatever house you enter, first say, "Peace to this household!" And if a person of peace lives there, your peace will rest upon him. But if not, it will return to you. And stay in that same house, eating and drinking what they offer you: for the laborer is worthy of his wages. Do not keep moving around from house to house.
>
> Into whatever town you enter, and they welcome you, eat whatever is set before you. And heal the sick in it, and tell them, "The kingdom of God has come close to you." But whatever town you enter, and they do not welcome you, go out into its streets and announce, "Even the dust of your town, which clings to our feet, we wipe off in public protest against you! Nevertheless, be certain of this: the kingdom of God has come close to you." I tell you: on "that day" it will be more tolerable for Sodom than for that town!
>
> Woe to you, Chorazin! Woe to you, Bethsaida! For if the miracles of power performed in you had been performed in Tyre and Sidon,

they would have repented long ago, sitting in sackcloth and ashes. Yet at the judgment, it will be more tolerable for Tyre and Sidon than for you! And you, Capernaum, will you be exalted to heaven? No! you will be hurled down to the depths of hades!

Whoever listens to you, listens to me. And whoever rejects you, rejects me. And whoever rejects me, rejects the one who sent me.

Luke 10:1–16

CELEBRATING THE SEVENTY

THE 70 RETURNED JUBILANTLY REJOICING. "Lord," they reported, "even the demons submit to us in the power of your name!"

Then he replied by saying to them, **"Yes, I watched Satan fall like a lightning bolt from heaven! Now you recognize that I have given you authority to tread upon snakes and scorpions, and to trample over all the power of the enemy, and nothing at all shall ever harm you! However, do not rejoice in this — that the spirits submit to you — but rejoice that your names are registered in heaven!"**

In that same hour he rejoiced in the Holy Spirit and exclaimed,

I praise You, Father, Lord of heaven and earth, that you have concealed these things from the wise and the clever, and have revealed them to the childlike. Yes, Father, for such was your gracious will, for this is well pleasing in your sight.

All things have been entrusted to me by my father. And no one knows who the Son is except the Father, or who the Father is except the Son, and those to whom the Son chooses to reveal him.

Then turning to the disciples, he privately said, **"Blessed are the eyes that see what you see! For I tell you that many prophets and kings desired to see what you see, but did not see it, and to hear what you hear, but did not hear it."**

Luke 10:17–24

THE GOOD SAMARITAN

JUST THEN A CERTAIN LAWYER — an expert in the Mosaic law — stood up to test him. "Teacher," he asked, what must I do to inherit eternal life?"

"What is written in the Law?" He replied to him. **"What do you read there?"**

Then he responded by answering: "You shall love the Lord your God with all your heart, and with all your soul, and with all your strength, and with all your mind. And, love your neighbor as yourself."

"You have answered correctly!" Jesus said to him. **"Do this and you will live forever!"**

But wanting to justify himself, he asked Jesus, "Who is my neighbor?"

In reply, Jesus answered, **"A certain man was going down from Jerusalem to** **Jericho, and fell victim to robbers. They stripped him, and beat him, and went away leaving him half dead.**

"Now as it happened, a certain priest was going down that same road. But when he saw him, he passed by on the other side. And so similarly a Levite also, when he came to the place and saw him, passed by on the other side.

"But a certain Samaritan, who was on a journey, came to where he was. And when he saw him, he had compassion. He went over to him, and bandaged his wounds, after pouring oil and wine on them. Then he set him on his own beast, and brought him to an inn, and took care of him.

"Then on the next day, he took out two *denarii* [the equivalent of two day's wages or about two hundred dollars] **and gave them to the innkeeper. 'Take care of him,' he instructed. 'And when I return, I will reimburse you whatever extra you spend.'**

"Which of these three, do you think, proved a neighbor to the man who fell among the robbers?"

"The one who showed him mercy!" he answered.

Then Jesus told him, **"You go and do the same!"**

Luke 10:25–37

HOSPITALITY OF MARY AND MARTHA

NOW AS THEY CONTINUED ON THEIR OWN JOURNEY, he entered a certain village where a woman named Martha welcomed him into her home. And she had a sister called Mary, who sat herself at the Lord's feet, listening to what he was teaching.

But Martha was distracted by her many tasks. So she went up to him and asked, "Lord, do you not care that my sister has left me to do all the serving by myself? Then tell her to help me!"

But the Lord replied to her by responding, **"Martha! Martha! You are worried and distracted by so many things. But of a few things that are important, only one is essential. For Mary has chosen what is more advantageous, which will not be taken away from her."**

Luke 10:38–42

NOW IT OCCURRED THAT ONCE, when he had finished praying in a certain place, one of his disciples said to him, "Lord, teach us to pray, just as John also taught his disciples."

Then he said to them, **"When you pray, say:**

> **'Father: May your name be held holy.**
> **May your kingdom come.**
> **Give us each day our daily bread.**
> **And forgive us our sins,**
>> **for we ourselves also forgiven everyone who sins against us.**
> **And let us not be lead into temptation.' "**

Then he said to them, **"Suppose one of you has a friend to whom you go in the middle of the night, and say to him, 'My friend, lend me three loaves of bread. For a friend of mine who is on a journey has just arrived, and I have nothing to serve him.' Then he says in response from within, 'Do not disturb me! The door has already been locked, and my children are with me in bed. I cannot get up and give you anything.'**

"I guarantee you, even though he will not get up and give him anything out of their friendship, at least because of his persistence, and to preserve his reputation, he will get up and give him as much as he needs.

"So this is what I am saying to you:

> **Keep asking, and it will be given to you.**
> **Keep searching, and you will find.**
> **Keep knocking, and the door will be opened to you.**

> **For everyone who asks, receives.**
> **And anyone who searches, finds.**
> **And anyone who knocks, the door will be opened.**

"Now suppose one of you fathers is asked by his son for a fish. He will not give him a snake instead of a fish, will he? Or if he asks for an egg, will he give him a scorpion? If you then, evil as you are, know how to give good gifts to your children, how much more shall your Heavenly Father give the Holy Spirit to those who ask him!"

Luke 11:1–13

DO NOT WORRY: YOUR TREASURE IS IN HEAVEN

circa A.D. 29

THEN HE SAID TO HIS DISCIPLES:

For this reason I am telling you:
Do not worry about your life, what you will eat;
Or about your body, what you will wear;
　　for life is more than food,
　　and the body more than clothing.
Consider the ravens: for they neither sow nor reap,
　　and they have neither storehouse nor barn,
　　and yet God feeds them.
Of how much greater value are you than the birds!
And by worrying, can any of you add a cubit [a half yard] to his height?
　　or a moment to his life?
Then since you are not able to do such a little thing as that,
　　why do you worry about the rest?

Consider the lilies how they grow:
　　they neither spin nor weave.
Yet I am telling you:
Not even Solomon in all his splendor was adorned like one of these!
But, if God so adorns the wildflowers,
　　which today are alive in the field
　　and tomorrow are thrown into the oven,
How much more will he adorn you!

O you of little faith! and as for you:
Do not keep constantly striving
    for what you are to eat,
    and what you are to drink.
And do not keep worrying!
For the pagan nations of the world
    greedily strive after all such things,
    and your Father already knows that you need them!
Instead, strive for his kingdom,
    and these things will be supplied to you as well.
Do not be afraid, little flock!
For it is your Father's good pleasure to give you the kingdom.
Sell your possessions
    and give to charity for those in need.
Make yourselves purses that do not wear out —
    an inexhaustable treasure in heaven,
    where no thief reaches, and no moth ruins.
For wherever your treasure is,
    there will your heart be also.

Luke 12:22–34

ALWAYS BE VIGILANT: THE SON OF MAN WILL COME UNEXPECTEDLY

BE DRESSED FOR ACTION
    with your belts fastened,
    and have your lamps lit.
Be like men who are waiting for their master
    to return from the wedding banquet —
So they may immediately open the door for him
    when he comes and knocks.
Blessed are those bondservants
    whom the master finds vigilant when he comes.
I guarantee this truth: He will gird himself to serve,
    and have them recline at the table,
    then he will come and serve them!
Whether he comes in the second watch before midnight,
    or even in the third watch after midnight,
    and finds them vigilant,
Blessed are those servants.

But be assured of this:
That if the owner of the house had known
    at what hour the thief was coming,
    he would not have allowed him to be break into his house.
You must likewise always be vigilant!
For the Son of Man is coming at an hour you do not expect!

"Lord, are you addressing this parable to us," Peter then asked, "or to everyone else as well?"

Then the Lord replied:

Who then is the faithful and prudent steward, whom his master will put in charge of his household servants, to give them their food rations at the proper time? Blessed is that slave whom the master finds doing just that when he arrives!

I can guarantee you this truth: he will put him in charge of all of his properties. But if that slave says to himself in his heart, "My master is delayed in coming," Then he begins to beat the other slaves — both men and women, and to eat and drink and get drunk.

The master of that slave will return on a day when he does not expect him, and at an hour that he does not know, and will tear him apart, and assign him a place with the unfaithful unbelievers.

And that slave who knew his master's will but did not make preparations, nor act according to his will, he will receive a severe beating with many lashes.

But the one who did not know, and committed deeds deserving a flogging, will receive fewer lashes.

From everyone to whom much has been given, much will be required. And from the one to whom much has been entrusted, even more will be demanded.

Luke 12:35–48

SORROW AHEAD: NOT PEACE BUT DIVISION

I HAVE COME TO CAST FIRE upon the earth — and how I wish it were already kindled! But I have a baptism to undergo — and how greatly anguished I am until it is accomplished!

Do you suppose that I have come to bring peace on earth? No, I tell you, but rather division!

For from now on five in one household will be divided, three against two, and two against three. They will be divided, father against son, and son against father; mother against daughter, and daughter against mother; mother-in-law against her daughter-in-law, and daughter-in-law against mother-in-law.

Luke 12:49–53

DISCERN THE TIMES: JUDGE WHAT IS RIGHT

HE ALSO SAID TO THE CROWDS:

When you see a cloud rising in the west, immediately you say,
    "It is going to shower!" and so it does.
And when you see a south wind blowing, you say,
    "It is going to be a scorcher!" and so it is.
You hypocrites! You frauds!
You know how to interpret the appearance of the earth and the sky,
    but why do you not know how to interpret this present time?
And why on your own initiative
    do you not judge for yourselves what is right?
For example, when you are going with your accuser
    to appear before the magistrate,
    on your way there make a diligent effort to settle the case
    and be rid of him.
Otherwise he may drag you before the judge,
    and the judge turn you over to the bailiff,
    and the bailiff throw you in jail!
I can guarantee you: You will never get released out of there
    until you have paid the very last cent.

Luke 12:54–59

GREAT CALAMITIES: NOT THE RESULT OF GREATER SINS

circa A.D. 29

N OW AT THAT VERY SAME OCCASION there were some present who reported to him about the Galileans whose blood Pilate had mingled with that of their sacrifices. He responded to them by replying:

> Do you suppose that because these Galileans suffered in this way
>   they were worse sinners than all other Galileans?
> No, I guarantee you!
> But unless you repent by changing the way you think and live,
>   you will all perish as they did!
> Or those 18 who were killed when the Tower of Siloam
>   fell on them —
> Do you suppose that they were worse offenders
>   than all others living in Jerusalem?
> No, I guarantee you!
> But unless you repent by changing the way you think and live,
>   you will all perish just as they did!

Luke 13:1–5

THE FRUITLESS FIG TREE: ONE MORE YEAR

T HEN HE TOLD THEM THIS PARABLE:

> A certain man had a fig tree planted in his vineyard. and he kept looking for fruit on it, and found none.

So he said to the gardener, "Look, for three years now I have come looking for fruit on this fig tree without finding any. Cut it down! Why should it be using up the soil?"

Then he responded and said to him, "Sir, let it alone for one more year, until I dig around it and work in manure. Then if it bears fruit next year, well and good. But if not, you can cut it down."

Luke 13:6–9

HEALING ON THE SABBATH: HUMILIATING HIS OPPONENTS

NOW HE WAS TEACHING ON THE SABBATH in one of the synagogues. And just then there appeared a woman, who for 18 years had been crippled by a spirit, a demon of sickness. She was hunched over, and utterly unable to straighten herself up or look up at all.

Then when Jesus saw her, he called her over and said to her, **"Woman, you are set free from your disability!"**

Then he laid his hands upon her, and immediately she stood up straight again, and she began praising God.

But the leader of the synagogue was indignant because Jesus had healed on the Sabbath. "There are six days in which work ought to be done," he began telling the crowd in response. "So come on those days to get healed, and not on the Sabbath day!"

Then the Lord in response replied to him, **"You hypocrites! Does not each of you on the Sabbath untie his ox or his donkey from the manger stall, and lead it away to water? Then ought not this woman, a daughter of Abraham whom Satan has bound for 18 long years, be released from this bondage on the Sabbath day?"**

As he said these things, all his opponents were humiliated. But all the crowd of people were rejoicing over all the glorious things that were being done by him.

Luke 13:10–17

THE FESTIVAL OF HANUKKAH: ACCUSATION OF BLASPHEMY

THE FESTIVAL OF THE DEDICATION took place at that time at Jerusalem. It was winter. And Jesus was walking in the temple courtyard, in the Portico of Solomon (or Solomon's Colonnade).

So the Jews encircled him, and began asking him, "How long will you keep us in suspense? If you are the Messiah, tell us plainly!"

Jesus answered them:

> **I have told you, and you do not believe.**
> **The miraculous works that I do**
> > **in the authority of my Father's name,**
> > **these bear witness of me.**
> **But you do not believe,**
> > **because you are not from among my sheep!**
> **My sheep recognize my voice,**
> > **and I know them, and they follow me.**
> **I give eternal life to them, and they shall never perish — ever!**
> > **and no one shall snatch them out of my hand.**
> **My Father, who has given them to me,**
> > **is stronger and greater than all;**
> > **and no one shall snatch them out of the Father's hand.**
> **I and the Father are one!**

The Jews once again picked up stones to stone him. But Jesus addressed them: **"I have shown you many good works from the Father. For which of them are you going to stone me?"**

"It is not for a good work that we are stoning you," the Jews retorted, "but for blasphemy — because you, although merely a man, make yourself out to be God!"

Jesus answered them:

> **Has it not been written in your own Law, "I said, you are gods!"?**
> **If he called them "gods" to whom the word of God came —**
> > **and the Scripture cannot be annulled —**
> **Do you say of him**
> > **whom the Father consecrated and sent into the world,**
> > **"You are blaspheming" because I said "I am the Son of God"?**
> **If I am not doing the works of my Father,**
> > **then do not believe me!**
> **But if I do them, even though you do not believe me,**
> **Believe the miraculous works,**
> > **so that you may know and recognize that the Father is in me,**
> > **and I in the Father.**

Then again they attempted to seize him, but he eluded their grasp.

John 10:22–39

BEYOND JORDAN: JESUS WITHDRAWS TO BETHANY

circa A.D. 29–30

THEN HE WENT AWAY AGAIN, back across the Jordan to the place where John had at first been baptizing, and he remained there.

And many people came to him and were saying, "John performed no miraculous sign, yet all that John predicted about this man was true!"

And many believed in him there.

John 10:40–42

WARNINGS ABOUT SALVATION: ENTER THROUGH THE NARROW DOOR

THEN HE PASSED THROUGH ONE TOWN and village after another, teaching as he made his way to Jerusalem. Someone asked him, "Lord, are just a few going to be saved?"

Then he replied to them:

> **Strive to enter through the narrow door:**
> > **for many, I guarantee you,**
> > **will attempt to enter and will not be able.**
> **When once the owner of the house gets up and closes the door,**
> > **and you stand outside and repeatedly knock on the door,**
> > **pleading, "Lord, open up for us!"**
> **Then he will reply and say to you,**
> > **"I do not know who you are, or from where you have come!"**

Then you will begin to protest,
    "We ate and drank with you in your company,
        and you taught in our streets!"
But he will reply, "I tell you, I do not know who you are,
        or from where you have come!
        Depart from me, all you who do evil!"
There will be wailing and grinding of teeth there
        when you see Abraham and Isaac and Jacob
        and all the prophets in the kingdom of God,
        but you yourselves being cast out and banished!
And people will come from the east and west,
        and from north and south,
        and will recline at the table in the kingdom of God.
Pay attention to this! Some are now last who will be first,
        and some are now first who will be last.

Luke 13:22–30

Warnings about Herod and against Jerusalem

JUST AT THAT VERY SAME TIME some Pharisees came and said to him, "Go away and depart from here, because Herod is determined to kill you!" Then he replied to them:

Go and tell that fox, "Take notice of this! I cast out demons
        and perform healings today and tomorrow,
And the third day I will finish my objectives."
Yes, I must journey on today, tomorrow,
        and the day following that,
Because it would not be right that a prophet
        should be killed outside of Jerusalem.
O Jerusalem! Jerusalem!
        the city that murders the prophets and stones those sent to her!
How often I have yearned to gather your children together,
        as a hen gathers her brood under her wings
        but you were not willing!
Pay close attention! Your house is abandoned to you —
        empty, desolate — and I tell you,
You shall not see me until the time comes when you say,
        "Blessed is he who comes in the name of the Lord!"

Luke 13:31–35

THEN ON ONE OCCASION ON A SABBATH, when he went into the house of one of the leaders of the Pharisees to eat dinner, the dinner guests were watching him closely. Right there in front of him was a certain man suffering from dropsy (abnormal swelling in his arms and legs.)

Then in response, Jesus addressed the experts on the Law, and the Pharisees, asking, **"Is it lawful to heal on the Sabbath, or not?"** But they remained silent.

So he took hold of him, and healed him, and sent him away. Then he said to them, **"Who among you, having a son or an ox that has fallen into a well on a Sabbath Day, will not immediately pull him out?"** And they could not respond to this.

Luke 14:1–6

PARABLE OF THE AMBITIOUS GUESTS AND THE BEST SEATS

HAVING OBSERVED HOW THE INVITED GUESTS had been selecting the places of honor at the table, he then began telling them a parable. This is what he said to them:

> **When you are invited by someone to a wedding banquet,**
> > **do not take the place of honor,**
> **In case someone more distinguished than you**
> > **may have been invited by him.**
> **Then he who invited both of you shall come and say to you,**
> > **"Give this place to this person!"**
> **Then in humiliating embarrassment**
> > **you would have to proceed to take the least important place.**
> **But when you are invited,**
> > **go and recline at the lowest place.**
> **Then, when the one who has invited you comes he may tell you,**
> > **"Friend, move up higher to a more important place!"**
> **Then you will be honored in the presence**
> > **of all who are reclining at the table with you.**
> **For everyone who honors himself shall be humbled,**
> > **and he who humbles himself shall be honored.**

Then he also said to the one who had invited him, **"When you give a luncheon or a dinner, do not just invite your friends or your brothers or sisters, or your other relatives or your wealthy neighbors, in case they invite you in return, and so you would be repaid. Instead, when you host a banquet, invite the poor, the disabled, the lame, and the blind. Then you will be blessed, since they do not have the means of repaying you. For you will be repaid at the resurrection of the righteous."**

Luke 14:7–14

PARABLE OF THE GREAT BANQUET AND THE COST OF BEING TOO BUSY

WHEN ONE OF THOSE WHO WAS RECLINING at the table with him heard this, he said to him, "Blessed is everyone who will eat bread in the kingdom of God!"

Then he responded to him:

A certain man was giving a great banquet, and he invited many guests. Then at the dinner hour he sent his slave to announce to those who had been invited, "Come, everything is now ready!" but without exception they all began to excuse themselves.

The first one said to him, "I have just bought a piece of land, and I need to go out and examine it. Please convey my apologies."

Then another one said, "I have just bought five pairs of oxen, and I am on my way to evaluate them. Please convey my apologies."

Still another one said, "I have just recently married a wife, and for that reason I cannot come."

So the slave returned and reported this to his master.

Then the owner of the house became angry and told his slave, "Go out at once into the main streets and back lanes of the town and bring in the poor, the disabled, the blind, and the lame!"

Then the slave reported, "Master, what you have ordered has been completed, and there is still room!"

Then the master said to the slave, "Go out into the highways and along the hedges, and urge people to come in, so that my house may be filled. For I promise you, not one of those who were initially invited will even taste my banquet!"

Luke 14:15–24

NOW VAST CROWDS WERE TRAVELING with him, and he turned and spoke to them:

> Whoever comes to me, and does not hate his father and mother,
>> and wife and children, and brothers and sisters —
>> yes, and even his own life itself — cannot be my disciple.
> Whoever does not persevere in carrying his own cross
>> and follow after me — cannot be my disciple.
> For which one of you, intending to construct a tower,
>> does not first sit down and estimate the cost,
>> to see whether he has sufficient to complete it?
> Otherwise, when he has laid a foundation and is unable to finish,
>> all who see it will begin to ridicule him, saying,
>> "This man began to build and was not able to finish."
> Or what king, when he sets out to encounter another king in battle,
>> will not first sit down and take counsel,
>> whether he is strong enough with ten thousand
>> to oppose the one coming against him with twenty thousand?
> And if not, while the other is still a great way away,
>> he sends a delegation and determines terms of peace.
> So in the same way, any one of you who does not renounce
>> all that he has cannot be my disciple.
> Salt is good, but if salt has lost its taste,
>> how shall its saltiness be restored?
>> It is fit neither for the soil nor for the manure pile.
>> It is thrown away! He who has ears to hear, let him listen.

Luke 14:25–35

PARABLES OF ASSOCIATING WITH SINNERS: THE LOST SHEEP, THE LOST COIN, AND THE PRODIGAL SON

NOW THE TAX COLLECTORS AND the most notorious sinners were all drawing near to listen to him. And both the Pharisees and the scribes (the teachers of the Law) kept complaining. "This man," they grumbled, "entertains the worst sinners, and even eats with them!"

So he told them this parable, saying:

Suppose one among you has a hundred sheep, and has lost 1 of them. Does he not leave the 99 in the open pasture, and go after the 1 that is lost until he finds it? Then when he has found it, he lays it on his shoulders, rejoicing!

And when he arrives home, he calls together his friends and neighbors. "Let's celebrate!" he says to them. "Rejoice with me, for I have found my sheep which was lost!"

I promise you that in the same way, there will be joy in heaven over one sinner who repents and changes his heart and life, than over 99 righteous persons who have no need of repentance.

Or suppose a woman has ten silver *drachmas*, and loses one *drachma* coin. Does she not light a lamp and sweep the house and search relentlessly until she finds it? Then when she has found it, she calls her friends and neighbors together. "Let's celebrate!" she says. "Rejoice with me, for I have found the *drachma* which was lost!"

I promise you that, in the same way, there is joy in the presence of the angels of God over one sinner who repents.

Then he continued:

A certain man had two sons. The younger of them said to his father, "Father, give me the share of the estate that is coming to me."

So he divided his property between them.

Then not many days after that, the younger son gathered together all that was his, and set off on a journey into a distant country, and there squandered his inheritance in reckless living.

Now when he had spent everything, a severe famine spread throughout that country, and he began to be in need.

So he went and hired himself out to one of the citizens of that country who sent him into his fields to feed pigs. And no one was giving him any food, to the point that he would have gladly filled his stomach with the carob pods that the pigs were eating.

But when he finally came to his senses, he reflected, "How many of my father's hired men have enough food to spare? but I am dying here of hunger! I will get up and go to my father, and I will say to him, "Father, I have sinned against heaven, and against you. I am no longer worthy to be called your son. Make me as one of your hired men."

So he got up and went to his father.

But while he was still a long way off, his father saw him, and was filled with compassion.

Then he ran and threw his arms around his neck, and kissed him.

Then the son said to him, "Father, I have sinned against heaven and against you. I am no longer worthy to be called your son."

But the father ordered his slaves: "Hurry! Bring out a robe — the finest one, and put it on him. And put a ring on his finger and sandals on his feet. And take the fattened calf and slaughter it, and let us feast and celebrate!

For this, my son, was dead and has come to life again! He was lost and has been found!" So they started to celebrate!

Meanwhile, the older son was in the field. And when he returned and was approaching the house, he heard music and dancing. So he summoned one of the servant boys to him, and began inquiring, "What is going on here?"

Then he replied to him: "Your brother has returned! And your father has slaughtered the fattened calf, because he has received him back safe and sound."

But then he became angry, and refused to go in.

So his father came out and began pleading with him.

But he retorted by saying to his father, "Look! For all these years I have been slaving for you, and I have never once disobeyed your orders. Yet you have never even given me a kid goat, so that I might celebrate with my friends.

"But when this son of yours comes back — who squandered your wealth with prostitutes — you killed the fattened calf for him!"

Then he said to him, "My son, you have always been with me. And everything that is mine is yours. But we had to celebrate and express our joy! For this brother of yours was dead and has come back to life! He was lost and has been found!"

Luke 15:1–32

PARABLE OF THE DISHONEST MANAGER: YOU CANNOT SERVE GOD AND WORLDLY WEALTH

THEN HE ALSO CONTINUED saying to his disciples:

There was a certain rich man who had a business manager; and accusations were brought to him that this manager was squandering the man's possessions. So he summoned him and asked him, "What is this that I am hearing about you? Turn in an account of your stewardship, for you cannot be my manager any longer."

Then the business manager thought to himself: *What should I do now? My master is taking the stewardship away from me! Dig? I am not strong enough! Beg? I am too ashamed! I know what I will do — so that when I am dismissed as manager, people will welcome me into their homes!*

So he summoned each of his master's debtors, one by one. Then he asked the first, "How much do you owe my master?"

"One hundred *batous* (about 875 gallons) of olive oil," he replied.

Then he said to him, "Take your promissory agreement, quickly, sit down, and write 50."

Then to another he said, "And how much do you owe?"

"One hundred *korous* (about 900 bushels) of wheat," he replied.

To him he said, "Take your promissory agreement, and write 80."

Then his master commended the dishonest manager because he had acted shrewdly. For the children of this age are more shrewd in dealing with their own kind than are the children of light.

And I tell you this: Although worldly wealth is often used in dishonest ways, you should rightly use it to benefit others and make friends for yourselves, so that when it fails they may welcome you into their eternal tents.

Whoever is honest in a very little is also honest in much. And whoever is dishonest in a very little is also dishonest in much.

If then you have not been honest with dishonest worldly wealth, who will trust you with the genuine riches? And if you have not been honest with what belongs to another, who will give you what is your own?

No slave can serve two masters. Either he will hate the one and love the other; or he will be devoted to one and despise the other. You cannot serve God and worldly wealth.

Luke 16:1–13

REBUKING THE PHARISEES: GOD'S LAW CANNOT BE ALTERED

NOW THE PHARISEES, WHO WERE lovers of money, heard all this, and they were ridiculing him with sarcastic remarks.
So he said to them:

You are those who publicly justify yourselves in the sight of others:
    but God knows your hearts.
For what is considered highly esteemed among men
    is a detestable abomination in the sight of God.
The Law and the Prophets were in effect until John;
    since then the gospel of the kingdom of God is being proclaimed,
    and everyone is trying to force his way into it.
But it is easier for heaven and earth to disappear
    than for one stroke of the letter of the Law to be dropped.
Anyone who divorces his wife and marries another
    commits adultery; And he who marries a woman divorce
    from her husband commits adultery.

213

Luke 16:14–18

PARABLE OF THE RICH MAN AND LAZARUS: THE DANGER OF WEALTH

NOW THERE WAS A CERTAIN RICH MAN who habitually dressed in regal purple and fine linen, and feasted sumptuously and lived lavishly every day.

And at his gate was regularly laid a certain destitute man named Lazarus, covered with ulcerated sores, and longing to eat whatever scraps fell from the rich man's table.

Moreover, even the dogs would come and lick his sores.

Then it so happened that the destitute man died, and he was carried away by the angels into Abraham's embrace.

And the rich man also died and was buried.

And in hades, where he was in constant torment, he lifted up his eyes and saw Abraham far away in the distance, with Lazarus in his embrace.

Then he cried out and shouted, "Father, Abraham, have mercy on me! And send Lazarus to dip the tip of his finger in water, and cool off my tongue. For I am in ceaseless agony in these flames!"

But Abraham replied, "My child, remember that during your life you received your soft comforts, while Lazarus in like manner hardships. But now he is being comforted here, while you are in agony.

"And besides all this, between us and you a great chasm has been fixed, so that those who wish to go over from here to you may not do so, nor may anyone cross over from there to us."

And he responded, "Then, father, I beg you to send him to my father's house — for I have five brothers — so that he may solemnly warn them, so that they may also not come to this place of torment!"

But Abraham replied, "They have Moses and the Prophets. Let them listen to them!"

To which he responded, "Oh no, Father Abraham! But if someone from the dead goes to them, they will repent — they will completely change the way they think and live!"

But then Abraham said to him, "If they do not listen to Moses and the Prophets, neither will they be convinced — even if someone rises from the dead!"

Luke 16:19–31

LESSONS ON DISCIPLESHIP: FORGIVENESS, FAITH, AND DUTY

THEN HE TOLD HIS DISCIPLES:

Situations that cause people to stumble and sin are inevitable,
   but woe to that person through whom they occur!
It would be better for him if a millstone were hung around
   his neck, and he were hurled into the sea,
   than for him to cause one of these humble ones to stumble.
So watch yourselves! Be on your guard! Be careful how you live!
   Always look out for one another!
If your brother sins, rebuke him.
And if he repents, forgive him.
And even if he wrongs you seven times a day,
   and returns to you seven times a day,
   saying, "I am sorry! I repent!"
You must forgive him.

Then one day the Apostles said to the Lord, "Give us more faith!"
To that the Lord replied:

If you had faith even the size of mustard seed, you could say to this mulberry tree, "Pull yourself up by the roots and plant yourself in the sea!" and it would obey you!

Suppose one of you has a slave who has just come in from the field, who has been plowing, or tending sheep. Would you say this to your slave? "Come in here at once, and take your place at the table, and sit here and eat."

Would you not more likely say this to him? "Prepare dinner for me, and change your clothes, and serve me while I eat and drink. After you have served me, you may eat and drink."

Does he thank the slave because he did what he was ordered to do?

So also with you, when you have done everything that you were ordered to do, say, "We are unworthy slaves; we have only done what was our duty."

Luke 17: 1–10

THE DEATH OF LAZARUS: VICTORY OVER DEATH

NOW A CERTAIN MAN NAMED LAZARUS WAS GRAVELY ILL. He was from Bethany, the village where Mary and her sister Martha lived. (This Mary was the one who anointed the Lord with perfumed ointment, and wiped his feet with her hair.) It was her brother Lazarus who was now so ill. So the sisters sent a message to him that said, "Urgent, Lord! The man whom you greatly love is gravely ill!"

But when Jesus heard this message, he said, **"This illness is not to end in death. Rather it is for the glory of God, so that through it the Son of God may be glorified."**

Now even though Jesus loved Martha and her sister and Lazarus, when he heard that Lazarus was so ill, he remained two days more in the place where he was. Then after this interval, he said to the disciples, **"Let us go to Judea again."**

"Rabbi!" the disciples responded to him. "The Jews — the Jewish leaders — were just recently seeking to stone you to death! And are you really going back there again?"

Jesus replied,

> **Are there not 12 hours in the daytime?**
> **If anyone walks during the daytime, he does not stumble,**
>   **because he sees by the light of this world.**
> **But if anyone walks in the night, he does stumble,**
>   **because the light is not in him.**

After saying this, he then said to them, **"Our friend Lazarus has fallen asleep. But I am going to awaken him out of his sleep."**

The disciples then responded to him, "Lord, if he has fallen asleep, he will recover."

Now Jesus had spoken of his death, but they thought that he was speaking of natural sleep. So then Jesus told them plainly, **"Lazarus is dead! And for your sake I am glad that I was not there, so that you may believe. But let us go to him."**

Thomas, who was called Didymus (or Twin)**,** said to his fellow disciples, "Let us go as well, that we may die with him!"

So when he arrived, Jesus found that Lazarus had already been in the tomb for four days. Now Bethany was near Jerusalem, only about fifteen *stadia* (or two miles) away, and many of the Jews had come to Martha and Mary, to console them about their brother.

When Martha heard that Jesus was coming, she went out to meet him. But Mary sat still at home. Martha then said to Jesus, "Lord, if you had been here, my brother would not have died! But even now I know that whatever you ask of God, God will give you!"

"Your brother shall rise again," Jesus replied to her.

Martha responded to him, "I know he will rise again in the resurrection on the Last Day."

"I am the resurrection and the life," Jesus replied to her. **"Whoever believes in me, even if he dies, will live. And everyone who is alive and believes in me will never die. Do you believe this?"**

"Yes, Lord," she told him, "I do believe you are the Messiah, the Son of God, the one who was to come into the world."

Then after she had said this, she went back and called her sister Mary, privately whispering to her, "The Master is here and is asking for you." And when Mary heard this, she quickly sprang up and went to meet him. Now Jesus had not yet entered the village, but was still at the same place where Martha had met him.

When the Jews who were with Mary in the house, consoling her, noticed how hastily she rose up and went out, they followed her, presuming that she was going to the tomb to mourn there.

Now when Mary arrived where Jesus was and saw him, she collapsed at his feet. "Lord, if you had been here," she said to him, "my brother would not have died!"

Then when Jesus saw her weeping, and the Jews who had come along with her also wailing, he was deeply moved in spirit, and was visibly distressed. **"Where have you laid him?"** he then asked.

"Come and see, Lord," they replied.

Jesus wept.

So then the Jews said, "See how much he loved him!" But some of them questioned, "Could not he, who opened the eyes of a blind man, also have prevented this man from dying?"

Then Jesus, once again deeply moved within, came to the tomb. Now it was a cave, and a boulder was lying across it. **"Remove the stone!"** Jesus directed.

"But Lord!" Martha, the sister of the dead man, exclaimed, "By this time there will be a terrible stench, for he has been there four days."

Jesus responded to her, **"Did I not promise you that if you believe, you would see the glory of God?"**

So then they removed the stone. Then Jesus raised his eyes, and said,

> **Father, I thank you that you have heard me.**
> **I myself have known that you always hear me.**
> **But I have said this**
> > **for the benefit of the people standing around here,**
> > **so that they may believe that you did send me!**

Then when he had said this, he cried out with a loud voice, **"Lazarus, come out!"**

The dead man came out! His hands and his feet were bound with linen strips. And his face was wrapped around with a burial headcloth.

Jesus instructed them, **"Unbind him, and let him go!"**

John 11:1–44

THE FALLOUT: THE PLOT TO KILL JESUS

AS A RESULT, MANY OF THE JEWS who had come with Mary, and had seen what Jesus had done, believed in him. But some of them went back to the Pharisees and reported to them what Jesus had done.

Then the ruling priests and the Pharisees convened a meeting of the Sanhedrin council. "What are we going to do?" they asked. "For this man is performing numerous miraculous signs. If we let him go on like this, everyone will believe in him, and the Romans will come and destroy both our place and our nation."

But a certain one of them, Caiaphas, who was designated chief priest that year, declared to them, "You comprehend nothing at all! You fail to grasp that it is expedient for you that one man should die for the people, so that the whole nation should not perish!"

Now this he did not say on his own initiative, but being chief priest that year, he prophesied that Jesus was going to die for the nation, and not only for the nation, but also to gather the dispersed children of God and unite them as one.

So from that day on they plotted together to put him to death. Consequently, Jesus no longer continued to walk about openly in public among the Jews. Instead, he withdrew from there to a town called Ephraim, in the region near the desert wilderness. And there he remained with his disciples.

John 11:45–54

HEALING TEN OF LEPROSY: ONLY ONE SHOWS GRATITUDE

circa A.D. 30

N OW IT CAME ABOUT, when it was almost time for the Jewish Passover, that Jesus traveled along the border between Samaria and Galilee, on his way to Jerusalem. As he entered a certain village, ten leprous men approached him. Keeping their distance, they raised their voices, shouting, "Jesus! Master! Take pity, have mercy on us!"

Immediately when he saw them, he said to them, **"Go at once! Show yourselves to the priests!"** And it came about that as they were on their way, they were cleansed.

Now one of them, when he saw that he had been healed, turned back, praising and glorifying God, shouting at the top of his voice. And he threw himself on his face at Jesus' feet, giving thanks repeatedly to him. (And he was a Samaritan!)

Then Jesus responded and asked, **"Were there not ten made clean? But the other nine, where are they? Was none of them found to return and give praise and glory to God, except this foreigner?"** Then he said to him, **"Get up, and go on your way. Your faith has made you well!"**

Luke 17:11–19; John 11:55

THE SUDDENNESS OF THE COMING KINGDOM: THOSE NOT PREPARED WILL BE LEFT BEHIND

L ATER, HAVING BEEN QUESTIONED BY THE PHARISEES as to when the kingdom of God was coming, Jesus responded to them by saying:

The kingdom of God is not coming with observable signs.
Nor will there be announcements:
    "Look! Here it is!" or, "There it is!"
For take notice! The kingdom of God is among you.
    It is within you.

Then he said to his disciples:

The days are coming when you will long to see
    one of the days of the Son of Man.
But you will not see it.
Then they will say to you, "Look there!" "Look here!"
Do not leave where you are,
    and do not run after them in pursuit.
For just as when the lightning flashes,
    and lights up the sky from one horizon to the other,
    so will the Son of Man be in his day.
But first he must endure terrible suffering,
    and be utterly rejected by this generation!
And just as it was in the days of Noah,
    so it also shall be in the days of the Son of Man!
People were eating; they were drinking;
    they were marrying; and they were being given in marriage
    — right up to the day Noah entered the ark.
Then the flood came and destroyed them all!
It was just the same as happened in the days of Lot.
People were eating; they were drinking; they were buying;
    they were selling; they were planting; they were building.
But on the day Lot left Sodom,
    fire and burning sulphur rained down from heaven,
    and destroyed them all!

It will be precisely the same on the day
    that the Son of Man is revealed!
On that day, let not the one who is on the housetop,
    and has possessions in the house,
    go down to carry them away.
And likewise, let not the one who is the field turn back —
    remember Lot's wife!
Whoever attempts to secure his life shall lose it;
    and whoever loses his life shall secure it.

> I guarantee you: On that night there will be two in one bed;
> one will be taken, and the other will be left.
> There will be two women grinding grain at the same place;
> one will be taken, and the other will be left.

Then, in response, they asked him, "Where, Lord?"
He responded to them,

> Where the corpse is, there also the vultures will be gathered.

Luke 17:20–37

TWO PARABLES ON PRAYER: THE PERSISTENT WIDOW AND THE PHARISEE AND THE TAX COLLECTOR

THEN JESUS BEGAN TELLING THEM A PARABLE to illustrate that at all times they should pray and not lose heart — and never give up. This is what he said:

> In a certain city there was a judge who had no reverence for God, and who had no respect for man. And there was a widow in that city who kept coming to him, saying, "Grant me justice and legal protection from my adversary."
> And for a while he refused, but he eventually said to himself, "Even though I have no fear of God nor respect for man, yet because this widow keeps pestering me, I will grant her justice and legal protection, so that she does not wear me out by her continual visits."

Then the Lord added:

> Pay attention to what the unjust judge says!
> Now will not God grant justice to his chosen ones
>   who cry to him day and night?
> Will he delay long in helping them?
> Will he keep putting them off?
> I can guarantee you: He will quickly grant justice to them!
> However, when the Son of Man comes,
>   will he find persistent faith on earth?

Then he also addressed this parable to those certain ones who trusted in themselves that they were righteous, and regarded others with scornful contempt:

Two men went up to the temple courtyard to pray, one a Pharisee, and the other a tax collector.

The Pharisee, standing up, was praying this prayer to himself:

> God, I thank you that I am not like other people —
>   extortionists, cheaters, adulterers,
>   or even like this tax collector here!
> I fast by giving up eating twice a week.
> I tithe by giving away a tenth of my entire income.

But the tax collector, standing some distance away, was even unwilling to lift his eyes to heaven, but instead continued beating on his chest, saying, "God, be merciful to me, for I am a sinner!'

I can guarantee you: This man, rather than the other, went down to his home justified. For everyone who exalts himself shall be humbled, but he who humbles himself shall be exalted.

Luke 18:1–14

CONFLICT WITH THE PHARISEES: TEACHINGS ON DIVORCE

NOW IT CAME ABOUT THAT when Jesus had finished speaking these words, he departed from Galilee and entered the region of Judea, on the other side of the Jordan.

Again vast multitudes accompanied him, and thronged around him. And as he usually did, he taught them. And he healed them there.

Then some Pharisees came to him to trap him. "Is it lawful for a man to divorce his wife for any reason at all?" they asked.

Then he responded to them by saying:

> What did Moses command you?
> Have you never read, that he who created them at
>   the beginning of creation "made them male and female"?
> And he said, "For this reason shall a man leave
>   his father and mother,
>   and shall be joined inseparably to his wife,
>   and the two shall become one body."
> Consequently they are no longer two bodies, but one body.
> Therefore, what God has joined together, let man not separate.

"Why then," they asked him, "did Moses command to 'give a written certificate of divorce, and divorce her'?"

But Jesus replied to them:

> Moses permitted you to divorce your wives
>   because of your hardness of heart.
> That is why he wrote you this commandment.
> But from the beginning it has not been so ordained.
> Now I say to you, whoever divorces his wife,
>   except for sexual immorality,
>   and marries another woman, commits adultery.

The disciples responded to him, "If that is the only grounds for a man with his wife, it is better not to marry!"

But he replied to them:

> Not all men can accept this statement,
>   but only those to whom it has been gifted.
> For there are eunuchs who were born that way
>   from their mother's womb;
> And there are eunuchs who were made eunuchs by others;
> And there are also eunuchs who made themselves eunuchs
>   for the sake of the kingdom of heaven.
> He who is able to accept this, let him accept it.

Then in the house the disciples again began questioning him about this. So he said to them, **"Whoever divorces his wife, and marries another woman, commits adultery against her. And if she herself divorces her husband, and marries another man, she is committing adultery."**

Matthew 19:1–12; Mark 10:1–12

CHRIST AND THE CHILDREN: FOR OF SUCH IS THE KINGDOM OF HEAVEN

SOME CHILDREN WERE BROUGHT TO HIM so that he might place his hands on them and pray. And people were even bringing their babies to him, so that he might touch them and bless them. But when the disciples saw it they began rebuking those who brought them.

But when Jesus saw this, he was indignant. He called for them, saying, **"Let the little children come to me, and stop hindering them. For it is to such as** these that the kingdom of heaven belongs. **I guarantee you this truth: Whoever does not receive the kingdom of God like a little child will never enter it at all!"**

Then he took them in his arms and embraced them. And after laying his hands upon them, and tenderly blessing them, he went on from there.

Matthew 19:13–15; Mark 10:13–16; Luke 18:15–17

THE RICH YOUNG OFFICIAL: THE POSSESSION OF POSSESSIONS

NOW, AS HE WAS STARTING out on the road again, a certain official of the council came running up to him. And he knelt in front of him, and began questioning him. He asked, "Good teacher, what good deed must I do to inherit eternal life?"

Then Jesus addressed him in response:

> **Why do you ask me about what is good,**
> **and why do you call me good?**
> **There is only One who is perfectly good;**
> **no one is perfectly good except God alone!**
> **But if you want to enter into life,**
> **continually observe the commandments.**

"Which ones?" he inquired.

Then Jesus replied:

> **You know the commandments!**
> *You shall not commit murder.*
> *You shall not commit adultery.*
> *You shall not steal.*
> *You shall not give false evidence.*
> *You shall not defraud or cheat.*
> *Honor your father and mother,* **and also**
> *You shall love your neighbor as yourself.*

"Teacher, all these things I have carefully observed ever since my childhood," the young man declared to him. "What am I still lacking? What more is required?"

When Jesus heard this, Jesus felt a love for him. Then looking straight at him, Jesus told him:

You still lack one thing! If you want to be perfect, go and sell all your possessions and give it all to the poor, and you will have riches in heaven. Then come and follow me!

But when the young man heard this commandment, he was stunned. His countenance fell and he went away grieving and sorrowful, for he was extremely wealthy and owned many possessions.

Then Jesus, looking away as he watched him leave, said to his disciples:

I tell you the truth:
It will be very difficult for a rich man —
> **or anyone who is rich —**
> **to enter into the kingdom of heaven.**
And again I tell you:
It is easier for a camel to go through the needle's eye,
> **than for someone who is rich**
> **to enter the kingdom of God.**

The disciples were utterly amazed at his words. So then again he said to his disciples, **"Children, how difficult it is to enter the kingdom of God!"**

When the disciples heard this, they were even more astonished. "Then who can be saved?" they asked him.

But Jesus, looking at them intently, said to them, **"This is impossible with men, but not with God. For all things are possible with God!"** And again he said, **"What is humanly impossible is possible with God!"**

Then Peter began to say to him in reply, "Look, we have given up everything we own and followed you! What then will there be for us? What will we have?"

Then Jesus addressed them, by replying:

I can assure you this truth:
At the renewal of all things,
> **when the Son of Man is seated on his glorious throne,**
You, yourselves, who have followed me
> **shall also sit upon 12 thrones,**
> **judging the 12 tribes of Israel.**
And everyone who has left houses or farms or wife
> **or brothers or sisters or mother or father or children**
> **for my sake, or for the sake of the gospel,**
> **or for the sake of the kingdom of God,**
Shall certainly receive many times as much —
> **a hundred times as much!**

Now at this time, in this present age,
>
> they shall receive houses and farms,
>
> and brothers and sisters, and mothers and children —
>
> along with persecutions!
>
> And in the age to come, they shall inherit eternal life.
>
> However, many who are first will be last,
>
> and many who are last will be first.

Matthew 19:16–30; Mark 10:17–31; Luke 18:18–30

SOVEREIGNTY OF THE ESTATE OWNER: PARABLE OF THE VINEYARD LABORERS

FOR THE KINGDOM OF HEAVEN is like an estate owner who went out at daybreak to hire laborers for his vineyard. After agreeing with the laborers for a *denarius* for the daily wage, he sent them into his vineyard.

Then when he went out about the third hour, at nine in the morning, he saw others standing idle in the market place. So he said to them, "You, too, go into the vineyard, and I will pay you whatever is right." And so they went.

When he went out again about the sixth and the ninth hours, at about noon and three in the afternoon, he did the same thing.

About the 11th hour, at five in the afternoon, he went out and found others standing around. And he asked them, "Why have you been standing here idle all day long?"

"Because no one has hired us," they replied to him.

"You also go into the vineyard!" he responded to them.

Then when evening came, the owner of the vineyard said to his foreman, "Summon the laborers and pay them their wages, beginning with the last group, then ending with the first."

When those hired about the eleventh hour, at about five, came, each one received one *denarius,* the usual daily wage. Then when those hired first came, they assumed they would receive more. But each of them also received a *denarius*, the normal daily wage.

And when they received it, they protested to the estate owner, saying, "These last have worked only one hour, and you have treated them equal to us who have borne the burden of the day and the scorching heat."

But he answered by responding to one of them, "My friend, I am doing you no wrong. Did you not agree with me for a *denarius*? Take what is your pay and go your way. But I choose to give to this latecomer the same as I give to you. It is not against the law to do what I choose with what belongs to me. Or are you envious because I am generous? Do you begrudge my generosity?"

Thus, in this way, the last will be first, and the first will be last.

227

Matthew 20:1–16

JESUS' THIRD PREDICTION: HIS DEATH AND RESURRECTION

NOW AS JESUS WAS GOING on up to Jerusalem, they were all walking on the road. Jesus was walking on ahead of them, leading the way. And the Twelve were dismayed, while those who followed were afraid.

Then once again Jesus took the Twelve aside, and on the way privately began to tell them what was going to happen to him. **"Listen!"** he said to them. **"Pay attention! We are going up to Jerusalem, and all the things, which are written through the prophets about the Son of Man, will be accomplished.**

"The Son of Man will be betrayed and delivered to the ruling priests and to the scribes — those experts in religious Law. And they will sentence him to death, and turn him over to the Gentiles. Then they will ridicule him, and flog him, and spit upon him. And after they have scourged him, they will execute him. They will crucify him! And after three days he will rise again. On the third day he will be raised up — resurrected — brought back to life!"

But they did not understand anything about any of this. The meaning of what he was saying was concealed from them, and they did not grasp anything of what he was talking about.

Matthew 20:17–19; Mark 10:32–34; Luke 18:31–34

LEADERSHIP AND SERVICE: WARNING AGAINST AMBITIOUS PRIDE

THEN THE MOTHER OF James and John, the sons of Zebedee, came forward to him with her two sons. She knelt respectfully before him, wishing to make a request of him, to ask him for a favor.

"Teacher, we want you to do for us whatever we ask of you," the two sons said to him.

"**What do you want me to do for you?**" he asked them. And to their mother he asked, "**What is it that you wish to request?**"

"Command that in your kingdom, these two sons of mine may sit, one on your right and one on your left," she responded to him. "Yes, grant we may sit, one on your right, and one on your left, in your glory!" they replied to him.

But Jesus responded and said to them, "**You do not realize what you are asking! Are you able to drink the cup that I am about to drink, or to be baptized with the baptism with which I am baptized?**"

"Yes, we are able!" they then responded to him.

Then Jesus said to them, "**My cup of sorrow that I drink you shall certainly drink. And you shall be baptized with the baptism of suffering with which I am baptized. But to sit on my right and on my left, this is not mine to grant. Rather, it is for those for whom it has been planned and prepared by my Father.**"

When the ten heard this, they began to feel irritated and indignant. Then they became angry with the two brothers, James and John.

But Jesus summoned them to him, and said to them, "**You know that among the Gentiles, those who are acknowledged as rulers lord it over them with absolute despotic power, and their highest officials exercise absolute tyrannical authority over them. But it shall not be so among you! Rather, whoever wishes to become great among you shall be your servant; and whoever wishes to be most important among you shall be your slave and slave of all — just as the Son of Man did not come to be served but to serve, and to give his life a ransom price for many.**"

Matthew 20:20–28; Mark 10:35–45

JERUSALEM:

THE FINAL COUNTDOWN —
THE WEEK THAT CHANGED THE WORLD

6

SECTION SIX

HEALED BY FAITH:
TWO BLIND MEN RECEIVE THEIR SIGHT

9th of Nissan, A.D. 30

THEN THEY REACHED JERICHO. And as he was approaching Jericho with his disciples, a huge crowd followed him. It so happened that there, by the roadside, two blind men were sitting, begging. One of them was Bartimaeus (that is, son of Timaeus). Now when they heard a huge crowd going by, Bartimaeus began to inquire as to what it all meant. "What is happening?" he asked. And they told him, "Jesus of Nazareth is passing by."

So he shouted out, saying, "Jesus, Son of David, have mercy on me!" Then together, at the top of their voices they shouted, "Lord, please pity us, Son of David!"

Then many of those who led the way at the front of the crowd rebuked them. "Be quiet!" they sternly warned them. But they kept crying out all the more. "Son of David! Have mercy on us! Pity us!" they kept shouting even louder.

Then Jesus stopped and ordered that the man be brought to him. **"Call him,"** he directed them. **"Bring them both here,"** he added. So they called the blind men, saying to them, "Take courage! Get up! He is calling for you!"

So throwing his coat aside, Bartimaeus jumped up, and came to Jesus. And when they had both come near, Jesus answered them by questioning them. **"What do you want me to do for you?"** he asked.

"Rabboni, my teacher, I want to see again!" Bartimaeus pleaded. "Lord, we want our eyes to be opened!" they answered him.

Then deeply moved with compassion, Jesus touched their eyes. **"Go your way,"** Jesus said to them. **"Receive your sight! Your faith has made you well!"**

Instantly they regained their sight. Then they began following him on the road, glorifying God. And when all the people saw it, they gave praise to God.

Matthew 20:29-34; Mark 10:46-52; Luke 18:35-43

PREPARING FOR PASSOVER: LOOKING FOR JESUS

NOW THE PASSOVER OF THE JEWS was at hand. So before Passover, many from out of the countryside went up to Jerusalem to purify themselves with ceremonial cleansing.

Then as they were standing around in the temple courtyard, they kept looking for Jesus. They kept asking each other, "What do you think? Will he avoid coming to the Festival? Surely he will not come at all, will he?"

The ruling priests and the Pharisees by now had given orders that anyone who knew where Jesus was must immediately inform them, so that they could arrest him.

John 11:55-57

ZACCHAEUS AT JERICHO: SEEKING AND SAVING THE LOST

JESUS ENTERED JERICHO and was passing through. There lived a man named Zacchaeus, a high-ranking tax collector, who was very wealthy.

Zacchaeus wanted to see who Jesus was. But he could not get a good view because of the crowd, for he was of small build. So he ran on ahead and climbed up into a sycamore tree so he could see Jesus from that vantage point, for Jesus was coming that way.

When Jesus reached that place, he looked up and said, **"Zacchaeus, come down quickly! For I must be your houseguest today."**

Zacchaeus scrambled down and welcomed him gladly, and they went to his home.

Shocked, the bystanders began to grumble, muttering their disapproval. "He has gone to be a house guest of a man who is a sinner!"

Zacchaeus stopped and said to the Lord, "Listen, Lord! I've decided to give half of everything I own to the poor. And if I've defrauded anyone out of anything, I will refund him four times as much."

Jesus responded, **"Salvation has come to this house today! Zacchaeus, you also are a true son of Abraham! It was the lost that the Son of Man came to seek and to save."**

Luke 19:1-10

W HILE THEY WERE STILL DIGESTING what he had just said, Jesus (knowing full well that they were expecting the kingdom of heaven to be established immediately when they arrived in Jerusalem) told them a parable:

233

> A certain nobleman was commissioned to go into a distant country to receive a kingdom for himself, and then return. Before he left, he summoned ten of his servants and gave them each a *mina* coin (equivalent to about three years' wages). And he instructed them to "Invest these *minas* for me until I return."
>
> But his own citizens hated him, and sent a delegation after him, to tell the person who was to appoint him king, "We do not want this man to rule over us!"
>
> He was granted the kingdom nevertheless, and subsequently returned home where he immediately summoned those servants to whom he had given the money. He wanted an accounting of how they had invested it.
>
> The first servant of the ten entered and reported, "Your *mina*, sir, has made you ten times more." And he said to him, "You did well, you are a good servant. Because you have been proven trustworthy of this small amount, you shall have charge over ten cities."
>
> The second servant came, saying, "Your *mina*, sir, has made five *minas*." Similarly he said to him, "You are to govern five cities."
>
> Then another came, saying, "Here is your *mina*, sir, which I kept put away in a napkin; for I was afraid of you, because you are an exacting man. You withdraw what you never invest, and you harvest what you did not plant."
>
> The king said to him, "You worthless servant! I will judge you by your own words! You know I am an exacting man, taking interest out on what I had not deposited, and harvesting what I did not plant. If you knew that, why did you not deposit the money in the bank? At least I would have earned the interest!"
>
> To those who stood by, the king said, "Take the *mina* away from him, and give it to the one who has ten *minas*." And they responded to him, "Sir, he already has ten *minas*!"
>
> "I will guarantee you this: That to everyone who has, more will be given. But from the one who does not have much, even what he has

will be taken away! Now for the enemies of mine, who do not want me to rule over them, bring them here and slay them in my presence."

When Jesus finished giving these illustrations, he continued pressing on ahead, toward Jerusalem.

Luke 19:11–28

SIXTH DAY BEFORE PASSOVER

FRIDAY SUNSET
TO SATURDAY SUNSET

JESUS ANOINTED BY MARY

10th of Nissan, A.D. 30

THE FOLLOWING DAY, six days before the Passover, Jesus then came to Bethany. Bethany is where Lazarus lived, whom Jesus had raised from the dead.

There Martha, Mary, and Lazarus prepared a supper for him in his honor. Martha served, but Lazarus was one of those reclining at the table with him. His disciples were also there.

Then Mary took a whole pound of very costly ointment, oil of pure nard, and anointed the feet of Jesus, and toweled them dry with her hair, until the whole house was filled with the fragrance of the nard.

But Judas Iscariot, one of his disciples (the one who would soon betray him) said, "Why was this ointment not sold? It is worth three hundred *denarii* (or thirty thousand dollars)! The money could have been given to the poor." (He said this, not that he was concerned for the poor, but because he was a thief; and since he was in charge of the money box, he would periodically take out some of what was put into it.)

Jesus responded to Judas, **"Leave her alone. Let her keep this for the day of my burial. You will always have the poor with you. But you will not always have me."**

When a great throng of the people learned that he was there, they came, not only that they might glimpse Jesus, but also to see Lazarus, whom he had recently raised from the dead.

The ruling priests then resolved to also put Lazarus to death. Because of his resurrection, many of the people were turning away from the Jewish leaders, and believing in Jesus.

John 12:2–11

THE DONKEY AND HER COLT — *11th of Nissan, A.D. 30*

WHEN THEY APPROACHED Jerusalem and had reached Bethpage and Bethany, near Mount Olivet, the Mount of Olives (as it is called), then Jesus sent two of his disciples on ahead.

He said to them, **"Go into the village ahead of you, and immediately as you enter it you will find a donkey tethered there, and her unbroken colt beside her, on which no one has ever sat. Untie them, and bring them to me. Should anyone say anything to you, and ask you, 'Why are you doing this?' you say, 'The Lord needs them and will return them right away.' And immediately that person will send them with you."**

All this occurred to fulfill what was spoken through the prophet saying:

> Tell the daughter of Zion,
> "Fear not,
> Behold, your king is coming to you,
>   humble and gentle, and riding on a donkey's colt,
>   the foal of a beast of burden."

So the disciples went and did just what Jesus had directed them, and found a colt tied to a gate, outside a house on a street corner, and began to untie it.

As they were untying the colt, its owners and some of the bystanders asked them, "What are you doing, untying the colt?" The disciples responded to them, just as Jesus had directed, "The Lord needs it." So they gave their permission and let them go.

Then they brought the donkey and her colt to Jesus, and put their garments on them. And Jesus mounted the colt, and sat on the garments.

Matthew 21:1–7; Mark 11:1–7; Luke 19:29–36; John 12:12

PROPHECY

Rejoice, greatly,
O daughter of Zion;
Shout,
O daughter of Jerusalem:

Behold your king
is coming unto you:
He is just,
and having salvation;
Lowly,
and riding on an ass,
and upon a colt,
the foal of an ass.

Written by the prophet Zechariah, year c. 520 B.C.
Zechariah 9:9

THE TRIUMPHAL ENTRY

THEN MOST OF THE LARGE crowd that had come to the Passover festival heard that Jesus was coming to Jerusalem. They spread their own garments on the road. Many others cut straw from the fields and leafy frond branches from the palm trees and spread them on the road.

As he was riding along and was approaching the descent of the Mount of Olives, the crowds that preceded him and those that followed after were all praising God joyfully with a loud voice for all the miracles they had seen, shouting:

Hosanna to the Son of David!
Blessed is the King of Israel of our father David,
the one who comes in the name of the Lord!
Peace in heaven!
Hosanna in the highest heaven!

His disciples did not understand the significance of these prophecies and of all these things at first. But when Jesus was glorified, then they remembered that these things were written in the Scriptures about him! And that these things had been done to Him. And that they had participated in fulfilling the prophecies!

Some of the Pharisees in the multitude said to him, "Teacher, reprove your disciples!" But Jesus responded, **"I tell you, that if they kept quiet, the very stones would shout!"**

The Pharisees therefore said to each other, "You see there is nothing you can do! Look, the whole world is running after him!"

The multitude who were with him when he called Lazarus from the tomb, and raised him from the dead, kept talking about it. The reason the throngs went out to meet him was because they had heard that he had performed this miracle.

As he approached and saw the city, he wept over it saying, **"If even today you only recognized the conditions for peace! But now they are hidden from your eyes. For the days shall come upon you when your enemies will build a rampart against you and surround you and hem you in from every side. They will level you and your children within you to the ground, and they will not leave even one stone upon another in you, because you did not recognize when God himself visited you."**

Then he entered Jerusalem, and went into the temple courtyard.

By the time he entered Jerusalem, the whole city was stirred. "Who is this?" they were asking. "This is Jesus the prophet," the crowds were saying, "from Nazareth in Galilee."

Then having looked around at everything, and since it was already late, he returned to Bethany with the Twelve.

Matthew 21:8–11; Mark 11:8–11; Luke 19:36–44; John 12:12–19

You dare to come and stand in my presence,
    in the house that is called by name!
And say "Now we are safe to indulge
    in all these detestable things!"
Has this house that is called by my name
    become a cave of thieves?
Look, I can see all that you are doing!
    declares the Lord.

Written by the prophet Jeremiah, year c. 625 B.C.
Jeremiah 7:10-11

FOURTH·DAY BEFORE PASSOVER

SUNDAY SUNSET
TO MONDAY SUNSET

THE FIG TREE

12th of Nissan, A.D. 30

WHEN THEY DEPARTED from Bethany in the morning the next day, to return to the city, Jesus became hungry. Seeing a lone fig tree along the roadside in the distance, he went up to it to see if he might find anything on it. But when he got to it, he found nothing but leaves, for it was not the season for figs.

Then addressing the tree, so that his disciples heard him, Jesus said to it, **"Never again shall there ever be any fruit from you!"**

Immediately the fig tree withered up from its roots! Seeing it, the disciples marveled. "How does the fig tree wither so suddenly like that?" they asked.

Matthew 21:18–20; Mark 11:12–14

JESUS CLEARS THE TEMPLE

THEN JESUS CAME TO JERUSALEM, and entered the temple courtyard, and began to cast out all those who were selling and buying in the temple. He overturned the tables of the moneychangers, and the chairs of those who sold doves. He would not even permit anyone to carry a container across the temple courtyard.

He told them, **"It is written in the Scriptures, 'My house shall be called a house of prayer for all the nations!' But you are making it a den of robbers!"**

He was teaching daily in the temple courtyard. The blind and the lame came to him and he healed them. But when the ruling priests, and the scribes, and the leaders of the people heard what Jesus taught, and saw the wonderful things that he had done, and that children were crying out in the temple, "Hosanna to the

Son of David!" they became indignant, and began looking for some way to destroy him. But as hard as they tried, they could find no way to accomplish their purpose, for they were afraid of him, for the crowds were spellbound at his teachings and hung onto his every word. They asked him, "Do you hear what these children are saying?"

"Yes, I do," replied Jesus. **"Have you never read?
'Out of the mouths of infants and nursing babies
You have perfected praise for yourself.' "**

When evening came, he left them and with the Twelve went out of the city to Bethany, where Lazarus, whom he had recently raised from the dead, lived. There he lodged for the night.

Matthew 21:12–17; Mark 11:15–19; Luke 19:45–48

THIRTY-THREE

THIRD DAY BEFORE PASSOVER

MONDAY SUNSET TO TUESDAY SUNSET

FAITH THAT MOVES MOUNTAINS *13th of Nissan, A.D. 30*

A S THEY WERE PASSING early the next morning, they saw the fig tree withered from the roots up.

Peter said to Jesus, "Master, look! The fig tree that you cursed has shriveled up! How did it dry up so quickly?"

Jesus replied: **"Believe me when I say to you, if you have faith in God, and have no doubts at all, you will be able to not only do what was done to this fig tree, but even if you say to this mountain, 'Be uprooted and throw yourself into the sea,' it will happen!**

"He that does not doubt in his heart, but believes that what he says will happen, then it will happen for him. That is why I tell you, if you have faith, everything you ask in prayer, believing that you have received it, you will receive it!

"And whenever you pray, you must forgive anything you have against anyone. Then your Heavenly Father will also forgive you your transgressions."

Matthew 21:20–22; Mark 11:19–26

JESUS' AUTHORITY CHALLENGED

T HEN WHEN THEY CAME INTO JERUSALEM again, when he had entered the temple courtyard, the ruling priests and the scribes, along with the elders of the people, came up to him. As he was teaching and preaching the good news of the gospel they said, "By what authority are you doing these things, and who gave you this authority to do them?"

Jesus replied to them: **"I, too, will ask you one question. And if you answer it for me, then I will also tell you by what authority I do these things.**

"The baptism of John — did it come from heaven, or from humans? Tell me that!"

They argued it out among themselves. "If we say, 'from heaven,' He will say to us, 'Why then did not you believe him?' But if we say 'from humans,' we fear the multitude, for they are all convinced that John was a real prophet, and they will stone us to death!"

So they answered Jesus, "We do not know."

"**Then neither will I tell you by what authority I am doing these things,**" Jesus responded.

Matthew 21:23–27; Mark 11:27–33; Luke 20:1–8

THE TWO SONS

BUT WHAT DO YOU THINK about this?" Jesus asked them.

"**A man had two sons, and he went to the first and said, 'Son, go work in the vineyard today.' And he answered, 'I will not!' but later he regretted it and went. The father went to the second son and said the same thing, and he responded, 'Yes sir, I will go,' but did not. Which of the two did what their father wanted?**"

"The first," they responded.

"**Believe me when I tell you this,**" Jesus retorted. "**Tax collectors and prostitutes will get into the kingdom of God ahead of you. For John came to you and showed you the way of righteousness, but you did not believe him. Yet the tax collectors and prostitutes believed him. And even after seeing this, you still did not change your minds and believe him.**"

Matthew 21:28–32

THE WICKED TENANTS

THEN JESUS BEGAN TO TELL the people this parable:

Listen to another parable! There was once a man, a landowner, who planted a vineyard, and built a fence around it, and hewed out a winepress in it, and dug a vat under the winepress, and built a watchtower. Then he leased it out to tenant vinegrowers and went on a journey into another country for a long time.

When the vintage harvest time approached, he sent his servants to the tenants to collect his rightful share of the grapes from his vineyard. And the tenants took his servants and beat one, murdered another, and stoned a third, and sent them away empty-handed.

Again he sent another group of servants, more than the first, And they did the same to them, wounding one in the head, and treating them all shamefully, and sending them away empty-handed.

And he kept sending others, and some they beat, and others they killed, and others they cast out.

Finally, the owner of the vineyard had one more to send — his beloved son. So he said, "What shall I do? I will send my beloved son!"

So he sent his son to them, thinking, *They will respect my son.*

Yet when the tenants saw the son, they said to each other, "This is the heir. Come on, let us kill him and seize his inheritance!" So they seized him, and hurled him out of the vineyard, and murdered him.

Now when the owner of the vineyard returns, what will he do to those tenants?

"He will come and put those evil workers to a miserable death!" they responded, "and will lease out the vineyard to other tenants who will pay him his share of the grapes when they are ripe."

But they added, "God forbid! May it never be so!"

But Jesus looking straight at them, said to them,

Have you never read the Scriptures?
"The very stone which the builders rejected has
    become the main cornerstone;
This was the Lord's doing and
    it is marvelous for us to see!"
Therefore I guarantee you,
The kingdom of God will be taken away from you,
    and will be given to a nation
    who will give back their fair share of the fruit they produce.
And whoever falls upon that stone
    will be broken to pieces.
But if it falls on anyone,
    it will crush him to powder
    and scatter him like dust.

When the ruling priests and the Pharisees heard these parables, they realized that he was speaking the parables about them. However, although they wanted to try to get their hands on him and arrest him that very hour, they feared the crowd, who regarded him to be a prophet.

So they left him, and went away.

Matthew 21:33–46; Mark 12:1–13; Luke 20:9–19

THIRD DAY BEFORE PASSOVER

The Wedding Feast

AND AGAIN, JESUS SPOKE to them in parables. He said:

The kingdom of heaven may be compared to a king who planned a wedding reception for his son. He sent his servants out to summon those who were invited to the wedding feast. And they refused to come.

Again, he sent other servants, saying, "Tell those whom we invited, I have prepared my dinner. My bull and fat calves have been butchered, and everything is ready. Come to the wedding!"

But they paid no attention to it, and went their individual ways, one to his own farm, another to his place of business, while the rest seized his servants and brutally attacked them and murdered them.

The king was furious! And he sent his troops and destroyed those murderers and set their city on fire.

Then he said to his servants, "The wedding feast is ready, but those who were originally invited have proven unworthy. So go out to the main thoroughfares, and invite everyone you find to my wedding reception."

So those servants went out into the streets, and gathered together all they could find, good and bad alike. And the reception hall was filled with guests.

But when the king came to see his guests, he saw there a man not dressed in wedding clothes. So he asked him, "My friend, how did you get in here without a wedding garment?" The guest was speechless!

Then the king said to the attendants, "Bind him hand and foot, and throw him outside into the darkness. There he can cry and grind his teeth!"

For although many are invited, few are chosen to stay.

Matthew 22:1–14

The Pharisees' Tax Trap

THEN THE PHARISEES, watching for their opportunity, went and plotted together how they might trap him in his own words. Eventually they sent their own disciples to him along with some of Herod's party as spies. They were to pretend to be sincere, so they could trap him in some statement, so they could turn him over to the authority and jurisdiction of the governor.

So they asked him, "Master, we know that you are honest, impartial, and do not defer to anyone else's opinion, but instead faithfully and truthfully speak and teach the way of God. So tell us what you think. Is it lawful to pay Caesar a poll tax, or not? Should we pay it, or should we not?"

But Jesus, perceiving their treachery, hypocrisy, and malice, responded to them, **"Why put me to the test? You hypocrites! Show me the coin used for paying the poll tax. Let me see it!"**

They brought him a *denarius,* and Jesus inquired further, **"Whose likeness and inscription is this?"**

"Caesar's," they responded.

Then Jesus said to them, **"Then pay to Caesar what belongs to Caesar, and pay God what belongs to God!"**

They were amazed at him, and marveled at his reply, and that they could not trip him up publicly with his own words. So they went away, and left him alone, and had nothing more to say.

Matthew 22:15–22; Mark 12:13–17; Luke 20:20–26

THE SADDUCEES' TRICK
RESURRECTION QUESTION

O N THAT SAME DAY, some Sadducees, who deny there is a resurrection, asked him a question.

"Master, Moses wrote for us, 'If a man dies childless, and leaves behind a wife, his brother as next of kin should marry his widow, and have children with her for his brother.'

"Now there were seven brothers among us. The first married and died, and having no offspring, left his wife to his oldest brother. The second brother also died, leaving no children; and the third likewise, down to the seventh who also died. None of the seven brothers had any children. And last of all the woman herself died.

"In the resurrection, therefore, whose wife of the seven will the woman be? For all seven married her!"

"You are way off the mark," Jesus answered.

"Is this not the reason you are mistaken? Because you do not understand the Scriptures, nor the power of God! People in this world marry and are given in marriage. But after the resurrection, when those who are worthy rise from the dead, and come back to life, there is no such thing as 'being married' or 'being given in marriage.' Men cannot die anymore, but are like angels in heaven. For being children of the resurrection, they are children of God.

"But as for the resurrection of the dead, have you not read in the book of Moses? The passage about the burning bush, that which was spoken to you by God says:

> I am the God of Abraham,
>   and the God of Isaac,
>   and the God of Jacob.
> God is not the God of the dead,
>   but of the living.
> For all are alive, as God sees us.
> That is where you are badly mistaken!

Then some of the scribes (the experts of the Law) answered him and said, "Master, you have spoken the truth well!" For they did not have the courage to question him any further about anything.

And when the crowds heard this, they were astounded at his teaching.

Matthew 22:23–33; Mark 12:18–27; Luke 20:27–39

THE GREATEST COMMANDMENT

WHEN THE PHARISEES HEARD that he had silenced the Sadducees, they joined forces together to silence him. One of them, a scribe and expert of the Mosaic law, who had been listening to the discussion with the Sadducees, and recognizing how well Jesus answered them, asked him this test question: "Master, what is the Law's most important commandment?"

Jesus answered him,

> **The first is this:**
>   *"Hear O Israel, The Lord our God is one;*
>   *And you shall love the Lord your God with all your heart,*
>   *and with all your soul, and with all your mind,*
>   *and with all your strength."*
> **This is the greatest and foremost commandment.**
> **And a second is like it:**
>   *"You shall love your neighbor as yourself."*
> **All of the Law and the Prophets depend on**
>   **these two commandments.**
>   **No other commandments are greater than these.**

"You are absolutely right, Master!" responded the scribe. "You have accurately stated that *'He is one: and no other God exists but him. To love him with the whole heart, and the whole intelligence, and with the whole strength, and to love one's neighbor as oneself"* is much greater than all the burnt offerings and sacrifices."

Recognizing that he had answered wisely, Jesus said to him, **"You are not far from the kingdom of God!"**

After this, no one ventured to ask him any more questions.

Matthew 22:34–40; Mark 12:28–34

MESSIAH, SON OF DAVID

W HILE THE PHARISEES were still huddled together in the temple, Jesus asked them, **"What is your opinion of the Messiah? Whose son is he?"**

"The son of David!" they replied.

"Then how is it," Jesus continued, **"that David, inspired by the Spirit, calls him Lord when he says:**

> **The Lord said to my Lord,**
> **Sit at my right hand, until I put my enemies under your feet.**
> **and make them a footstool for your feet.**

"So if David thus calls him Lord, how can he be David's son?"

Not one of them could answer him a word, and from that day on no one dared ask him any further questions. But the great crowd was delighted with what they heard Jesus say.

Matthew 22:41–46; Mark 12:35–37; Luke 20:41–44

DENUNCIATION OF THE PHARISEES

T HEN, WHILE ALL THE PEOPLE were still listening, Jesus turned to his disciples and said:

> **The scribes and the Pharisees sit in Moses' seat, giving themselves power and authority. So everything they tell you, do and observe, but do not do what they do! For they do not practice what they preach!**
> **They pile heavy, back-breaking burdens on the shoulders of others, yet they themselves will not raise a finger to move them.**
> **Whatever they do is to be seen, for effect. They walk around in long robes, and increase the size of the religious insignias they wear,**

and lengthen the tassels of their shawls. They devour widows' houses and cover it up by making long prayers. They will receive the most severe condemnation!

They love the place of honor at banquets, the best seats in the synagogues, and respectful salutations at the market places, being called "Rabbi" or "Teacher" by others.

But as for you, do not look for others to call you "Rabbi," for you have one Teacher, and you are all brothers and equals. And do not call anyone on earth "Father," for you have only one Father, and he is in heaven. And do not be called "Master," for only one is your Master, the Messiah.

The greatest among you shall be your servant. Whoever exalts himself shall be humbled. And whoever humbles himself shall be exalted.

Matthew 23:1–12; Mark 12:38–40; Luke 20:45–47

HYPOCRISY OF THE PHARISEES

BUT WOE UNTO YOU, you hypocritical scribes and Pharisees!
>Because you lock people out of the kingdom of heaven!
For you will not go in yourselves,
>nor will you allow those who are trying to enter to do so.
Woe unto you, you hypocritical scribes and Pharisees!
For you travel about on sea and land to make one proselyte,
>and when he becomes your convert,
>you make him twice as fit for hell as you yourselves are!
Woe unto you, you blind guides who say,

>Whoever swears an oath by the temple, that is nothing.
>But whoever swears by the gold of the temple, he is obligated.

You blind fools! Which is greater?
>The gold, or the temple that makes the gold sacred?
Or again you say,

>If anyone swears by the altar, that is nothing.
>But if anyone swears by the offering that is on it,
>>he must keep his oath!

You blind men! Which is more important?
>The offering, or the altar that makes the offering holy?
Therefore, he who swears an oath by the altar,
>swears by it and everything on it.

And he who swears by the temple,
  swears by it and by him who dwells in it.
And he who swears by heaven,
  swears by the throne of God and by him who sits on it.
Woe unto you, fraudulent scribes and Pharisees!
For you tithe with one-tenth of your mint and dill and cumin,
  but you have neglected the weightier demands of the Law —
  to be just, merciful, and faithful.
These are the things you should have observed,
  without neglecting the others.
You blind guides!
You strain out insects, but gulp down whole camels!
Woe unto you, you hypocritical scribes and Pharisees!
For you clean the outside of the cup and dish,
  but inside they are full of the filth of your greed
  and self-indulgence.
You blind Pharisees!
First, clean the inside of the cup and the dish,
  so that the outside may be also cleansed.
Woe unto you, you biblical scholars and Pharisees, you hypocrites!
You are like whitewashed graves,
  which look beautiful on the outside,
  but inside are full of dead people's bones
  and every kind of decay.
So you, too, outwardly appear righteous unto men,
  but inside you are a mass of hypocrisy and wickedness.
Woe unto you, scribes and Pharisees! Hypocrites!
For you build tombs for the prophets
  and adorn the monuments of the righteous, and say,
  "If we had lived in the days of our forefathers,
  we would never have participated with them
  in shedding the blood of the prophets."
Consequently, you testify against yourselves
  that you are descendants of those who murdered the prophets
Then fill up to the brim the cup of your forefathers' guilt!
You snakes! You brood of vipers!
  How can you escape being condemned to the sentence of hell?
That is why I have been sending you
  prophets, sages, and teachers of the Scriptures,
  some of whom you kill and crucify,
  and others whom you flog in your synagogues
  and persecute from city to city.

As a result, on your hands is all the innocent blood
spilled on this earth, from the blood of innocent Abel
to the blood of Zachariah, Barachiah's son,
whom you murdered between the sanctuary and the altar.
Believe me when I tell you,
This generation who is living now will bear the guilt of all!

Matthew 23:13–36

JESUS MOURNS OVER JERUSALEM

OH JERUSALEM, JERUSALEM!
You murder the prophets
and stone the messengers who are sent to you.
How often have I longed to gather your children together
as a hen gathers her brood under her wings,
and you would have none of it!
Now your house is abandoned by me and left desolate.
For I tell you, from now on you will not see me again until you say:
"Blessed be he who comes in the name of the Lord."

Matthew 23:37–39

THE WIDOW'S PENNY

THEN JESUS SAT DOWN opposite the treasury and watched the rich people as they dropped their money into the collection box. Many rich people were putting in large amounts. Then a poor widow came and put in two small copper coins, both of them together worth a cent.

Calling his disciples to him, he said to them, **"Believe me when I say to you, this poor widow put in more than all the others who were contributing to the treasury. For they all contributed out of their surplus, but she, out of her poverty, put in everything she had — all that she had to live on!"**

Mark 12:41–44; Luke 21:1–4

THE MESSIAH GLORIFIED

AMONG THOSE WHO HAD COME to worship at the Passover feast were some Greeks. They approached Philip (who was from Bethsaida in Galilee), and requested of him, "Sir, we want to see Jesus." Philip went and told Andrew; then Andrew and Philip both went and told Jesus.

Jesus responded: **"The time has come for the Son of Man to be glorified. Believe me when I tell you, unless a grain of wheat falls into the earth and dies, it will be just one kernel. But if it dies, it yields much grain.**

"The man who lives his life will end up losing it. But he who disregards his life in this world will preserve it for eternal life.

"If any man wants to serve me, he must follow me. Where I am, my servant will also be. If any man wants to serve me, the Father will honor him.

"Now my soul is troubled! And what can I say? 'Father, save me from this hour?' No! For it was for this very purpose that I came — for this very hour! 'Father, glorify your name!' "

Then there came a voice out of heaven:

I have both glorified it! And I will glorify it again!

The crowd who stood around heard it and said that it had thundered. Others said, "An angel has spoken to him."

Jesus responded, **"This voice came for your benefit, not for mine. Now is the judgment of this world! Now shall the ruler of this world be thrown down and expelled! And when I am lifted up from the earth, I will draw all to myself."** (He said this to indicate the kind of death he would die, death by crucifixion.)

The crowd answered him, "We have heard from the Law that the Messiah is to remain here forever. How then can you say that the Son of Man must be 'lifted up'? Who is this 'Son of Man'?"

At this, Jesus answered them, **"For a little longer the light is still with you. Walk while you still have the light, so that darkness does not overtake you. For he who walks in the dark does not know where he is going. While you have the light, believe in the light so that you may become sons of light."**

When Jesus had said this, he left and secluded himself from them.

In spite of all the miraculous signs he had performed before them, they still did not believe in him. It was that the words spoken by the prophet Isaiah might be fulfilled:

> Lord, who has believed our message?
> And to whom has the arm of the Lord been revealed?

For this reason they could not believe. For again Isaiah also said:

> He has blinded their eyes, and hardened their heart;
>> lest they should see with their eyes,
>> and perceive with their heart,
>> and turn for me to heal them.

Isaiah said this because he saw Jesus' glory, and spoke of him.

Yet in spite of all this, many even of the authorities did believe in him. But they would not admit it publicly for fear of the Pharisees, in case they would be excommunicated from the synagogues. For they loved the approval of men more than the approval of God.

Jesus cried out and said,

> He who believes in me does not believe in me only,
>   but in him who sent me,
>   and he who sees me, sees him who sent me.
> I have come as light into the world,
>   that whoever believes in me need not remain in the dark.
> If anyone hears my teachings and does not keep them,
>   it is not I who judges him.
> For I did not come to judge the world, but to save it.
> Everyone who persistently rejects me
>   and refuses to accept my teachings has a judge.
> At the last day, the very words that I have spoken
>   will be his judge!
> For I have not spoken on my own authority.
> The Father who sent me has himself instructed me
>   what to say and how to speak.
> And I know that his orders are eternal life.
> Therefore, all that I say
> I speak only in accordance with what the Father has directed me.

John 12:20–50

PROPHECY

As a deer longs for flowing streams, so my soul longs for you, O God.
My soul thirsts for God, for the living God.

When may I go and see the face of God?
My tears are my food, day and night,
   while people taunt me all day long,

      Where is your God!
      Where is your God!

This I recall as I pour out my soul, how I walked with the throng
   in procession to the house of God
   amid shouts of praise and songs of thanksgiving
   with the multitudes celebrating Festival.

Why are you in despair, O my soul,
   and why have you become disturbed within me?
Put your hope in God!
   for I will still praise him.
He is my Savior and my God!
O my God, my soul is in despair within me.

Written by the sons of Korah, year c. 950 B.C..
Psalm 42:1–6

N OW AS SOME OF THE DISCIPLES were talking about the temple, how it was adorned with beautiful stones and various votive offerings, Jesus said, **"As for these things which you see, I guarantee that the days will come when there will not be left one stone upon another which will not be torn down."**

And they questioned him, asking, "Master, when will this happen, and what will be the sign when this is about to occur?"

And he said, **"Be careful that you are not misled. For many will come using my name, saying, 'I am he!' and 'The time is very near now.' Do not go after them!**

"And when you hear of wars and revolutions, do not be terrified. For these things must indeed occur first; but the end does not follow immediately."

Then he continued by saying to them,

Nation will rise against nation, and kingdom against kingdom. There will be terrible earthquakes, and plagues, and famines in various places. And there will be terrifying sights, and great miraculous signs coming from the sky.

But before all these things occur, they will seize you and persecute you, and turn you over to the synagogues and prisons, bringing you before kings and governors because of my name. This will offer you opportunity to tell them the truth. So make up your minds not to prepare your defense beforehand, because I will personally give you such ability and wisdom to speak, that none of your opponents combined will be able to resist or refute you!

You will even be betrayed by parents and brothers, and relatives, and friends; and they will put some of you to death! You will be hated by everyone everywhere because of your allegiance to me. And yet not a single hair on your head will be lost. By your endurance you will save your souls!

But when you see Jerusalem surrounded by armed forces, then realize that her devastation has arrived! Then it is time for those who are in Judea to flee to the mountains, and those who are within the city to escape. Do not let those who are in the country come back into town, because these are the days of vengeance when all that was written in the Scriptures will come true.

Woe to pregnant women and to those who are still nursing their babies in those days. For there will be bitter distress on this country, and great punishment on these people. They will fall by the edge of the sword, and be taken off as prisoners of war unto all nations; and Jerusalem will be trampled underfoot by the heathen Gentiles, until the times of the Gentiles are completed.

And there will be miraculous signs in the sun and moon and stars. On earth there will be despair among the other nations, perplexed at the roaring and surge of the sea.

People will faint with terror when they begin realizing what is coming upon the world. For the celestial powers will be shaken.

Then they will see the Son of Man coming in a cloud with great power and great splendor! Now when these things begin to occur, stand confidently erect and look upwards, because your redemption is drawing near.

Then he told them a parable as an illustration:

Look at the fig tree — or indeed all trees. As soon as you see them come out in leaf, you know for yourselves, without being told, that the summer is now near. Similarly, when you see these things happening, be equally sure that the kingdom of God is near.

Believe me when I say to you, this present generation will not all pass away until all this takes place. The sky and earth will pass away, but my words will never pass away.

Be on your guard! Do not let your hearts be weighed down with dissipation, drunkenness, and the worries of this life, and that day suddenly spring on you like a trap. For it will surprise all who inhabit the face of the earth anywhere. But be vigilant at all times, always on the alert, praying that you will have the strength to escape all of this that will occur, so that you will stand in the presence of the Son of Man.

Luke 21:5–36

JESUS' DAILY PRACTICE

NOW DURING THE DAYTIME, Jesus was teaching in the temple courtyard. But at evening he would leave, and spend the night on Mount Olivet, as it was called.

And all the people would rise early each morning, and return to the temple courtyard to listen to him.

Luke 21:37–38

Jesus Forecasts the Future: The "Olivet Discourse"

A S JESUS WAS LEAVING the temple courtyard and was going away, his disciples came up to him and pointed to the temple buildings.

One of his disciples said to him, "Just look at those massive stones, Teacher! What magnificent buildings!"

Jesus asked them: **"You see all these buildings, do you not? I guarantee you this truth: Not one stone will be left upon another. All will be torn down!"**

A little later, when he was sitting alone on the Mount of Olives, facing toward the temple, his disciples Peter, James, John, and Andrew asked him privately, "Tell us, when will all this happen? What will be a signal of your coming, when all these things are to be accomplished? When will the world come to an end?"

Jesus began to answer them:

> Be careful that no one misleads you! Because many will come in my name saying, "I am the Messiah." And they will mislead many people.
>
> You will hear of wars and rumors of wars. See to it that you are not frightened, for these things must happen, but it will not be the end yet. Nation will go to war against nation, and kingdom against kingdom. There will be numerous famines and earthquakes in various places. But these are just the beginning of birth pangs.
>
> Then they will hand you over to be tortured, and executed, and you will be hated by all nations on account of your allegiance to me.
>
> Be on your guard! Watch out for yourselves! They will hand you over to the local courts. You will be beaten in the synagogues. You will be arraigned before governors and kings on account of me, as evidence to them.
>
> At that time many will turn away from the faith, and will betray one another, and hate each other. And many false prophets will appear, and deceive many. Because of the spread of lawlessness, most people's love will grow cold.
>
> Whenever they arrest you and bring you to trial, do not worry beforehand about what to say. Just say whatever is given you at the time. For it will not be you who will speak, but the Holy Spirit!
>
> Brother will deliver brother to death, and a father his child. Children will rebel against their own parents and condemn them to death. And you will be hated by all because you are committed to me.
>
> But the one who endures to the end will be saved.

And the gospel of the kingdom will first be proclaimed as evidence to all nations. Then the end of the world will come!

Therefore when you see the "Abomination of Desolation" (which Daniel the prophet mentioned) **usurping the Holy Place, where it should not be!** (let the reader comprehend) **then let those of you in Judea flee to the mountains.**

Anyone on the housetop must not waste time and go down, or enter the house, or take anything out. Anyone in the field must not return to get a coat.

How horrible for expectant women and nursing mothers in those days! Pray that your escape will not take place in winter or on a Sabbath.

For at that time there will be great tribulation, such misery as has never been equaled from when the world was created until now, nor ever will be again.

If the Lord would not shorten those days of troubles, no one could survive. But for the sake of God's own people, whom he has chosen, those days will be reduced.

And if at that time anyone says to you, "Look! Here is the Messiah!" or "Look! There he is!" do not believe it.

For false messiahs and false prophets will appear and perform spectacular signs and miracles to deceive even the elect, if that were possible.

So be on your guard! Remember this, that I have told you everything in advance.

So if they tell you, "Look! He is out in the wilderness," do not go out there. Or "He is hiding in the inner rooms," do not believe it.

For just as lightning that comes out of the east flashes so that it is visible in the west, so will the coming of the Son of Man.

Wherever there is a carcass, there the vultures will gather. But in those days, immediately following that tribulation, the sun will be darkened.

The moon will stop shining. The stars will come falling from the sky. The powers of the universe will be shaken.

Then all the people of the earth will see the sign of the Son of Man in the heavens, and will mourn when they see the Son of Man coming in the clouds with overwhelming power and glory.

And then he will send his angels with a loud trumpet blast, and gather together his chosen from the four points of the compass, from the furthest bounds of the earth to the furthest bounds of the heavens.

Now learn this lesson from the fig tree: As soon as its branches become tender and sprout leaves, you know that summer is near. In the same way when you see all these things happening, you recognize that he is near, right at the very gates!

I can guarantee this truth: This generation will certainly not disappear until all these things take place. The heavens and earth will disappear, but my words will never disappear!

No one knows about that actual day or hour, not even the angels in heaven, nor the Son, but the Father alone!

For the coming of the Son of Man will be just as in the days of Noah. For in the days before the flood, people were eating and drinking, marrying and giving in marriage, up to the day that Noah entered the ark. They did not understand what would happen until the flood came and swept them all away.

That is how it will be at the coming of the Son of Man. Two men will be out in the field; one will be taken and the other left. Two women will be grinding together at the mill; one will be taken and the other left.

Therefore be on guard! Be on the alert! Because you do not know on which appointed day your Lord is coming.

But be certain of this: If the owner of the house had known what time of the night the burglar would arrive, he would have stayed awake and would not have allowed anyone to break into his house.

For this same reason you must continue to be prepared, for at a time you are not expecting, the Son of Man will arrive.

Who then is like the trusted and trustworthy servant who, when the master leaves on a trip, is placed in charge of the other household servants, to manage their food allowances at the proper times? Each servant is assigned his responsibility, and the guard at the door is told to continually keep watch.

It would be fortunate for that servant if the master finds him doing precisely that when he returns! I tell you the truth: He will put him in charge of everything else he owns.

But suppose that servant is dishonest and says to himself, "My master is delayed," and then begins to bully his fellow servants, and to eat and drink with drunkards. The master will come back on a day when that servant does not expect him, and at an hour of which he is unaware, and will lash him to shreds, and assign him the same fate as the hypocrites where there will be wailing and grinding of teeth.

Therefore keep alert, because you do not know when the owner of the house will return. It could be in the evening, or at midnight, or at daybreak when the rooster crows, or in the morning. Make sure he does not come unexpectedly and find you asleep. What I say to you, I say to everybody: "Keep alert!"

Matthew 24:1–51; Mark 13:1–37

TEN BRIDESMAIDS

AT THAT TIME the kingdom of heaven will be like ten bridesmaids who took their lamps and went out to meet the bridegroom. Five of them were foolish, and five were sensible.

When the foolish ones took their lamps, they did not take any extra oil with them, whereas the sensible ones took oil in flasks as well as with their lamps. The bridegroom was delayed a long time in coming, and they all became drowsy and fell asleep.

At midnight the cry rang out: "Look! Here comes the bridegroom! Come out to meet him!"

Then all of the bridesmaids woke up and trimmed their lamps. The foolish ones said to the sensible, "Give us some of your oil, for our lamps are going out."

"Oh, no," the prudent replied. "There may not be enough for both us and you. Instead, you had better go to those who sell oil and buy some for yourselves."

But while they had gone away to buy the oil, the bridegroom arrived, and those who were ready went with him into the wedding reception. And the door was locked shut.

Later the other bridesmaids also came, saying, "Lord, Lord, open the door for us!" But he replied, "I tell you the truth, I do not know you."

Therefore keep on the alert, for you do not know the day nor the hour.

Matthew 25:1–13

FIVE HUNDRED THOUSAND DOLLARS

AGAIN, IT WILL BE LIKE a man about to go abroad, who called his staff and entrusted them with his resources.

To the one he gave five *talents* or about five hundred thousand dollars, to another two thousand, and to another one thousand, each proportioned to his individual ability. Then he left on his trip. (A *talent* was worth between 15 and 20 years wages for a laborer.)

The one who had received the five hundred thousand dollars immediately invested it, and gained five hundred thousand more in profit. Similarly, the one who had the two hundred thousand dollars gained two more. But the one who had received the one hundred thousand dollars went off, dug a hole in the ground, and buried his master's money.

After a long time the master returned and settled accounts with his staff.

The one who had received the five hundred thousand dollars came forward and brought the other five. "Sir," he said, "you entrusted me with five hundred thousand dollars. See, I have gained five hundred thousand more."

His master replied to him, "Well done, my good and reliable servant! You have been faithful and trustworthy over a little; I will put you in charge of much. Come and share your master's happiness!"

The one with the two hundred thousand dollars also came forward. "Sir," he said, "you entrusted me with two hundred thousand dollars. See, I have gained two hundred thousand more." His master replied to him, "Well done, my good and reliable servant! You have been faithful and trustworthy over a little; I will put you in charge of much. Come and share your master's happiness!"

Then the one who had the one hundred thousand dollars came forward. "Sir," he said, "I knew you to be a demanding man, harvesting where you have not sown, and gathering where you have not winnowed. So I was afraid, and I went out and hid your hundred thousand dollars in the ground. See, here is what is yours."

His master replied to him, "You worthless and lazy servant! So you knew that I harvested where I have not sown, and gathered where I have not winnowed! Then you should have invested my money with the bankers, so that on my return, I would have received my principle with interest.

"Now, take the hundred thousand dollars away from him, and give it to the one who has the million dollars. For to all that have, more will be given, and will have more than enough. But from the ones who do not have, even what they do have will be taken away.

"As for this worthless servant, throw him outside into the outer darkness where there will be wailing and grinding of teeth!"

Matthew 25:14–30

WHEN THE SON OF MAN comes in his majestic splendor, and all his angels with him, he will then take his seat on his majestic throne, with all nations before him.

He will separate them into two groups, as a shepherd separates sheep from goats. He will put the sheep on his right and the goats on the left.

Then the King will say to those on his right, "Come, you who are blessed by my Father. Inherit the kingdom reserved for you from the creation of the world. For I was hungry and you gave me something to eat. I was thirsty and you gave me something to drink. I was lonely and you welcomed me into your home. I needed clothes and you gave me something to wear. I was sick and you took care of me. I was in prison and you came to visit me."

Then the truly upright will answer him, "Lord, when did we see you hungry and feed you, or thirsty and gave you something to drink? When did we see you lonely and welcome you into our home, or needing clothes and gave you something to wear? When did we see you sick or in prison and go to visit you?"

Then the King will answer and say to them, "Let me assure you this truth: Anything you did for one of these brothers of mine, however humble, you did it to me."

Then he will say to those on his left, "Depart from me! God has cursed you! Go into the everlasting fire prepared for the devil and his angels. For when I was hungry you gave me nothing to eat. When I was thirsty you gave me nothing to drink. When I was lonely you never made me welcome in your homes. When I needed clothes you did not give me anything to wear. When I was sick and in prison, you did not come to help me."

Then they, too, will ask, "Lord, when was it that we saw you hungry, or thirsty, or needing clothes, or sick or in prison, and never came to help you?"

Then he will answer them, "I guarantee you this truth: Anything you neglected to do to one of the seemingly least significant, you failed to do it for me."

Then they will go off to everlasting punishment, but the truly upright will enter into eternal life.

Matthew 25:31–46

Jesus Forecasts His Own Crucifixion

WHEN JESUS HAD FINISHED his full discourse, he said to his disciples, **"As you know, the Passover and Festival of Unleavened Bread will be celebrated in just two days. At that time the Son of Man will be handed over to be crucified!"**

At that very same time, the ruling priests, the scribes and teachers of the Law, and the elders of the people assembled together in the palace court of the high priest, whose name was Caiaphas. They were trying to devise some strategic scheme to arrest Jesus by treachery, and put him to death. "But not during the Festival," they kept repeating, "or there may be a riot among the people."

Matthew 26:1–5; Mark 14:1–2

CHAPTER

THIRTY-FOUR

SECOND DAY BEFORE PASSOVER

TUESDAY SUNSET
TO WEDNESDAY SUNSET

THE REANOINTING OF JESUS
14th of Nissan, A.D. 30

NOW JESUS WENT BACK to Bethany, as a guest in the house of a man known as Simon the Leper. While he was relaxing at the table, a woman came to Him with an alabaster jar of very expensive ointment made of pure nard. She broke open the jar and began pouring the ointment on his head.

When the disciples who were present saw this, they were very indignant. "Why this waste!" they said among themselves. "This ointment could have been sold for a large sum, perhaps three hundred *denarii* (a *denarius* being the equivalent of a day's wage) or thirty thousand dollars, and the money given to the poor." And they harshly rebuked her.

But Jesus, knowing what was going on, said to them, **"Leave her alone! Why are you troubling this woman? She has done a beautiful thing to me. For you will always have the poor with you and you can help them any time you want. But you will not always have me. She has done what she could. When she poured this ointment on me, she did it to prepare me for my burial. I tell you the truth: Wherever the gospel is proclaimed throughout the whole world, what she has done will also be spoken in remembrance of her."**

Matthew 26:6–13; Mark 14:3–9

THE ULTIMATE BETRAYAL

NOW THE FESTIVAL of Unleavened Bread called the Passover was drawing near, and the ruling priests and teachers of the Law were searching for some way to put him to death. However, they were afraid of the people.

Then Satan entered into Judas, surnamed Iscariot, one of the Twelve. He went to the ruling priests and the officers of the temple guard and discussed a plan with them about how he might betray him to them. He asked them, "What are you prepared to pay me if I betray him to you?"

They were delighted to hear this and contracted to pay him money. They offered him 30 silver coins. So he agreed, and from then on began looking for an opportunity to betray him to them when no crowd was present.

Matthew 26:14–16; Mark 14:10–11; Luke 22:1–6

PREPARATION FOR PASSOVER

THEN CAME THE FIRST DAY of the Festival of Unleavened Bread when it was customary for the Passover lamb to be sacrificed.

Jesus sent Peter and John, saying, **"Go and make preparations for us to eat the Passover meal."**

Jesus' disciples asked him, "Where do you want us to go and make preparations for you to eat the Passover?"

So in reply he sent the two of his disciples, telling them, **"Pay attention to this! Go into the city, and just as you enter the city a man carrying a jar of water will meet you. Follow him to the house that he enters, and say to the owner of the house, 'The Master says: My appointed time is near. Where in your house is the guest room where I might celebrate the Passover with my disciples?' He will show you to a large upper room. Make preparations for us there."**

Then the disciples left, went into the city, and found everything just as Jesus had told them. So they did as Jesus had directed, and prepared the Passover.

Matthew 26:17–19; Mark 14:12–16; Luke 22:7–13

LAST DAYS OF MESSIAH:

THE WEEKEND THAT
CHANGED THE WORLD

7

SECTION SEVEN

JESUS' LESSON IN HUMILITY — *15th of Nissan, A.D. 30*

NOW IT WAS just before the Passover feast. Jesus knew that the time had come for him to leave this world and go back to the Father. He loved his own who were in the world. He would now show them the full extent of his love, to the end.

The devil had already put into the heart of Judas, son of Simon Iscariot, to betray him.

When evening hour came, Jesus arrived and took his place reclining at the table with the Twelve. Supper was served.

Jesus was fully aware that the Father had put everything into his hands and under his power, and that he had come from God, and that he was now returning to God. With that knowledge, he rose from the table, laid aside his outer garments, and wrapped a towel around his waist. Then he poured water into a basin and began to wash his disciples feet, drying them with the towel he had wrapped around himself.

So he came to Simon Peter, who said to him, "Lord, are my feet to be washed by you?"

"You do not comprehend now what I am doing, but later you will understand," Jesus answered Peter.

"You will never wash my feet!" Peter said to him.

"Unless I wash you," Jesus answered him, **"you share no part with me."**

"Master, wash not just my feet, but my hands as well!" Simon Peter responded to him.

"Anyone who has had a bath needs only to wash his feet; then his whole body is clean," Jesus responded to him. **"And you are clean. But not all."** For he knew who was betraying him. That was why he added, **"Not all of you are clean."**

So when he had finished washing their feet, and had put on his outer garments again, and was again reclining at the table, he asked them, **"Do you understand what I have done for you? You call me 'Teacher' and 'Master,' and rightly so, for that is what I am.**

"So if I, your Master and Teacher, have washed your feet, you too ought to wash one another's feet. For I have set you an example, that you also should do as I have done to you.

"I guarantee you this solemn truth: No servant is greater than his master, nor is one who is sent greater than the one who sent him. Now since you know these things, you will be blessed if you do them.

"I am not referring to all of you. I know those whom I have chosen. But it is that the Scriptures be fulfilled: 'He who eats my bread has lifted his heel against me.'

"I am telling you now before it occurs, so that when is does happen, you will believe that I am who I say I am. I most solemnly guarantee you this truth: Whoever accepts anyone I send accepts me; and whoever accepts me, accepts the one who sent me."

Matthew 26:20; Mark 14:17; Luke 22:14; John 13:1–20

PROPHECY

All who hate me whisper together against me;
   they conceive the worst for me:

   A fatal disease has gripped him,
   He will never rise up again from where he lies.

Even my close friend, in whom I trusted, who ate my bread with me,
Has lifted his heel against me.

Written by King David, year c. 1000 B.C.
Psalm 41:7–9

THE LEADER AS SERVER

NOW A DISPUTE AROSE among them as to which of them was regarded to be the greatest.

But Jesus said to them, **"The kings of the heathen Gentiles lord it over them, and those who lord it over them call themselves 'benefactors.'**

"But not so with you! On the contrary, the greatest among you must become like the youngest, and the leader like the server. For who is greater, the one who reclines at the table, or the one who serves? Is it not the one who reclines at the table? But I am among you as the one who serves.

"You are those who have remained by me in my trials. Just as the Father has conferred on me a kingdom, so do I confer on you, so that you might eat and drink at my table in my kingdom, and sit on thrones, judging the 12 tribes of Israel."

Luke 22:24–30

JESUS REVEALS HIS BETRAYER

WHILE THEY WERE RECLINING at the table eating, Jesus was anguished in spirit and exclaimed, **"I must tell you this truth: One of you is about to betray me — one who is eating with you!"**

His disciples were deeply distressed, and kept staring at one another in bewilderment as to whom among them he meant. They began to question among themselves which of them might be he who would do this. Then they said to him, one after another, "Surely it is not I, Lord! Is it?"

One of them, the disciple whom Jesus loved, was reclining next to him. Simon Peter motioned to this disciple and said, "Ask him whom he means."

Leaning back close to Jesus' chest, John asked him, "Who is it, Lord?"

Jesus answered, **"It is one of the Twelve. The hand of the one betraying me is with mine on the table. One who has just dipped his hand into the same bowl with me will betray me! The one to whom I will give this bread when I have dipped it into the bowl.**

"The Son of Man will go just as it is decreed about him. But woe to that man who betrays the Son of Man! It would have been better for him if he had never been born!"

Then Judas, the one who would betray him, said, "Surely it is not I, Lord! Is it?"

Jesus said to him, **"The words are yours. You have said it yourself."**

Then dipping the piece of bread, he gave it to Judas, son of Simon Iscariot. As soon as Judas took the bread, Satan entered into him.

"What you are about to do, do quickly," Jesus told him.

But no one reclining at the table understood why Jesus had said this to him. Since Judas had charge of the money box, some supposed that Jesus was telling him to buy what was needed for the Festival, or that he should give something to the poor.

As soon as Judas had taken the bread, he immediately went out. And it was night.

Matthew 26:23–25; Mark 14:20–21; Luke 22:21–23; John 13:21–30

THE LORD'S SUPPER INSTITUTED

WHILE RECLINED AT THE TABLE with his disciples, Jesus said to them, **"I have earnestly desired to eat this Passover with you before I suffer. For I tell you, I will never again eat it until it finds fulfillment in the kingdom of God."**

Then taking the cup, and after giving thanks, He said, **"Take this and divide it among yourselves. For I tell you, from this moment I will never drink the fruit of the vine at all until the kingdom of God comes."**

While they were eating, Jesus took a loaf of bread, gave thanks and broke it, and gave it to his disciples, saying, **"Take and eat it. This is my body which is given for you. Do this in remembrance of me."**

Then in the same way, after the supper he took the cup, gave thanks, and offered it to them, saying, **"Drink from it, all of you."** And they all drank from it.

"This cup is my blood of the new covenant, which is poured out for you, and for many, for the forgiveness of sins. Do this, whenever you drink it, in remembrance of me. I solemnly tell you the truth: I will not drink again of this fruit of the vine from now on until that day when I drink it anew with you in my Father's kingdom — the kingdom of God."

For wherever you eat this bread and drink this cup, you give testimony to the Lord's death until he comes.

Matthew 26:26–29; Mark 14:22–25; Luke 22:19–23; 1 Corinthians 11:23–26

JESUS PREDICTS PETER'S DENIAL

WITH JUDAS HAVING GONE OUT, Jesus said:

"Now the Son of Man is glorified, and in him God has been glorified. If God has been glorified in him, God will also glorify him in himself, and will glorify him at once.

"Dear little children, I am to be with you only a little while longer. You will look for me, and just as I told the Jews — the people, so I now also tell you.

"Where I am going you are not able to come.

"A new commandment I am giving you, that you love one another. Even as I have loved you, so you too should love one another.

"By this everyone will recognize that you are my disciples, since you have love for one another."

Simon Peter asked him, "Master, where are you going?"

Jesus replied, **"Where I am going, you cannot follow me now. But you shall follow me afterward."**

Peter responded to him, "Master, why can I not follow you now? I will lay down my life for you!"

Then Jesus replied, **"Will you really lay down your life for me? I most solemnly tell you this truth: Before a rooster crows, you will have disowned me three times!**

"Simon, Simon, listen! Satan has demanded that all of you be given up to him, to sift you all as wheat. But I have prayed, especially for you Peter, that your faith may not fail. And when you yourself have returned again, you in turn must strengthen your brothers."

But Peter replied, "Master, I am prepared to go with you, both to prison, and to death!"

Jesus answered, **"I tell you, Peter, the rooster will not crow today until you have three times denied that you even know me!"**

Luke 22:31–34; John 13:31–38

PROPHECY

Therefore I shall give him his portion among the great,
and he shall divide the spoils with the mighty:
Because he poured out his life unto death,
and he was numbered with the transgressors.
For he bore the sin of many,
and interceded for the transgressors.

Written by the prophet Isaiah, year c. 700 B.C.
Isaiah 53:12

THE DISCIPLES' FIRST COMMISSION

T HEN JESUS ANSWERED THEM, **"When I sent you out without a wallet, travel bag, or sandals, you did not lack anything, did you?"**

"No, nothing!" they replied.

Then he said to them, **"But now, let the one who has a wallet take it, and likewise a travel bag. And let the one who has no sword sell his cloak and buy one. For I tell you, that which is written is about to be fulfilled in me: 'And he was numbered with the transgressors.' For what is written about me is now coming to fulfillment."**

Then they said, "Look, Lord, here are two swords."

"It is enough!" he replied to them.

Luke 22:35–38

Do NOT LET YOUR HEARTS be troubled! Believe in God; Believe also in me!

> In my Father's house are many dwelling places.
> If it were not so would I have told you
>> that I am going there to prepare a place for you?
> And since I am going to prepare a place for you,
>> I shall return again, and will take you back with me,
>> so that you will also be where I am.
> And where I am going, you know the way.

Thomas said to him, "Lord, we do not even know where you are going! So how can we know the way?"

Jesus said:

> I am the way, the truth, and the life.
> No one comes to the Father, except through me.
> If you had known me —
>> who I really am —
>> you would also have known my Father.
> From now on you know him and have seen him.

Philip said, "Lord, show us the Father, and that will be enough for us." Jesus responded to him,

> Have I been among you for so long a time, Philip,
>> and you still do not know who I am?
> Whoever has seen me has seen the Father!
> Then how can you say, "Show us the Father?"
> Do you not believe that I am in the Father,
>> and the Father is in me?
> The words that I speak to you
>> I do not speak on my own authority.
> Rather it is my Father, living in me,
>> who is doing his own works.
> Believe in me when I say that
>> I am in the Father,
>> and the Father is in me.
> Or else accept on the evidence
>> of the works themselves.
> I guarantee you this truth:

Anyone who believes in me
    will also do the works that I do,
    and will do even greater works than these,
    because I am going to the Father.
And I will do whatever you ask in my name,
    that the Father may be glorified in the Son.
If you ask me for anything in my name, I will do it.
If you love me, you will keep my commandments.
And I shall ask the Father and he will give you
    another advocate who will live with you forever —
The Spirit of Truth whom the world cannot accept
    because it neither sees nor recognizes him.
You know him, because he lives with you,
    and will be in you.
I shall not leave you deserted.
I shall come back to you.
In a little while the world will no longer see me,
    but you will see that I live.
Because I will continue to live,
    you will also live.
When that time comes you shall realize
    that I am in my Father, and you in me,
    and I in you.
Whoever has received and obeys my commandments
    is the person who loves me.
And whoever loves me will be loved by my Father;
    and I shall love him, and reveal myself to him.

Judas, not Iscariot, asked him, "Master, how is it that you will reveal yourself to us, and not to the world?"

Jesus replied to him:

If anyone loves me he will keep my word;
And my Father will love him; and we will come to him;
    and make our dwelling place in him.
Anyone who does not love me does not keep my words.
And the word which you hear is not mine,
    but comes from the Father who sent me.
I have told you these things
    while I am still dwelling with you.

But the Advocate, the Holy Spirit,
    whom the Father will send in my name,
    will teach you all things,
    and cause you to recollect everything that I have told you.
Peace I leave with you.
My own peace I give to you.
    Not as the world gives give I unto you.
Do not let your hearts be troubled
    and do not be fearful.
You have heard me tell you, "I am going away
    and I am coming back to you."
If you loved me, you would have rejoiced
    that I am going to the Father,
    because the Father is greater than I.
And I have told you this now, before it occurs,
    so that when it does happen, you will believe.
I will not speak much longer with you,
    for the prince of this world is on his way.
He has no power over me.
But the world must be shown that I love the Father,
    and that I do exactly what
    the Father has commanded me.
Come now! Rise up! Let us leave here!

And after singing a hymn, Jesus left for the Mount of Olives, as was his custom. And his disciples also accompanied him.

Matthew 26:30; Mark 14:26; Luke 22:39; John 14:1–31

THE LAST CONVERSATION ON THE WAY TO GETHSEMANE

I AM THE TRUE VINE, and my Father is the vinedresser.
Every branch in me that bears no fruit he cuts away.
While every branch that does bear fruit he constantly prunes
    so that it will bear even more fruit.
You are already pruned by the word I have spoken to you.
Remain living in me, as I in you.
Just as the branch can bear no fruit by itself
    unless it remains united with the vine,

Neither can you bear fruit
  unless you remain united with me.
I am the vine. You are the branches.
Whoever remains living in me, and I in him,
  bears fruit abundantly.
For severed from me you can do nothing.
If anyone does not remain in me he is thrown away
  like a broken off branch, and he withers.
Such branches are gathered up
  and thrown onto the fire and are burned.
If you remain living in me
  and my words remain living in you,
You may ask whatever you please
  and it shall be done for you.
By this my Father is glorified: when you bear much fruit
  and show yourselves to be my disciples.
I have loved you just as the Father has loved me.
Remain living in my love.
You will remain in my love
  if you keep my Father's commandments,
  just as I have kept my Father's commandments
  and remain in his love.
I have told you these things so that my own joy may be in you,
  and that your joy may be complete.
This is my commandment:
Keep loving one another, as I have loved you.
No one has greater love
  than to lay down his own life for his friends.
You are my friends if you keep doing what I command you.
I shall no longer call you servants or slaves,
  because a servant or slave does not know
  his master's confidence.
Instead I have called you friends,
  because I have disclosed to you
  everything that I have learned from my Father.
No, it was not you who have chosen me:
  it was I who have chosen you,
  and I have appointed you to go out and bear fruit,
  fruit that will remain living;
So that whatever you ask the Father in my name
  he may give it to you.

This is what I am commanding you:
    Keep loving one another!
If the world hates you,
    know that it hated me before it hated you.
If you belonged to the world,
    the world would love you as its own.
But because you do not belong to the world,
    but I have chosen you out of the world,
    the world therefore hates you.
Do you remember the word that I spoke to you?
    "A servant is not greater than his master!"
If they persecuted me,
    they will persecute you as well.
If they followed my teachings,
    they will also follow yours.
But it will be because of me
    that they will treat you this way;
Because they do not know
    the one who sent me.
If I had not come and spoken to them,
    they would not have been guilty of sin.
But now they have no excuse for their sin.
Whoever hates me also hates the Father.
If I had not accomplished among them
    the miracles which no one else had ever done,
    they would not have been guilty of sin.
But now they have seen these miracles,
    and yet they have hated both me and my Father.
But this is all done in order that the word may be fulfilled
    that is written in their Law:

        They hated me without reason.
        They hated me without cause.

When the Advocate comes,
    whom I will send to you from the Father,
    the Spirit of truth who comes from the Father,
    he will testify about me.
And you also must testify about me,
    because you have been with me from the beginning.

John 15:1–27

Let not those gloat over me who are enemies without cause.
Let not those who hate me without reason maliciously leer at me.

Those who hate me for no reason outnumber the hairs of my head.
Numerous are those who seek to destroy me;
    my treacherous enemies accuse me without cause.

Written by King David, year c. 1000 B.C.   279
Psalm 35:19 & 69:4

LAST WORDS ABOUT THE FUTURE

I HAVE TOLD YOU all this
    so that you will not stumble and go astray.
They will expel you from the synagogue.
Indeed, a time is coming when anyone who kills you
    will think that he is offering a holy service to God.
They will do these things
    because they have not known the Father or me.
But I have told you these things now,
    so that when the time for them occurs,
    you will remember what I warned you.
I did not tell you these things at the beginning,
    because then I was with you,
    but now I am going to him who sent me.
Yet none of you asks me, "Where are you going?"
But because I have said these things to you,
    sorrow has filled your hearts.
Nonetheless, I am telling you the truth:
    it is to your advantage that I am going away.
For if I do not go away,
    the Advocate will not come to you.
Whereas if I do go, I will send him to you.
When he comes, he will convict the world
    of guilt concerning sin,
    and righteousness, and judgment:
Concerning sin, because they refuse to believe in me;
Concerning righteousness, because I go to the Father,
    and you will see me no longer;

Concerning judgment, because the prince of this world
    now stands condemned.
I still have much more to say to you,
    but you cannot bear them now.
However, when the Spirit of Truth comes,
    he will guide you into all truth.
For he will not speak on his own authority,
    but will only tell you what he hears,
    and he will disclose to you the things to come.
He will glorify me because he will draw upon what is mine,
    and disclose it to you.
Everything that belongs to the Father is mine,
    which is why I said:
That he will draw upon the things that are mine,
    and will disclose it to you.
In a short time you will no longer see me,
    and again, a short time, you will see me.

Some of his disciples then questioned one another, "What does he mean when he tells us, 'In a short time, you will no longer see me, and then a short time later you will see me,' and 'because I go to the Father'?" And they continued questioning, "What does he mean by 'a short time'? We do not understand what he is saying."

Jesus knew that they wanted to question him, so he said to them,

Are you asking one another what I meant when I said,
"In a short time you will no longer see me,"
    and again, "a short time, and you will see me"?
I most solemnly assure you this truth:
You will weep and mourn,
    but the world will rejoice.
You will be anguished,
    but your anguish will be turned to joy.
A woman in labor suffers, because her time has come;
But when she has given birth to the child,
    she no longer remembers the agony,
    in her joy that a child has been born into the world.
So it is with you.
Now you are anguished.
But I will see you again,
    and your hearts will be full of joy
    and no one will be able to rob you of that joy.

And in that day
>you will no longer need to ask me anything.

I most solemnly assure you this truth:

If in my name you ask the Father for anything,
>he will give it to you.

Until now you have not asked for anything in my name.

Ask and you will receive,
>so that your joy will be complete.

I have said these things in figurative language.

A time is coming when I will
>no longer speak figuratively,
>but will tell you about the Father in plain words.

When that day comes, you will ask in my name.

And I am not saying to you
>that I will plead the Father on your behalf,

For the Father himself loves you
>because you have loved me,
>and have believed that I emanated from the Father.

I emanated from the Father
>and have come into the world.

Now I am leaving the world,
>and I am again returning to the Father.

His disciples said, "Ah, now you are speaking plainly to us, without figurative language! Now we realize that you know all things, and have no need to be even asked questions. Because of this, we believe that you came from God."

Jesus answered them:

Do you finally believe?

Be forewarned!

The time is coming —
>in fact it has already come!

When all of you will be scattered,
>each going your own way and leaving me alone.

Yet, I am not alone, because the Father is with me.

I have told you all these things
>so that in me you may have peace.

In the world you will have trouble!

But be courageous!

I have conquered the world!

John 16:1–33

AFTER JESUS HAD FINISHED speaking, lifting his eyes upward toward heaven, he prayed:

Father, the hour is come!
Glorify your Son so that your Son may glorify you.
For you have granted him sovereignty over all people,
    so that he may give eternal life
    to all whom you have given him.
Now eternal life is this:
    to know you as the only true God,
    and to know Jesus, whom you have sent as Messiah.
I have brought glory to you on earth
    by completing the work which you gave me to do.
Now, Father, glorify yourself, and me in your presence
    with the glory which I had with you before the world existed.
I have manifested your name — your very self,
    to the men whom you gave me out of the world.
They were yours, and you gave them to me,
    and they have obeyed your word.
Now, at last, they recognize
    that everything you have given me
    belongs to and comes out from you.
For I have given them the message that you gave me;
And they have understood with certainty
    that I came out from you;
And they now believe and are convinced
    that it was you who sent me.
It is for them that I am praying.
I am not praying for the world,
    but for those whom you have given me,
    because they belong to you.
All that I have is yours,
    and all that is yours is mine,
    and through them I have been glorified.
And now I am no longer in the world,
    but they themselves are still in the world
    and I am coming to you.
Holy Father: Protect them in your name which you have given me,
    that they may be one, even as we are.

While I was with them,
I protected them in your name
   which you had given me.
I guarded them and not one of them was lost
   except for the son of destruction —
   that the Scriptures might be fulfilled.
But now I am coming to you
   and I say these things while I am still in the world
So that they may experience
   the complete measure of my joy within them.
I have given them your word
   and the world has hated them
   because they are not of the world
   anymore than I am of the world.
I am not asking that you take them from the world
   but that you protect them from the evil one.
They do not belong to the world
   even as I do not belong to the world.
Sanctify them by the truth.
Your word is truth.
As you sent me into the world,
   I likewise have sent them into the world.
And for their sake I sanctify myself
   that they also will be sanctified in truth.
It is not for them alone that I pray.
I also pray for those who through their teaching
   will come to believe in me —
That all of them may be one
   even as you, Father, are in me, and I am in you;
That they may also be in us,
   that the world may believe that it was you who sent me.
I have given them the glory you have given me,
   that they may be one the same way as we are one.
I in them, and you in me;
So that they may be perfected in unity
So that the world may know that you did send me
   and that you have loved them
   the same way as you have loved me.
Father! I also want those whom you have given me
   to be with me where I am,
So that they may see my glory which you have given me;

For you have loved me
> from before the foundation of the world.
O righteous Father!
Although the world does not know you,
> yet I have known you;
And these men know you that you did send me.
I have made your name known to them,
> and will continue to make you known,
So that the love which you have had for me
> may be in them, and I may be in them.

John 17:1–26

PROPHECY

Even my close friend, in whom I trusted,
> who ate my bread at my table,
> has lifted his heel against me.
But You, O Lord, have mercy on me.
Raise me up, that I may repay them.

Written by King David, year c. 1000 B.C.
Psalm 41:9–10

PETER'S DESERTION PREDICTED AGAIN

WHEN HE HAD FINISHED praying all this, Jesus left with his disciples across the Kidron ravine. There was a garden there, which he and his disciples entered.

Then Jesus said to them, **"This very night, you will all fall away as deserters on account of me, for it is written:**

I shall strike down the shepherd,
> **and the sheep of the flock shall be scattered.**

"But after I am raised up, I will go ahead of you into Galilee."

But Peter replied to him, "Even though all others may fall away as deserters on account of you, I never will fall away!"

"I most solemnly declare this truth to you," Jesus replied. **"This day, this very night, before a rooster crows twice, you yourself will disown me three times."**

But Peter emphatically and repeatedly insisted, "Even if I have to die with you, I will never disown you!" And all the other disciples kept saying the same.

Matthew 26:31–35; Mark 14:27–31; John 18:1

Declares the Lord Sabaoth, the Lord of Hosts:

Awake, O sword, against my shepherd,
    against the man who is my associate.
Strike the shepherd that the sheep may be scattered,
    and I shall turn my hand against the little lambs.

Written by the prophet Zechariah, year c. 520 B.C.
Zechariah 13:7

THE GRIEF OF GETHSEMANE

THEN JESUS WENT with them to a place called Gethsemane, and on reaching the place he told his disciples, **"Sit down here while I go over there and pray. Continue to pray that you will not enter into temptation."**

He took Peter, and the two sons of Zebedee (James and John), along with him, and he began to be overwhelmingly grieved and anguished.

Then he said to them, **"My soul is overwhelmed with sorrow to the point of death. Remain here, and keep watch with me. Stay awake!"**

Going a little farther, he withdrew about a stone's throw beyond them, and fell on his face to the ground. Then he knelt, and began to pray that if it were possible, the hour might pass him by.

"Abba, my Father!" he prayed. **"Everything is possible for you! If it is possible, if you are willing, may this cup pass me by. Remove this cup from me! Yet not as I want, but as you want. Not my will, but always yours be done."**

Then he returned to his disciples and found them sleeping, and he said to Peter, **"What! Simon! Could you men not stay awake with me for one hour? You must stay awake! And keep praying! So that you will not enter into temptation! The spirit indeed is willing, but the body is weak."**

Once again, he went away and prayed the same words, **"My Father, if it is not possible for this cup to pass me by, unless I drink it, may your will be done."**

And when he came back, he again found them sleeping, because their eyes were heavy. They did not know how to answer him. So he left them there and went away and prayed the third time, saying the same words as before.

Then an angel from heaven appeared to him, strengthening him. And being in anguish, he was praying more earnestly; and his perspiration became like drops of blood, falling to the ground. *(This paragraph is not in all ancient manuscripts.)*

When he rose from prayer, he returned the third time to his disciples and found them asleep, exhausted from sorrow.

"Are you still sleeping and resting?" he asked them. "Enough! Get up, and keep praying that you will not enter into temptation. Pay attention! The hour is at hand, and the Son of Man is being betrayed into the hands of sinners. Arise! Let us be going! See, my betrayer is at hand!"

Matthew 26:36–46; Mark 14:32–42; Luke 22:40–46

THE BETRAYAL AND ARREST

NOW ONE OF THE TWELVE, Judas, who was betraying him, knew of the place because Jesus had often met there with his disciples. So just as Jesus was speaking, Judas, with a detachment of soldiers and some officials from the ruling priests and the Pharisees whom he was guiding, suddenly came there with lanterns and torches and weapons. With him was the large crowd armed with swords and clubs, sent from the ruling priests, and the scribes — those protectors of the Law, and the elders of the people.

Now the betrayer had arranged a signal with them: "The one I kiss is the man. Seize him and lead him away securely."

Then Jesus, knowing all that was going to happen to him, went out to meet them.

Going immediately to Jesus, Judas said, "Greetings, Rabbi!" and kissed him.

But Jesus asked him, **"Judas, are you betraying the Son of Man with a kiss? Do what you came to do, friend!"**

To the rest he asked, **"Who is it that you want?"**

"Jesus the Nazarene," they replied.

"I am," Jesus said. (And Judas the betrayer was standing there with them.)

As Jesus said to them, **"I am,"** they drew back and fell to the ground.

Again he asked them, **"Who is it you want?"**

And they said, "Jesus the Nazarene."

"I told you that I am he," Jesus answered. **"So if it is I whom you seek, then let these men go their way."**

This happened so that the words he had spoken were fulfilled: **"Of those whom you have given me, I have not lost even one."**

Then the men stepped forward, seized Jesus, and arrested him.

When those who were around him saw what was happening, they asked, "Lord, shall we strike with the sword?"

Then with that, Simon Peter, one of those who was standing near with Jesus, instantly reached for the sword he was wearing, drew it, and struck the servant of the ruling priest, cutting off his right ear. (The servant's name was Malchus.)

At this, Jesus commanded Peter, **"Stop! No more of this! Let them have their way! Put your sword back in its sheath. For all who draw the sword will die** by the sword. Do you not think that I cannot appeal to my Father, and he will promptly put at my disposal more than 12 legions of angels? But how then would the Scriptures be fulfilled if it should happen this way? The cup which the Father has given me, shall I not drink it?"

Then he touched the man's ear and healed him.

At that moment, Jesus then said to the crowd — the ruling priests, the officers of the temple guard, and the elders — who had come for him, **"Am I leading a rebellion, that you have to come out with clubs and swords to apprehend me as against a robber? Every day I customarily sat with you, teaching in the temple courts, and you did not lay a hand on me, let alone apprehend me. But this is your hour when the power of darkness reigns. For this has all taken place so that the Scriptures, the writings of the prophets, must be fulfilled."**

Then all the disciples deserted him and fled.

A certain young man, who was following Jesus, was wearing nothing but a linen garment over his naked body. They seized him, but he left the garment behind and fled away, naked.

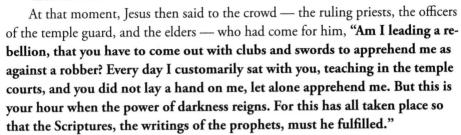

287

Matthew 26:47–56; Mark 14:43–52; Luke 22:47–53; John 18:2–11

PROPHECY

This is the will of him who sent me:
   that I should lose none of them whom he has given me,
   but that I should raise them up on the last day.

Spoken by Messiah, year c. A.D. 30
John 6:36

PROPHECY

While I was with them I protected them
   and kept them safe. I guarded them by
   your name which you have given me.

Not one has been lost, except the one destined to be lost
   so that the Scriptures would be fulfilled.

Spoken by Messiah, year c. A.D. 30
John 17:12

THE NIGHT TRIAL BY ANNAS

THEN SEIZING HIM, the detachment of soldiers with its commander and the Jewish officials arrested Jesus. They bound him and led him away, first to Annas who was the father-in-law of Caiaphas, the chief priest that year. It was

Caiaphas who had counseled the Jews that it was expedient that one man should die for the sake of the people.

Meanwhile, the chief priest interrogated Jesus about his disciples and about his teaching.

"I have spoken openly for all the world to hear," Jesus replied. **"I have always taught in a synagogue or at the temple, where all the Jews congregate; and I have spoken nothing in secret. Why question me? Question those who have heard what I said to them. Surely they know what I said."**

And when he had said this, one of the officers standing nearby struck Jesus with his open hand. "Is that the way you answer the chief priest?" he demanded.

"If I have said anything wrong," Jesus responded, **"testify to the wrong. But if I spoke rightly, why do you strike me?"**

Then Annas sent him, still bound, to the chief priest Caiaphas.

John 18:12–14,19–24

PETER IN THE COURTYARD OF THE CHIEF PRIEST

T HEN THOSE WHO HAD ARRESTED JESUS led him away to the house of Caiaphas, the chief priest, where all the ruling priests, the teachers of the Law, and the elders were assembled.

Now Simon Peter and another disciple were following Jesus at a distance. Since John, that other disciple, was known to the chief priest, he entered with Jesus into the chief priest's courtyard. But Peter had to wait, standing outside the gate.

So the other disciple, who was known to the chief priest, went out and spoke to the maid who was watching the gate, and brought Peter inside.

Now it was cold, and the servants and the officers were standing around a charcoal fire they had kindled in the middle of the courtyard, warming themselves. Peter was also standing with them, warming himself.

And when the officers sat down together around the fire to see the outcome, Peter joined them and sat down with them, intending to see how it would end.

Matthew 26:57–58; Mark 14:53–54; Luke 22:54–55; John 18:15–16, 18

THE NIGHT TRIAL BY CAIAPHAS

N OW THE RULING PRIESTS and the whole Sanhedrin council kept trying to obtain false allegations and evidence against Jesus that would warrant execution. But they were not finding any. Even though many false witnesses were coming forward, giving false testimony against him, their statements were not consistent.

Eventually, two men stood up and came forward and alleged this false statement against him: "We heard him say," they declared, " 'By my power I will destroy this temple of God made by hand; and in three days will rebuild another, not made by man.' "

Then the chief priest stood up before the whole assembly, and took his place, and asked Jesus, "Have you no answer to make? What about this accusation that these men testify against you?"

But Jesus remained silent, and made no reply.

Again the chief priest was questioning him, and said to him, "By the living God, I order you under oath, tell us if you are the Messiah, the Son of the Blessed One, the Son of God!"

"You have said so! I am!" Jesus responded. **"More than that, I tell you: You will soon see the Son of Man seated at the right hand of the Almighty, and coming in the clouds of heaven."**

Then the chief priest tore his garments and exclaimed, "He has uttered blasphemy! What further need do we have of witnesses? There! You have all heard his blasphemy! What is your verdict?"

And they unanimously condemned him as guilty. "He deserves death!" they responded. "He must be put to death!"

Then the men who were guarding Jesus contemptuously began mocking and ridiculing and beating him. Some began to spit at him, in his face; and they struck him with their fists. Others blindfolded him, struck him with the palms of their hands, and said, "Prophesy to us, you, Messiah! Who is it who struck you?" And they said many other insulting things to him, blaspheming.

Then the guards took him and beat him with blows to his head and face.

Matthew 26:59–68; Mark 14:55–65; Luke 22:63–65

PROPHECY

The Lord Jehovah says to my Lord:

**Take your seat at my right hand
until I make your enemies your footstool.**

*Written by King David, year c. 1000 B.C.
Psalm 110:1*

PROPHECY

I saw there before me, coming with the clouds of heaven,
    one like a Son of Man.
And he approached the Ancient of Days,
    and was presented before him.
And to him was given dominion,
    and glory, and sovereign power,
That all the peoples, nations, and those of every language
    should serve and worship him.
His dominion is an everlasting dominion
    which will never be taken away.
And his sovereignty is one
    which will never be destroyed.

Written by the prophet Daniel, year c. 550 B.C.
Daniel 7:13–14

THE THREE DENIALS OF PETER

NOW PETER WAS SITTING outside in the courtyard below by the fire; and the maid of the chief priest, who was on duty at the gate, came to him. When she noticed Peter there, warming himself, she looked at him intently in the firelight and asked Peter, "You too were with Jesus the Galilean, from Nazareth! You are not also one of this man's disciples, are you? This man was with him, too!"

But he falsely denied it before them all. "I am not!" he retorted. "I do not know him, girl! I do not even know or understand what you are talking about!" And he went out onto the porches at the gate.

Another servant girl saw him and began saying to those who were standing around there, "You are also one of them! This fellow was with Jesus of Nazareth. He is one of them!"

And once again he denied it, with an oath saying, "I am not, my friend, I am not one of them! I do not know the man!"

Just then a rooster crowed.

Then a little later, after about an hour, those who were standing there went up to Peter and said, "Surely you are one of them who was with him! You are not also one of his disciples, are you? For you are a Galilean, too. For your dialect betrays you!"

One of the chief priest's servants, a relative of the man whose ear Peter had cut off, challenged him: "Did I not see you with him in the olive grove garden?"

Again, Peter denied it. Then he began to call down a curse upon himself and to swear to them, "I do not know the man about whom you are talking! I do not know what you are talking about!"

And at that moment, a rooster crowed for the second time!

The Lord turned and looked at Peter. Then Peter remembered the word which Jesus had spoken: **"Before the rooster crows twice today, you will disown me three times."**

And he went out, and broke down and wept bitterly.

Matthew 26:69–75; Mark 14:66–72; Luke 22:56–62; John 18:17,25–27

PROPHECY

I offered my back to those who struck me,
My cheeks to those who plucked out my beard.
I did not shield my face from mocking and spitting.

Written by the prophet Isaiah, year c. 700 B.C.
Isaiah 50:6

THE CONDEMNATION BY THE COUNCIL

EARLY IN THE MORNING, as soon as it was daybreak, the council of the elders of the people — the ruling priests, with the teachers of the Law, and the entire Sanhedrin council — assembled together. And Jesus was led into their council chamber before them.

They said: "If you are the Messiah, then tell us!"

But he replied to them, **"If I tell you, you will not believe me, and if I question you, you will not answer. But from now on, the Son of Man will be seated at the right hand of the power of God!"**

And they all asked, "Then are you the Son of God?"

And He replied to them, **"You are correct. As you say, I am."**

Then they exclaimed, "What further need do we have of testimony? For we have heard it ourselves from his own lips!"

Then they took counsel against Jesus to put him to death.

Matthew 27:1; Mark 15:1; Luke 22:66–71

JUDAS COMMITS SUICIDE

THEN WHEN JUDAS, who had betrayed him, saw that Jesus had been condemned, he was seized with remorse and returned the 30 silver coins to the ruling priests and the elders. "I have sinned! I have betrayed innocent blood!" he declared.

But they replied, "What is that to us? That is your own concern!"

Flinging the money into the temple sanctuary, he departed, and went away and hanged himself; and falling headlong, he burst open in the middle and all his intestines gushed out.

But the ruling priests picked up the silver coins and said, "It is not lawful to deposit these into the temple treasury, because it is the price of blood."

So after they had conferred together, with the price of his treachery and wickedness they purchased the Potter's Field as a burial place for foreigners, which is why to this day in their language it has been called *Hakaldama*, or Blood Acres.

Then that which was spoken through Jeremiah the prophet was fulfilled:

And they took 30 silver coins, the value of One on whom a price had been set, a price that was set by the people of Israel;

And they paid it out to them for the Potter's Field, just as the Lord directed me.

Matthew 27:3–10; Acts 1:18–19

PROPHECY

I knew that this was
    what the Lord directed.
So I bought the field
    from my cousin Hanamel of Anathoth,
And weighed out the silver to him:
    17 silver shekels — about seven ounces.

Written by the prophet Jeremiah, year c. 600 B.C.
Jeremiah 32:8–9

PROPHECY

So they weighed out my wages, 30 silver coins.
Then the Lord said to me:

    Throw it to the potter, that princely sum
    at which they have valued me.

So I took the 30 silver coins and threw them to the potter,
    into the house of the Lord.

Written by the prophet Zechariah, year c. 520 B.C.
Zechariah 11:12–13

THEN THE WHOLE ASSEMBLY rose. They bound Jesus, led jim away from Caiphas to the Praetorium, headquarters of the Roman governor, and handed him over to Pilate, the governor.

By now it was morning, and to avoid ceremonial defilement, the Jews themselves did not enter into the Praetorium, but stayed outside because they wanted to be able to eat the Passover.

So Pilate went out to them, and asked them, "What charge do you bring against this man?"

"If he were not a criminal," they retorted to him, "we would not have handed him over to you."

"Take him yourself," Pilate therefore responded, "and judge him according to your own law."

"We are not empowered to execute anyone," the Jews objected (thus fulfilling the words Jesus had spoken indicating what kind of death he was about to die).

And they began to accuse him, asserting, "We have found this man subverting our nation. He forbids paying taxes to Caesar, and claims that he himself is Messiah, a king!"

Pilate went back inside the Praetorium again, and summoned Jesus. Now Jesus was brought before the governor, and stood in front of him, and Pilate asked him, "Are you the king of the Jews?"

"Are you saying this of your own initiative?" Jesus responded, **"or did others tell you about me?"**

"What! Am I a Jew?" Pilate retorted. "It was your own people and their ruling priests who handed you over to me! What is it you have done?"

"My kingdom does not belong to this world," Jesus replied. **"If my kingdom were of this world, then my followers would have been fighting to prevent me from being surrendered to the Jews. But as it is, my kingdom is not from here."**

"So then you are a king?" Pilate therefore said to Him.

"You say it correctly," Jesus answered. **"I am a king! For this is why I was born, and for this reason I have come into the world, to testify to the truth. Everyone who is of the truth listens to my voice."**

"What is truth?" Pilate asked him.

And when he had said this, Pilate again went out to the Jews and said to the ruling priests and to the crowd, "I find no basis for a case against this man!"

But when the ruling priests and the elders kept harshly accusing him of many things, Jesus gave no answer.

Then Pilate again asked him, "Are you not going to answer? Do you not hear how many serious accusations they are testifying against you?"

But to the great amazement of the governor, Jesus made no defense, not even to a single charge.

But they kept insisting, saying, "He incites the people with his rhetoric all over Judea, from Galilee where he began, even all the way here to this place!"

Matthew 27:2,11–14; Mark 15:1–5; Luke 23:1–5; John 18:28–38

THE MESSIAH BEFORE HEROD

UPON HEARING THIS, Pilate asked whether the man was a Galilean. And when he learned that he belonged under Herod's jurisdiction, he remitted him to Herod, who himself was also in Jerusalem at that time.

Now Herod was very glad when he saw Jesus for he had wanted to see him for a long time. Because of what he had been hearing about him, he was hoping to witness some miraculous work performed by him. So he asked him many questions, but he gave him no answer. Meanwhile, the ruling priests and the scribes were standing there, vehemently accusing him.

Then Herod and his soldiers, after treating him contemptuously and mocking him, dressed him in an elegant robe and sent him back to Pilate. And although Herod and Pilate had before been at enmity, that very day they became friends with each other.

Luke 23:6–12

The Messiah Back before Pilate

PILATE THEN SUMMONED together the ruling priests, and the leaders, and said to them, "You brought this man before me as one who was inciting the people to rebellion. Now, take notice! After examining him before you, I have found no basis for your charges against this man, concerning your accusations against him.

295

"No! and nor indeed has Herod, for he sent him back to us. Take notice! Nothing deserving death has been done by him, I will therefore have him flogged and release him."

Luke 23:13–17

The Messiah or Barabbas

NOW IT WAS THE GOVERNOR'S custom on the occasion of the Feast to release any one prisoner requested by the people. And at that time there was in prison a notorious prisoner called Barabbas — Jesus Barabbas.

Now Barabbas was a revolutionary who had been thrown into prison on murder charges for an insurrection in the city. He was being held with other insurrectionists who had committed the murder in an uprising.

When the crowd thronged up to Pilate and began asking the governor to do as he had customarily done for them, Pilate replied, "As is your custom, I should release one prisoner at Passover. Which one do you want me to release for you: Jesus Barabbas, or Jesus who is called Messiah, 'The King of the Jews'?" For he knew it was out of envy and malice that the ruling priests had handed Jesus over to him.

Matthew 27:15–18; Mark 15:6–10: Luke 23:19; John 18:39–40

The Message from Pilate's Wife

AND WHILE PILATE was seated on the judgment bench, his wife sent an urgent message to him: "Have nothing to do with that innocent man! For this past night I have been extremely upset in a dream on his account."

Matthew 27:19

Crucify Him!

BUT THE RULING PRIESTS and the elders incited the crowd and persuaded them to ask Pilate to release Barabbas instead, and to have Jesus executed.

"Which of the two do you want me to release to you?" asked the governor.

"Away with this man! Release Barabbas to us," they all shouted together.

"But in that case, then," Pilate was asking them again, "what shall I do with Jesus who is called Messiah, the one you call 'King of the Jews'?"

"No, not this man, but Barabbas!" they all shouted back again in response. And in unison they shrieked, "Let him be crucified!" And, "Crucify him!"

"Why? What crime has he committed?" Pilate was asking them. "What evil has he done?"

But they shouted all the louder, "Let him be crucified!" And, "Crucify him!"

Matthew 27:20–23; Mark 15:11–14; Luke 23:18–19; John 18:40

The Messiah Mocked

SO THEN PILATE TOOK Jesus and had him flogged. And the soldiers platted a crown of thorns, and placed it on his head.

They threw a purple cloak around him, and kept coming up to him, one after another, saying, "Hail! King of the Jews!"

And they struck him repeatedly in the face with the palms of their hands.

John 19:1–3

No Case against Him

WANTING TO RELEASE JESUS, Pilate appealed to them again, but they kept shouting back, "Crucify him! Crucify him!"

Once again, for the third time, Pilate came out and spoke to the Jews. "Take notice! I am bringing him out to you to let you know that I find no cause for a charge against him!"

So Jesus came outside, wearing the crown of thorns and the purple cloak. And Pilate said to them: "Behold, here is the man!"

Immediately at the sight of him, the ruling priests and their guards shouted out, "Crucify! Crucify!"

"Why? What crime has this man committed? I have found in him no cause for capital punishment! I will therefore have him flogged, and then release him."

But shouting at the top of their voices they insistently demanded that he be crucified. And their shouts kept getting louder, "Crucify! Crucify!"

"Take him yourself and crucify him!" Pilate retorted. "As for me, I find no case against him!"

Luke 23:20–23; John 19:4–6

No Friend of Caesar

T HE JEWS ANSWERED HIM instantly, "We have a Law, and according to that Law he ought to die because he has claimed and made himself to be the Son of God!"

So when Pilate heard this statement, he was even more afraid than ever, and he went back into the Praetorium again, and said to Jesus, "From where have you come?"

But Jesus gave him no answer.

"Do you not speak to me?" Pilate therefore demanded! "Do you not realize that I have the authority to release you, or the authority to crucify you?"

"You would have no authority whatsoever over me at all," Jesus answered, **"unless it were given you from above. For this reason the one who delivered me up to you has a greater sin."**

Consequently, Pilate made efforts to release him, but the Jews kept shrieking, "If you release this man you are no friend of Caesar! Anyone who makes himself out to be a king opposes Caesar!"

John 19:7–12

No King but Caesar

H AVING HEARD THIS, Pilate brought Jesus out and sat down on the judgment seat at a place called the Stone Pavement (which in Aramaic is *Gabbatha*).

Now it was the day of Preparation of Passover, and it was about the sixth hour (Roman time, or about six A.M.).

"This is your king!" Pilate said to the Jews.

"Take him away!" they shouted. "Take him away! Crucify him!"

"Am I to crucify your king?" Pilate asked.

"We have no king but Caesar!" the ruling priests answered.

John 19:13–15

Capitulation

S O WHEN PILATE saw that he was getting nowhere, but rather that a riot was about to erupt, he took water and washed his hands in front of the crowd. "I am innocent of this man's blood," he said. "See to it yourselves — it is your responsibility!"

Then the people in unison responded, "Let his blood be on us and on our children!"

And their shouting prevailed, so that Pilate, wanting to placate the crowd, finally pronounced sentence — that their demand should be granted.

Then he released Barabbas to them — the one for whom they had continued to ask, who had been thrown into prison for insurrection and murder.

But he had Jesus flogged. Then he handed him over to them as they wished, to be crucified.

Matthew 27:24–26; Mark 15:15; Luke 23:24–25; John 19:16

THE SOLDIERS MOCK JESUS

THEN THE GOVERNOR'S SOLDIERS took charge of Jesus, led him away, and took him into the interior of the governor's palace that is the Praetorium.

They then assembled together the whole Roman batallion which gathered around him.

They stripped him and put a purple robe on him. They twisted together a crown of thorns and set it on his head. They put a staff in his right hand and knelt in front of him and mocked him. They jeered at him, "Hail, your majesty! King of the Jews!"

Again and again they spit on him, and took the staff and repeatedly struck him on his head. Falling to their knees, they bowed down before him making mock homage to him.

And after they had finished mocking him, they took off his purple robe, and put his own garments on him.

Then they led him away to crucify him.

Matthew 27:27–30; Mark 15:16–19

TO GOLGOTHA VIA DOLOROSA

SO THEY TOOK JESUS and led him away. He went out, bearing his own cross himself, to the place called the Skull (which in Aramaic is *Golgotha*).

As they led him away, they seized a certain man from Cyrene named Simon, the father of Alexander and Rufus, who was passing by on his way in from the country. They put the cross on him, and forced him to carry it behind Jesus.

A large number of people followed him, including women who mourned and wailed for him. But Jesus, turning toward them, said:

Daughters of Jerusalem,
    do not weep for me!
But weep for yourselves and for your children.
Pay attention to this!
For the days are coming when they will say,

    Blessed are the barren women,
        the wombs that never bore,
        and the breasts that never nursed!

Then they will begin to say to the mountains,
    "Fall on us!"
And to the hills,
    "Cover us!"
For if this is what is done when the wood is green,
    then what will happen when it is dry?

Then they brought Jesus to the place Golgotha, which to the Roman is Calvary, which means the Skull. There they offered him vinegar wine to drink, mixed with gall or myrrh, but after tasting it, he refused to drink it.

Matthew 27:31–34; Mark 15:20–23; Luke 23:26–31; John 19:16–17

PROPHECY

Then will they cry out to the mountains,
    "Cover us!"
And to the hills,
    "Fall on us!"

Written by the prophet Hosea, year c. 750 B.C.
Hosea 10:8

PROPHECY

They put gall in my food
And for my thirst gave me vinegar.

Written by King David, year c. 1000 B.C.
Psalm 69:21

CRUCIFIED WITH CRIMINALS
ABOUT NINE A.M.

15th of Nissan, A.D. 30

TWO OTHER MEN, both criminals, were also led out with him to be executed at the same time.

When they reached the place called the Skull (called *Calvary* by the Romans, and *Golgotha* in Aramaic), they crucified him there along with the two criminals — one on his right, the other on his left — with Jesus in the middle.

And Jesus was praying, **"Father, forgive them, for they do not know what they are doing!"**

Matthew 27:38; Mark 15:27; Luke 23:32–34; John 19:18

PROPHECY

Therefore I shall give him his portion among the great,
    and he shall divide the spoils with the mighty;
Because he exposed himself to death,
    and was numbered with the transgressors;
For he himself bore the sin of many and interceded for the transgressors.

Written by the prophet Isaiah, year c. 700 B.C.
Isaiah 53:12

THE NOTICE

AND PILATE ALSO WROTE a notice on a placard. The soldiers fastened the notice to the cross, above his head. And the notice giving the charge against him read:

THIS IS JESUS FROM NAZARETH
THE KING OF THE JEWS

And many Jews read this placard, because the place where Jesus was crucified was near the city; and the notice was written in Aramaic, in Latin, and in Greek.

Then the ruling priests of the Jews protested to Pilate, "Do not write 'The King of the Jews' but 'He claimed that he is king of the Jews'."

Pilate replied, "What I have written, I have written!"

Matthew 27:37; Mark 15:26; Luke 23:38; John 19:19–22

GAMBLING FOR GARMENTS

T HEN WHEN THE SOLDIERS crucified Jesus, they took his outer garments, and divided them into four parts, one share for each soldier, with the tunic undergarment remaining. Now the tunic was seamless, in one piece from the top throughout.

"Let us not tear it apart," they therefore said to one another. "But let us cast lots to decide whose it shall be."

This happened so that the Scriptures might be fulfilled:

> They divided my garments among themselves,
>   and for my clothing they cast lots.

So this is what the soldiers did. Then they sat down there to keep watch over him.

Matthew 27:35–37; Mark 15:24–25; Luke 23:34; John 19:23–24

PROPHECY

> They divided my garments among themselves,
>   and for my clothing throw dice.

Written by King David, year c. 1000 B.C.
Psalm 22:18

JEERING AT JESUS

N OW THE PEOPLE stood there, just watching. And those who were passing by jeered at him, wagging their heads, and taunting, "Ha! You who would destroy the temple and rebuild it in three days, rescue yourself from death! Come down from the cross if you are the Son of God!"

In the same way, the ruling priests, along with the scholars and teachers of the Law, and the elders, were also mocking him among themselves. "He rescued others from death," they scoffed and sneered at him, "but he cannot rescue himself! Indeed! Let this 'Messiah,' the 'King of Israel,' now rescue himself and come down from the cross! Then we might see and believe, if indeed he is the 'Anointed,' the 'Chosen One.' He put his trust in God? Let God rescue him now, if he will have anything to do with him! For did he himself not say, 'I am the Son of God!'?"

The soldiers also jeered at him, coming up to him, offering him sour vinegar wine, and taunting, "If you are the King of the Jews, rescue yourself from death!"

In the same way, the criminals who were being crucified along with him were also casting abuses at him.

One of the criminals who was hanging there kept deriding him, saying, "Are you not the Messiah? Then rescue yourself, and us, from death!"

But the other criminal rebuked him. "Since you are under the same sentence of condemnation yourself!" he said, "do you not even fear God? We are indeed being punished justly for we are receiving what we deserve for our crimes. But this man has done nothing wrong!"

Then he said, "Jesus! Remember me when you come into your kingdom!"

And Jesus answered him, **"I can guarantee you this truth: Today you shall be with me in Paradise!"**

Matthew 27:39–44; Mark 15:29–32; Luke 23:35–43

PROPHECY

I have become the object of their taunts.
At the sight of me, they wag their heads.

Written by King David, year c. 1000 B.C.
Psalm 109:25

PROPHECY

All they that see me laugh me to scorn;
     they insult me with their lip, they shake their head, saying,

He trusts in the Lord Jehovah, let him deliver him;
     since he delights in him.

They gape on me with their mouths,
     as a ferocious and roaring lion.
I am poured out like water;
     and all my bones are out of joint.
My heart is like wax; it is melted within me.

PROPHECY

My strength is dried up like broken pottery;
> and my tongue cleaves to my jaws;
> and you have brought me into the dust of death.
Dogs have surrounded me;
A wicked mob has encompassed me;
They pierced my hands and my feet.
I can count all my bones;
They look and stare upon my nakedness.
They divide my garments among themselves,
> and for my clothing throw dice.

Written by King David, year c. 1000 B.C.
Psalm 22:7–8 & 13–18

ENTRUSTING MARY

BUT MEANWHILE, standing near the cross of Jesus was his mother, his mother's sister Mary (the wife of Clopas), and Mary from Magdala.

Then when Jesus saw his mother there, and the disciple whom Jesus loved standing beside her, he said to his mother, **"Dear woman, see here is your son."**

Then he said to the disciple, **"See, here is your mother."**

And from that hour John, the disciple, took her unto his own home.

John 19:25–27

THE ENVELOPING DARKNESS
ABOUT NOON

NOW FROM THE SIXTH HOUR (which is about noon) until the ninth hour (which is about three in the afternoon), darkness enveloped the whole land, for the sun was obscured.

And about the ninth hour Jesus screamed out with a loud voice in Aramaic, ***"Eloi, Eloi, lema sabachthani?"*** which means, **"My God, my God, why have you abandoned me?"**

When some of those who were standing there heard this, they began saying, "Listen! This man is calling for Elijah."

After this, knowing that everything was now accomplished in fulfillment of the Scriptures, Jesus said, **"I am thirsty!"**

A jar of sour vinegar wine was there. So immediately someone ran, and taking a sponge, soaked the sponge with the sour wine, and put the soaked sponge on a hyssop stick. Then he lifted it to Jesus' mouth, and offered him a drink.

But the rest said, "Wait! Leave him alone! Let us see whether Elijah will come to take him down."

When Jesus had received the wine, he said, **"It is finished!"**

And then Jesus screamed out again in a loud voice, **"Father, into your hands I entrust my spirit."**

And having said this, his head fell forward, and he breathed his last, and gave up his life. Jesus died.

Matthew 27:45–50; Mark 15:33–37; Luke 23:44–46; John 19:28–30

PROPHECY

My God, my God, why have you abandoned me?
Why are you so far from helping me,
    and from the words of my roaring?

Written by King David, year c. 1000 B.C.
Psalm 22:1

PROPHECY

They gave me poison in my food,
    and for my thirst they gave me vinegar to drink.

Written by King David, year c. 1000 BC
Psalm 69:21

PROPHECY

Into your hands I commit my spirit.
You have redeemed me, O Lord, God of truth.

Written by King David, year c. 1000 B.C.
Psalm 31:5

THE CENTURION

SUDDENLY AT THAT MOMENT, the curtain in the temple sanctuary was torn in two, from top to bottom. And the earth shook, and the rocks were split open. The tombs broke open, and the bodies of many holy people who had died were raised to life. And coming out of their tombs, they went (after his resurrection) into the Holy City and appeared to many.

Now when the centurion who was standing right in front of him, and those with him who were guarding Jesus, witnessed the earthquake and all that was happening, and observed how he expired, they became terrified and exclaimed, "Certainly this was the Son of God!"

And the centurion glorified God, saying, "Certainly this man was innocent!"

Matthew 27:51–54; Mark 15:38–39; Luke 23:44–47

No Broken Bones

SINCE IT WAS THE DAY OF PREPARATION, and the next day was to be a special Sabbath, the Jews wanted to avoid having the bodies remaining on the cross on the Sabbath. They therefore requested Pilate to have the legs broken and the bodies removed.

So soldiers therefore came and broke the legs of the first man, then of the other who had been crucified with Jesus. But when they came to Jesus and discovered that he was already dead, they did not break his legs. Instead, one of the soldiers thrust a spear into his side, and a flow of blood and water immediately came out.

And this is the evidence of one who has seen it. As an eyewitness, this testimony is true! And he knows that he is telling the truth, so that you may come to believe as well.

For these things occurred so that the Scriptures would be fulfilled:

"Not one of his bones will be broken."

And again as another Scripture says:

"They will look upon the one whom they have stabbed."

John 19:31-37

PROPHECY

Do not break any of the bones.

Written by the patriarch Moses, year c. 1450 B.C.
Exodus 12:46

PROPHECY

They must leave nothing of it until morning,
    nor break any of its bones.
According to all the requirements of the Passover
    they shall observe it.

Written by the patriarch Moses, year c. 1425 B.C.
Numbers 9:12

The Lord protects all of his bones;
    not one of them will be broken.

Written by King David, year c. 1000 B.C.
Psalm 34:20

307

They will look upon the one
    whom they have thrust through.
And they will mourn for him
    as one mourns for an only son;
And grieve bitterly over him
    as one grieves for a firstborn.

Written by the prophet Zechariah, year c. 520 B.C.
Zechariah 12:10

WATCHING FROM A DISTANCE

WHEN ALL THE CROWDS who had congregated for this spectacle observed what had occurred, they returned to the city, beating their breasts. But all of his friends remained, standing at a distance, watching it all unfold.

Included were many women who had accompanied Jesus when he was in Galilee. Among them were Mary of Magdala, Mary the mother of the younger James and of Joseph, and Salome the mother of the sons of Zebedee. When he was in Galilee, these women had followed him, and had provided for him and looked after his needs.

Many other women who had come up to Jerusalem with him were also present.

Matthew 27:55–56; Mark 15:40–41; Luke 23:48–49

My loved ones and my friends
    shun my agony.
Even my relatives stand far away.

Written by King David, year c. 1000 B.C.
Psalm 38:11

PASSOVER SABBATH: MESSIAH'S BURIAL

THURSDAY SUNSET TO FRIDAY SUNSET

JOSEPH'S TOMB

16th of Nissan, A.D. 30

IT WAS PREPARATION DAY, the day before Passover. Then when it was almost evening, there came a rich man from Judea, from the town of Aramathea, named Joseph. A prominent member of the Sanhedrin Council, he had himself become a disciple of Jesus, but secretly, for fear of the Jews. A virtuous and upright man, he was living in hope of seeing the kingdom of God, and had not consented to the Council's decision and action. Daring the consequences, he gathered up courage and went boldly before Pilate, and asked if he could take away the body of Jesus.

But Pilate was surprised that Jesus was dead so soon. Summoning the centurion, he asked him if Jesus was already dead. And when Pilate ascertained this from the centurion, he granted permission and ordered that the body be given over to Joseph.

Joseph purchased a fine linen cloth, a shroud, and came and took the body down. He was also accompanied by Nicodemus who had at first come to Jesus at night, and who now came bringing a myrrh and aloes mixture — about 75 *litrai*, or about 100 pounds. So they took the body of Jesus away, and wrapped it first in the clean linen sheet or shroud, then bound it in strips of clean linen laced with the spices, as is the burial custom of the Jews.

Now at the place where Jesus was crucified there was a garden. And in the garden was Joseph's own new tomb or sepulcher that had been hewn out of the rock, one in which no one had ever been laid. Because it was the Jewish Day of Preparation, and the Sabbath was beginning, and the tomb was nearby, they laid Jesus there. Then Joseph rolled a large boulder against the entrance to the tomb, and they departed.

The women who had come with him from Galillee had followed closely behind them, and saw the tomb and how his body was laid in it.

Mary of Magdala and Mary the mother of Jesus were sitting there opposite the tomb, and were intently observing, and saw where he was buried.

Then they all returned home and prepared spices and perfume ointments. But on the Sabbath they rested in accordance with the commandment.

Matthew 27:57–60; Mark 15:42–47; Luke 23:50–56; John 19:31–42

He was assigned a grave with the wicked,
    yet in dying his tomb was with a rich man;
Although he had done no violence,
    nor was there any deception in his mouth.

Written by the prophet Isaiah, year c. 700 B.C.
Isaiah 53:9

Remember the Sabbath day
    by keeping it holy.
Six days you shall labor
    and do all your work,
But the seventh day is a Sabbath
    to the Lord your God.
On it you shall not do any work,
    not you, nor your son or daughter,
    nor your male or female servant,
    nor your livestock,
    nor the resident alien staying with you
    within your gates.

Recorded by the patriarch Moses, year c. 1450 B.C.
Exodus 20:8–10

THE SEPULCHER SECURED

THE NEXT DAY, which is the one after the Day of Preparation, the ruling priests and the Pharisees assembled before Pilate. "Your excellency," they said, "we recall that while he was still alive, that imposter said, 'After three days I will rise again.' Therefore give an order to have the tomb made secure until the third day. Otherwise, his disciples may come and steal him away and tell the people, 'He has been raised from the dead,' and the final fraud will be worse than the first."

"You may have a guard of soldiers," Pilate answered. "Go, make it as secure as you know how!" So they went and secured the tomb by putting a seal on the stone, and by posting the guard of soldiers.

Matthew 27:61–66

THIRTY-EIGHT

THE FIRST DAY OF THE WEEK

SATURDAY SUNSET TO SUNDAY SUNSET

THE WOMEN VISIT THE TOMB — *18th of Nissan, A.D. 30*

NOW AFTER THE SABBATH was over, on the first day of the week, very early in the morning while it was still dark, just as it began to dawn, Mary of Magdala and the other Mary (the mother of James), and Salome, went to take a look at the tomb. They had purchased spices and aromatic oils which they had prepared so that they might go to the tomb and anoint him.

They came to the tomb just as the sun had risen, and were wondering to one another, "Who will roll away the stone from the entrance to the tomb for us?"

Matthew 28:1; Mark 16:1–3; Luke 24:1; John 20:1

AN ANGEL OPENS THE TOMB

AND SUDDENLY there was a violent earthquake. For an angel of the Lord, descending from heaven, went forward and rolled the boulder back, and sat on it. His face was like lightning, and his garments whiter than snow.

Those keeping guard were so terrified at the sight of him that they trembled and collapsed like dead men.

When the women looked up, they saw that the stone, which was extremely large, had been rolled back and removed from the entrance to the tomb.

Matthew 28:2–4; Mark 16:4; Luke 24:2; John 20:1

VISITORS IN THE EMPTY TOMB

MARY OF MAGDALA immediately ran away and came to Simon Peter, and to the other disciple (John, the one whom Jesus loved), and said to them, "They have removed the Lord out of the tomb, and we do not know where they have laid him!"

But when the other women entered the tomb, they did not find the body of Jesus.

Instead, while they stood there confused and wondering about this, two men in gleaming garments suddenly were standing there beside them. One, a young man, clothed in a pure white robe, was suddenly sitting at the right side.

Terrified, the women bowed their faces to the ground.

Mark 16:5; Luke 24:3–5; John 20:2

THE MESSAGE FROM BEYOND

BUT THE ANGEL SAID to the women, "Do not be alarmed or afraid! For I know you are looking for Jesus the Nazarene, who has been crucified. But why do you search among the dead for the Living One?

"Come see the place where they had laid him. He is not here! He has risen! Just as he said!

"Remember how he spoke to you when you were still in Galilee? 'The Son of Man must be delivered into the hands of sinful men, and be crucified, and the third day rise again!' "

Then they recalled his words.

"Now then," he continued, "go quickly and tell his disciples, and Peter. 'He has risen from the dead and in fact is going ahead of you into Galilee! You will see him, there, just as he told you!'

"Now, this is the message that I had come to tell you."

So the women hastily departed from the tomb, trembling in amazement, for the shock had overwhelmed them. Afraid yet filled with great joy, they fled to report this to his disciples.

They said nothing to anyone, because they were so afraid.

Matthew 28:5–8; Mark 16:6–8; Luke 24:6–8; John 20:3

JESUS MEETS THE WOMEN

AS THE WOMEN WENT on their way, suddenly, coming to meet them, was Jesus! And they came to him, grasped his feet, and worshiped him!

Then Jesus said to them, **"Do not be afraid any longer! Go and tell my brothers, they must leave for Galilee. They will see me there!"**

Matthew 28:9–10

The Women Talk Nonsense

WHEN THE WOMEN RETURNED from the tomb, they recounted all these things to the 11, and to all the others. Now it was Mary of Magdala, Joanna, Mary the mother of James, and several others. The other women who accompanied them also were telling these things to the Apostles.

313

But this story of theirs seemed like nonsense to the men, and they did not believe the women.

Luke 24:9–11

Bribing the Soldiers

NOW WHILE THE WOMEN were on their way, some of the guards went into the city and recounted to the ruling priests everything that had occurred.

When the ruling priests had assembled with the elders and conferred together, they devised a plan. They gave a substantial amount of bribe money to the soldiers, telling them, "You are to say to the people, 'His disciples came during the night and stole him away while we were sleeping.' And if this should reach the governor's ears, we will appease him and keep you out of trouble."

So the soldiers took the money and did as they had been instructed. And this fabrication has been widely circulated among the Jews, to the present day.

Matthew 28:11–15

The Empty Shroud

THEN PETER HEADED OUT for the tomb with John, the other disciple. Both were running together, side by side, but the other disciple outran Peter and arrived at the tomb first. Stooping down, he peered in and saw the strips of linen wrappings lying there. But he did not enter.

Then Simon Peter, who was behind him, caught up and charged into the tomb. And he saw the strips of linen wrappings lying there, as well as the burial face napkin that had been around Jesus' head. It was not lying with the other linens, but was still rolled up in a place by itself.

Then the other disciple, John, who had reached the tomb first, also went in, and he too saw and believed. For until this moment, they still did not comprehend from the Scriptures that he must rise again from the dead.

Then the disciples returned to their homes.

John 20:3–10

For you will not abandon my soul
　　to Sheol — to the grave,
Nor will you allow your faithful Holy One
　　to see the pit of decay.

Written by King David, year c. 1000 B.C.
Psalm 16:10

STOP HOLDING ON!

B UT MARY WAS STANDING just outside the tomb, sobbing. And as she sobbed, she stooped and peered into the tomb, and she saw two angels in white garments, sitting where the body of Jesus had been lying, one at the head, and the other at the feet.

And they asked her, "Woman, why are you sobbing?"

"Because they have taken away my Lord," she responded to them, "and I do not know where they have laid him!"

On saying this, she turned around and noticed Jesus standing there. However, she did not realize that it was Jesus.

"Woman," he said to her, **"why are you sobbing so? For whom are you looking?"**

Supposing that he was the gardener, she replied to him, "Sir, if you have carried him away, tell me where you have laid him, and I will take him away."

Jesus said to her, **"Mary!"**

Turning around, she said to him, in Aramaic, *"Rabboni!"* — which means Teacher or Master.

"Stop holding on to me!" Jesus responded to her. **"For I have not yet ascended to the Father. But go instead to my brothers, and tell them, 'I am ascending to my Father and your Father, to my God and your God!'"**

Mary from Magdala went, and announced to the disciples, "I have seen the Lord!" and that he had said these things to her.

John 20:11–18

THE COUPLE FROM EMMAUS

N OW ON THAT VERY SAME DAY, two of them were traveling to the country to a village called Emmaus, which was about 60 *stadia* or about 7 miles from Jerusalem. And they were relating to each other about everything that had happened.

And as they were absorbed, talking together and discussing those things with each other, it came about that Jesus himself caught up with them, and began walking along with them. But because he appeared to them in another form, their eyes were prevented from recognizing him.

And he asked them, **"What is this discussion that you are exchanging with each other as you are walking along?"**

Then they stopped still, their faces downcast.

One of them, named Cleopas, answered him by asking, "Are you the only one person visiting Jerusalem who is not aware of the things that have occurred there in these last few days?"

"What sort of things?" he asked.

"The things about Jesus of Nazareth," they replied to him, "who was a prophet, powerful in work and word in the sight of God and of all the people. And how both the ruling priests and our leaders handed him over to be sentenced to death. And they crucified him!

"But we had been hoping that it was he who was going to liberate Israel.

"In fact, besides all this, it is now the third day since all these things occurred.

"In addition, some of our women astounded us! They were at the tomb early this morning. But they did not find his body! But they returned and told us that they had seen a vision of angels, who announced that he is alive!

"Then some of the men who were with us went to the tomb and found it exactly as the women had described. But him they did not see!"

Then he said to them both, **"How dull of mind to comprehend, and slow of heart to believe all that the prophets have declared! Was it not necessary for the Messiah to suffer all these things and then enter into his glory?"**

Then beginning with Moses and all the prophets, he interpreted to them all the passages in the Scriptures that referred to himself.

As they approached the village to which they were going, he gave the impression that he was going farther.

But they strongly urged him, "Remain with us! For it is nearly evening! The day is almost over."

So he went in to stay with them.

Now it occurred that while he was reclining at the table with them, he took bread, and giving thanks, he broke it and began giving it to them.

Then, with that, their eyes were opened, and they recognized him. But he vanished from their sight.

And they asked each other, "Were not our hearts burning within us while he was talking with us on the road, and as he was opening the meaning of the Scriptures to us?"

Mark 16:12; Luke 24:13–32

CHAPTER

THIRTY-NINE

39

THE NEXT DAY
AND ONE WEEK LATER

SUNDAY SUNSET TO
MONDAY SUNSET

BEHIND LOCKED DOORS

19th of Nissan, A.D. 30

THAT VERY SAME HOUR, on the evening of that same day, the first day of the week, the couple returned from Emmaus to Jerusalem where they found the 11, and those who were assembled together with them.

For fear of the Jews, the doors were locked where the disciples were gathered together.

The disciples were saying, "It is true! The Lord has really risen! And he has appeared to Simon!"

Then the two themselves began to relate their experiences on the road, and how he was recognized by them in breaking the bread. But the disciples did not believe them either.

While they were talking about this, Jesus himself came and stood among them, in their midst, and said to them, **"Peace to you!"** They were all so startled and terrified that they thought they were seeing a ghost.

And he said to them, **"Why are you troubled? And why do doubts arise in your hearts? Look at my hands and my feet, that it is I myself! Touch me and see for yourselves! For a ghost does not have flesh and bones as you see I have!"**

After he said this, he showed them his hands and his feet, and his side. And the disciples were overjoyed at recognizing the Lord.

While the disciples were still incredulous, for the sheer joy and amazement, he asked them, **"Have you anything here to eat?"**

They offered him a piece of boiled fish, which he took and ate in front of them. Then he said to them, **"This is what I meant in my words which I spoke to you while I was still with you: that everything which is written concerning me in the law of Moses, and in the Prophets, and in the Psalms, had to be fulfilled."**

Then he opened their minds so they could understand the Scriptures, and further said to them, **"This is what is written: that the Messiah would suffer, and on the third day would rise again from the dead; and that repentance bringing the forgiveness of sins would be proclaimed in his name to all nations, beginning from Jerusalem. You are witnesses of these things.**

"And note this! I am sending down upon you what my Father has promised. But you are to remain here in the city until you are clothed with power from on high."

Then Jesus again said to them, **"Peace to you! As the Father has sent me, so I am also sending you."**

After having said this, he breathed on them and said to them, **"Receive the Holy Spirit! If you forgive the sins of anyone, their sins have been forgiven them. If you retain the sins of anyone, they have been retained."**

Mark 16:13; Luke 24:37–49; John 20:19–23

PROPHECY

After two days he will revive us;
On the third day he will raise us up,
    that we may live in his presence.

Written by the prophet Hosea, year c. 725 B.C.
Hosea 6:2

DOUBTING THOMAS

BUT THOMAS, CALLED DIDYMUS, the Twin, one of the Twelve, was not with the other disciples when Jesus came. So the other disciples kept telling him, "We have seen the Lord!"

But he told them, "Unless I shall see in his hands the imprints of the nails, and put my fingers in those nailholes, and put my hand into his side, I will not believe."

John 20:24–25

NO DOUBT ABOUT IT!   *26th of Nissan, A.D. 30*

AFTER EIGHT DAYS, once again his disciples were inside the house, and Thomas was with them.

Although they were behind doors that were locked shut, Jesus came and stood among them and said, **"Peace to you!"**

Then he said to Thomas, **"Reach out your finger, and look at my hands. And reach out your hand here and put it into my side. No longer be unbelieving, but believe!"**

Thomas replied to him, "My Lord and my God!"

Then Jesus told them,

> **Because you have seen me,**
> **you have come to believe.**
> **Blessed are those who have not seen**
> **and have come to believe.**

Now Jesus performed many other miraculous works in the presence of his disciples, which are not recorded in this book. But these have been written so that you may come to believe that Jesus is the Messiah, the Son of God, and that through believing in his name you may have life.

John 20:26–31

40

FROM GALILEE TO GLORY: THE ASCENSION

THE FOLLOWING 40 DAYS

BREAKFAST WITH JESUS

A.D. 30

THEN, AS JESUS HAD DESIGNATED, the 11 subsequently proceeded to Galilee. There, by the Sea of Tiberius, Jesus again manifested himself to his disciples.

This is what happened.

Simon Peter, Thomas called Didymus, and Nathaniel from Cana in Galilee, and the sons of Zebadee, and two other of His disciples were together there.

"I am going fishing," Simon Peter said to the others.

"We are also coming with you," they responded to him.

So they went out, and got into the boat, but throughout the night they caught nothing.

Dawn was already breaking when Jesus stood on the shore. However, the disciples did not realize that it was Jesus.

So Jesus called out to them, **"Boys, you have no fish, do you?"**

"No!" they called back to him.

"Throw your net on the starboard of the boat," he then said to them, **"and you will find some."**

So they cast the net, and now they were unable to haul it in because of the great number of fish within it.

Then John, that disciple whom Jesus loved, said to Peter, "It is the Lord!"

And so, as soon as Simon Peter heard the words "It is the Lord!" he wrapped his fisherman's coat around him (for he had stripped down), and plunged into the sea.

But the other disciples came in the small boat, towing the net full of fish, for they were not far from shore, only about 200 cubits, or 90 meters or 100 yards away. When they landed and came ashore, they saw a fire already made, and fish lying on the charcoals, and bread.

Jesus said to them, **"Bring some of the fish which you have just now caught!"**

Simon Peter climbed aboard, and hauled the net ashore. It was full of large fish, 153 of them. But even with so many, the net was not torn.

"Come, have breakfast," Jesus invited them.

Now, none of the disciples dared ask Him, "Who are you?" They realized that it was the Lord.

Matthew 28:16; John 21:1–12

THE DEMANDS OF DEDICATION

JESUS CAME AND TOOK THE BREAD, and gave it to them, and did the same with the fish. This was now the third time Jesus had revealed himself to the disciples after he was raised from the dead.

So when they had finished eating, Jesus said to Simon Peter, **"Simon, son of John, do you devotedly love me more than these others do?"**

"Yes, Lord," he replied, "you know that I truly love you as my brother."

"Tend my lambs," Jesus responded to him.

Jesus said to him a second time, **"Simon, son of John, do you devotedly love me?"**

"Yes, Lord," he replied, "You know I truly love you as my brother."

"Shepherd my sheep," Jesus responded to him.

A third time Jesus asked him, **"Simon, son of John, do you truly love me as my brother?"**

Peter was deeply hurt because Jesus' third question to him was, **"Do you truly love me as my brother?"**

And he answered, "Lord, you know everything! You know that I truly love you as my brother!"

"Tend my lambs," Jesus responded to him. **"I guarantee you this solemn truth: When you were young, you dressed yourself, and fastened your own belt, and walked wherever you wanted to go.**

"But when you grow old, you will stretch out your hands, and someone else will put a belt around you, and take you where you do not want to go."

Now he said this to indicate by what kind of death Peter would glorify God. After this Jesus said to him, **"You must follow me!"**

John 21:13–19

PAY YOUR OWN PRICE

THEN PETER TURNED AROUND and noticed John, the disciple whom Jesus loved, following them. He was the one who at the supper had leaned close to the chest of Jesus and asked, "Lord, who is the one who is betraying you?"

On seeing John, Peter then asked, "Lord, but what about this man?"

"If I want him to remain alive until I return, what concern is that to you?" Jesus replied. **"You must follow me!"**

Because of this, the rumor spread among the brethren that this disciple would not die. But Jesus did not say that John would not die. He only said, **"If I want him to remain alive until I return, what concern is that to you?"**

John 21:20–23

THE GREAT COMMISSION

UNTIL THE DAY he was taken up, after his suffering he presented himself alive by many convincing evidences, appearing to them over a period of 40 days, and speaking to them about the kingdom of God.

Then, as Jesus had designated, the 11 proceeded to the mountain in Galilee. When they saw him there, they knelt before him and worshiped him.

But some were still doubtful.

Then Jesus led these Apostles, whom he had chosen, out near Bethany. He then approached them and through the Holy Spirit gave them instructions:

> **Full authority in heaven and earth has been committed to me.**
> **Go then and make disciples of all nations;**
> **Baptizing them in the name of the Father,**
> **and of the Son, and of the Holy Spirit;**
> **And teaching them to observe everything**
> **that I have commanded you.**
> **And remember!**
> **I am with you all the days even to the very end of the age.**

On one occasion, when he was eating with them he had given this command:

> **Do not depart from Jerusalem.**
> **But wait for the gift my Father promised,**
> **of which you have heard me speak.**
> **For John baptized with water.**
> **But you shall be baptized with the Holy Spirit**
> **not many days from now.**

So now, when they were assembled together, they asked him, "Lord, is this the time when you are restoring the kingdom to Israel?"

He responded to them:

> **It is not for you to know the times or dates**
>> **which the Father has established by his own authority.**
> **But you will receive power when the Holy Spirit comes upon you.**
> **And you shall be my witnesses, testifying in Jerusalem,**
>> **and in all Judea and Samaria,**
>> **and even to the remotest ends of the earth.**

Matthew 28:16–20; Luke 24:50; Acts 1:3–8

THE ASCENSION

AFTER HE HAD SAID these things, he raised his hands and blessed them. And it occurred that while he was blessing them, as they were watching, he parted from them and was lifted up, and a cloud received him out of their sight.

As he was departing and they were still intently gazing up into the sky, two men in white garments suddenly stood beside them.

"Men of Galilee," they said, "why do you stand there staring into the sky? This same Jesus, who has been taken from you into heaven, will come back in just the same way as you have watched him go into heaven!"

Then they returned to Jerusalem from the mount called Olivet, or Mount of Olives, which is near Jerusalem, a Sabbath day's walk or one thousand meters, about three quarters of a mile from Jerusalem.

When they entered the city, they went up to the upper room where they were staying. Those present were

> Peter and John and James and Andrew;
> Philip and Thomas;
> Bartholomew and Matthew;
> James son of Alphaeus; and
> Simon the Zealot; and
> Judas son of James.

All of these were continually with one accord devoting themselves to prayer, waiting together along with the women, and Mary the mother of Jesus, and his brothers.

And with great joy, they were constantly in the temple, praising God.

Luke 24:50–53; Acts 1:9–14

Therefore my heart is glad and my soul rejoices.
My body also will rest secure.
For you will not abandon me to Sheol — to the grave
Nor will you allow your faithful Holy One to see the pit of decay.

Written by King David, year c. 1000 B.C.
Psalm 16:9–10 325

MANY APPEARANCES

NOW I WANT TO REMIND YOU, my brothers, of the good news of the gospel which I proclaimed to you, which you have accepted, and on which you stand, by which you are also saved — if you hold firmly to the message I have proclaimed to you, unless you have come to believe in vain.

For what I also received I passed on to you as of primary importance: that Messiah died for our sins according to the Scriptures, and that he was buried, and that he was raised to life on the third day, according to the Scriptures, and that he first appeared to Cephas also known as Peter, and then afterward to the Twelve.

After that he appeared to more than five hundred of the brothers at one time, the majority of whom remain living until now, although some have fallen asleep in death.

Then he appeared to James, then to all the apostles, and last of all he appeared to Paul also, as to one abnormally born.

1 Corinthians 15:1–8

TRUE TESTIMONY

IT IS THE SAME DISCIPLE about which Jesus said to Peter, "If I want him to remain alive until I return, what concern is that to you?" who bears eyewitness to all these things. He has written them down, and we know that his eyewitness accounts are true.

And there are also many other things which Jesus did. If every one of them were individually written down in detail, I suppose that even the whole world itself would not have the room to contain the books that would be written!

John 21:23–25

FROM EMPTY TO EXALTATION

HAVE THE SAME ATTITUDE in yourselves that was also in Christ Jesus, who, though he was in the form of God, did not regard equality with God as something to be grasped.

Rather, he stripped himself of his privileges, taking the form of a bond servant — a slave, being made in human likeness.

And being found in appearance as a man, he further humbled himself by becoming obedient to death — even death on a cross!

For this, God also highly exalted him, and bestowed on him the name which is above every other name —

So that, at the name of Jesus, every knee must bow of those who are in heaven, and on earth, and under the earth,

And every tongue acknowledge that Jesus Christ is Lord to the glory of God the Father.

Philippians 2:5–11

PROPHECY

And to him was conferred dominion,
    and glory, and sovereign power.
That all peoples, nations, and those of every language
    should serve and worship him.
His dominion is an everlasting dominion
    which will never be taken away.
And his sovereignty is one which will never be destroyed.

Written by the prophet Daniel, year c. 550 B.C.
Daniel 7:14

PROPHECY

Turn to me and be saved all you ends of the earth.
For I am God, and there is no other!
By myself I have sworn in all integrity.
From my mouth the word has been uttered — it is an irrevocable word!
To me every knee shall bow; every tongue shall swear allegiance.
In the Lord alone, they will say of me, are righteousness and strength.
All who have raged against him will come to him and be put to shame.

Written by the prophet Isaiah, year c. 700 B.C.
Isaiah 45:22–24

STEPHEN'S VISION OF JESUS

STEPHEN, FILLED WITH THE HOLY SPIRIT, intently peered into heaven, and saw the glory of God, and Jesus standing in the position of authority at the right hand of God.

"Look!" he exclaimed, "I can see the heavens opened, and the Son of Man standing at the right hand of God!"

While they were stoning Stephen, he prayed, "Lord Jesus, receive my spirit!"

Then he fell on his knees, and shouted out in a loud voice, "Lord, do not hold this sin as a charge against them."

And having said this he fell asleep. That is, he died.

Acts 7:55–56, 59–60

PAUL'S VISION OF JESUS

NOW SAUL, still breathing murderous threats against the disciples of the Lord, went to the chief priest and asked for letters from him to the synagogues in Damascus, so that if he found any there belonging to "the Way," whether men or women, he might bring them as prisoners to Jerusalem.

With this authority and commission of the ruling priests, Saul journeyed, approaching Damascus at midday. Suddenly a light from heaven flashed around him.

To King Agrippa, Paul later recounted, "About noon, O King, as I was on the road, I saw a light from heaven, brighter than the midday sun blazing all about me and around those who were traveling with me.

"We fell to the ground, and I heard a voice saying to me in Aramaic, **'Saul, Saul, why are you persecuting me? It is dangerous for you, kicking against the thorns!'**"

Then Saul asked, "Who are you, Lord?"

"I am Jesus, whom you are persecuting," the Lord replied. **"Now get up and stand on your feet!**

"For this purpose I have appeared to you: to appoint you to serve as minister and as a witness, not only of this that you have seen of me, but also of other things in which I will appear to you.

"I will deliver you from your own people, and from the Gentiles to whom I am sending you — to open their eyes, so that they may turn from darkness into light, and from the dominance of Satan to God, in order that they may receive forgiveness of sins, and an inheritance among those who have been sacrificed, by faith in me.

"Now go into the city, and you will be told what you must do."

The men traveling with him stood speechless, having heard the sound but seeing no one. Then Saul got up from the ground, but although his eyes were opened, he could see nothing. So they led him by the hand into Damascus.

For three days he was blind, and did not eat or drink anything.

Now there was in Damascus a certain disciple named Ananias. The Lord spoke to him in a vision: **"Ananias!"**

"Yes, Lord?" he replied. "I am here!"

The Lord told him, **"Arise and go to Straight Street, and inquire at the house of Judas for a man of Tarsus named Saul. For at this moment he is praying. In a vision he has seen a man named Ananias come and lay his hands on him to restore his sight."**

But Ananias answered, "Lord! I have heard from many about this man, how much harm he has done to your holy ones at Jerusalem! And here he has the warrant from the ruling priests to shackle all who call upon your name!"

But the Lord said to Ananias, **"Go! This man is my chosen instrument, to carry my name before the heathen Gentiles, and to kings, and to the descendents of Israel. For I will show him how much he must suffer for the sake of my name."**

So Ananias departed to the house, and entered it. And he laid hands on Saul and said, "Brother Saul, the Lord Jesus, who appeared to you on the road as you were coming here, has sent me so that you may regain your sight, and be filled with the Holy Spirit."

Immediately something like fish scales fell from his eyes, and he regained his sight. He rose up, and was baptized. And after taking some food, he regained his strength.

Now for several days he remained with the disciples in Damascus, and immediately began proclaiming Jesus in the synagogues, declaring that "He is the Son of God!"

All those who heard were amazed, asking, "Is this not the very one who in Jerusalem destroyed those who called upon this name? Has he not come here for the express purpose of arresting and taking them bound in chains before the ruling priests?"

Yet Saul kept increasing more and more powerful, and continued baffling the Jews who lived in Damascus by proving that Jesus is the Messiah.

Acts 9:1–22; 26:12–17

Now the word of the Lord came to me saying:

Before I formed you in the womb I knew you.
And before you were born I consecrated you apart.
I appointed you as a prophet to the nations.

Then I said: "Alas, sovereign Lord,
Behold, I do not know how to speak,
    because I am only a youth."

But the Lord said to me:

Do not say "I am only a youth."
Because to all that I send you, you shall go.
And all that I command you, you shall speak.
Do not be afraid of confronting them,
        for I am with you to deliver you,"

declares the Lord.

Recorded by the prophet Jeremiah, year c. 600 B.C.
Jeremiah 1:5–8

JOHN'S VISION OF JESUS

I JOHN, YOUR BROTHER and partner in persecution, and in the kingdom, and in patient endurance, which are ours in Jesus, was on the island called Patmos (meaning *banished*), because of proclaiming the Word of God and giving testimony of Jesus.

I was in the Spirit's power on the Lord's Day, and I heard behind me a great voice like a war trumpet, saying:

"Write on a scroll what you see, and send it to the seven churches — to Ephesus, and to Smyrna, and to Pergamun, and to Thyatira, and to Sardis, and to Philadelphia, and to Laodicea.

"I am the Alpha and the Omega, the beginning and the end, who is and who was and who is to come — the Almighty!"

And then I turned around to see who was the voice that was speaking to me. And having turned I saw seven golden lampstands. And in the middle of the lampstands I saw one like a Son of Man, clothed in a robe reaching to his feet, and with a golden sash belted across his chest. His head and his hair were like snow-white wool; and his eyes were like blazing fire. His feet were like burnished bronze refined in the furnace; and his voice was like the roar of rushing waters. In his right hand he held seven stars; and out of his mouth came a double-edged sword. His face was ablaze like the full brilliance of the sun.

And when I saw him, I fell at his feet as if dead. But he laid his right hand upon me, saying,

> **Do not be afraid anymore!**
> **I am the Alpha and the Omega,**
> **the First and the Last.**
> **I am the Ever-Living One.**
> **I was once dead, and you see**
> **I am alive forevermore.**
> **And I have the keys of death and of hades,**
> **the realm of the dead.**

Then, in the right hand of him who sat on the throne, I saw a scroll written on the inside and on the back, sealed up with seven seals.

Then I saw a mighty powerful angel announcing in a loud voice, "Who is worthy to open the scroll and break its seals?"

But no one in heaven, or on the earth, or under the earth, was able to open the scroll, or to even examine its contents. And I began weeping bitterly because no one could be found who was worthy to open the scroll, or even to inspect it.

Then one of the elders said to me, "Stop weeping! Take notice! The Lion of the tribe of Judah, the Root of David, he has triumphed, enabling him to open the scroll and to break its seven seals."

Then I saw a Lamb, as though it had been slaughtered, standing in the center between the throne (encircled by the four living creatures) and the elders. He had seven horns and seven eyes — which are the sevenfold Spirit of God, sent out into all continents of the earth. He came forward and took the scroll out of the right hand of the One who sat on the throne.

When he had received the scroll, the four living creatures and the 24 elders prostrated themselves, falling down before the Lamb. Each one was possessing a lyre, and golden bowls full of incense (which are the prayers of the holy ones), and was singing a new song:

> Worthy are you to receive the scroll and to break its seals;
> Because you were slaughtered,

And with your blood you ransomed for God
>   people from every tribe and language and race and nation.
You make them a royal house of priests to serve our God,
>   and they shall reign as kings upon the earth.

Then I looked and heard the voice of an immense number of angels numbering myriads of myriads, and thousands of thousands. They were encircling the throne and the living creatures and the elders. In a single great voice they sang:

Worthy is the Lamb who was slaughtered
>   to receive power and riches and wisdom and strength
>   and honor and glory and praise.

Then I heard every living creature — everything in creation that lives in heaven, and on earth, and under the earth, and on the seas, and all things in them, singing together:

To the One seated on the throne and to the Lamb,
Be praise and honor and glory and power for ever and for ever.

And the four living creatures said "Amen!" And the elders prostrated themselves, and bowed down and worshiped him.

Revelation 1:9–18; 5:1–13

This is what the Lord says,
>   Israel's King and Redeemer,
>   the Lord of Hosts:

**I am the First and I am the Last;
There is no God except me.**

Recorded by the prophet Isaiah, year c. 700 B.C.
Isaiah 44:6

As I was watching,
Thrones were set in place
>   and the Ancient One took his throne.
His robe was snow white,
>   and the hair of his head like pure white wool.
His throne was a blaze of flames,
>   and its wheels were a burning fire.
A surging river of fire was flowing,
>   issuing from his presence.

Thousands upon thousands were attending him,
    and myriads upon myriads were stationed before him.
The court sat in judgment, and the books were opened.
As I kept gazing at the continuing night visions
    I saw before me, coming with the clouds of heaven,
        One like a Son of Man!
He approached the venerable Ancient of Days
    and was presented before him.
And on him was conferred dominion, glory and sovereign power
That all peoples, nations, and those of every language
    should serve and worship him.
His dominion is an everlasting dominion
    which will never pass away.
And his sovereignty is one which will never be destroyed.
I raised my eyes and looked up and this is what I saw:
Before me was a man dressed in linen
    with a belt of the purest gold around his waist.
His body was like yellow beryl chrysolite.
His face had the appearance of lightning.
His eyes were like flaming torches,
    his arms and feet like the gleam of burnished bronze,
    and his voice like the roar of a tumultuous multitude.

333

Written by the prophet Daniel, year c. 550 B.C.
Daniel 7:9–10, 13–14; 10:5–6

For a child has been born to us;
    a son has been given to us.
And the dominion of his government
    shall be born upon his shoulders.
And his title shall be called:
    Wonderful Counselor.
    Mighty God.
    Everlasting Father.
    Prince of Peace.
Of his vast government and of his boundless peace
    there shall be no end.
He will reign on the throne of David
    and over his kingdom,
Establishing and sustaining it
    with justice and righteousness,
From that time on and forevermore.

Written by the prophet Isaiah, year c. 700 B.C.
Isaiah 9:6–7

ISAIAH 53

Who has believed what we have heard?

   And to whom has the power of the Lord been revealed?

For he grew up like a tender shoot before him,

   like a root out of parched ground.

He has no stateliness or majesty that would make us look at him,

   nothing in his appearance that would make us be attracted to him.

He was despised and rejected by others,

   a man of sorrows and acquainted with suffering.

Like one from whom men avert their gaze,

   we despised him and we gave him no esteem.

Surely it was our infirmities he himself bore;

   it was our diseases he himself carried.

Yet we considered him stricken by God,

   struck down by him, and punished.

He was pierced through for our transgressions,

   crushed for our iniquities.

The punishment borne by him brought us peace,

   and by his scourging we are healed.

All of us like sheep have gone astray;

   each one of us has turned to our own way.

But the Lord has laid on him the iniquity of us all.

He was abused and he was afflicted,

   yet he never opened his mouth.

Like a lamb that is led to the slaughter,

And like a sheep that is silent before its shearers,

    so he never opened his mouth.

Arrested, he was taken away and condemned!

Who of his contemporaries would have imagined his fate?

    That from the world of the living he was cut off.

    For the transgressions of others he was struck dead.

He was assigned a grave with the wicked,

    yet in his dying his tomb was with a rich man.

Although he had done no violence,

Nor was there any deceit in his mouth,

    yet it was the will of the Lord

    to crush him and cause him to suffer.

Although the Lord caused him to give himself as a sin offering,

    he will see his offspring.

And he will prolong his days;

    and the will of the Lord will prosper in his hands.

Therefore I shall give him his portion among the great,

    and he shall divide the spoils with the mighty —

Because he exposed himself to death,

    and was numbered with the transgressors.

For he himself bore the sin of many,

    and interceded for the transgressors.

Written by the prophet Isaiah, year c. 700 B.C.
Isaiah 53:1–12

INDEX OF ANCIENT PROPHECIES FROM THE OLD TESTAMENT FULFILLED IN THE LIFE OF JESUS

Genesis 28:12–13 by the patriarch Moses, c. 1450 B.C. 53

Exodus 12:46 by the patriarch Moses, c. 1450 B.C. 306

Exodus 20:8–10 by the patriarch Moses, c. 1450 B.C. 310

Leviticus 12:8 from the law of Moses, c. 1440 B.C. 32

Numbers 9:12 by the patriarch Moses, c. 1425 B.C. 306

Numbers 24:17 from the law of Moses, c. 1400 B.C. 36

Deuteronomy 1:1, 3 by the patriarch Moses, c. 1500 B.C. 180

Deuteronomy 18:15 by the patriarch Moses, c. 1500 B.C. 180

Deuteronomy 18:15, 17–18 by the patriarch Moses, c. 1500 B.C. 141, 180

Deuteronomy 19:15 by the patriarch Moses, c. 1500 B.C. 170

2 Samuel 7:12–16 by the prophet Nathan to King David, c. 1000 B.C. 24

1 Chronicles 17:12–14 by the prophet Nathan to King David, c. 1000 B.C. 25

Psalm 2:7–8 by the Psalmist, c. 1000 B.C. 47

Psalm 16:9–10 by King David, c. 1000 B.C. 325

Psalm 16:10 by King David, c. 1000 B.C. 314

Psalm 22 by King David, c. 1000 B.C. 17

Psalm 22:1 by King David, c. 1000 B.C. 305

Psalm 22:7–8 and 13–18 by King David, c. 1000 B.C. 304

Psalm 22:18 by King David, c. 1000 B.C. 302

Psalm 31:5 by King David, c. 1000 B.C. 305

Psalm 34:20 by King David, c. 1000 B.C. 307

Psalms 35:19 and 69:4 by King David, c. 1000 B.C. 279

Psalm 38:11 by King David, c. 1000 B.C. 307

Psalm 41:7–9 by King David, c. 1000 B.C. 270

Psalm 41:9–10 by King David, c. 1000 B.C. 284

Psalm 42:1–6 by the sons of Korah, c. 950 B.C. 254

Psalm 69:21 by King David, c. 1000 B.C. 299, 305

Psalm 72:10–15 by King Solomon, c. 950 B.C. 34

Psalm 78:1–2 by the psalmist Asaph, c. 750 B.C. 122

Psalm 89:3–4 by the psalmist Ethan the Ezrahite, c. 1000 B.C. 180

Psalm 91:11–12 by the Psalmist, c. 1500 to 950 B.C. 51

Psalm 109:25 by King David, c. 1000 B.C. 303

Psalm 110:1 by King David, c. 1000 B.C. 289

Isaiah 6:8–10 by the prophet Isaiah, c. 700 B.C. 119

Isaiah 6:9–10 by the prophet Isaiah, c. 700 B.C. 155

Isaiah 7:14 by the prophet Isaiah, c. 700 B.C. 24

Isaiah 8:11, 13–15 by the prophet Isaiah, c. 700 B.C. 103

Isaiah 9:1–2 by the prophet Isaiah, c. 700 B.C. 70

Isaiah 9:2 by the prophet Isaiah, c. 700 B.C. 27

Isaiah 9:6–7 by the prophet Isaiah, c. 700 B.C. 333

Isaiah 29:18–19 by the prophet Isaiah, c. 700 B.C. 103

Isaiah 35:5–6 by the prophet Isaiah, c. 700 B.C. 103

Isaiah 40:1–5 by the prophet Isaiah, c. 700 B.C. 44
Isaiah 42:1 by the prophet Isaiah, c. 700 B.C. 162
Isaiah 42:1–4 by the prophet Isaiah, c. 700 B.C. 47, 83
Isaiah 42:6 by the prophet Isaiah, c. 700 B.C. 29
Isaiah 44:6 by the prophet Isaiah, c. 700 B.C. 332
Isaiah 45:22–24 by the prophet Isaiah, c. 700 B.C. 328
Isaiah 46:13 by the prophet Isaiah, c. 700 B.C. 29
Isaiah 49:6 by the prophet Isaiah, c. 700 B.C. 29
Isaiah 50:6 by the prophet Isaiah, c. 700 B.C. 291
Isaiah 53:1–12 by the prophet Isaiah, c. 700 B.C. 334–335
Isaiah 53:3 by the prophet Isaiah, c. 700 B.C. 163
Isaiah 53:4 by the prophet Isaiah, c. 700 B.C. 72
Isaiah 53:7 by the prophet Isaiah, c. 700 B.C. 294
Isaiah 53:9 by the prophet Isaiah, c. 700 B.C. 310
Isaiah 53:12 by the prophet Isaiah, c. 700 B.C. 273, 301
Isaiah 60:6 by the prophet Isaiah, c. 700 B.C. 34
Isaiah 61:1 by the prophet Isaiah, c. 700 B.C. 103
Isaiah 61:1–2 by the prophet Isaiah, c. 700 B.C. 69
Isaiah 66:22–24 by the prophet Isaiah, c. 700 B.C. 169
Jeremiah 1:5–8 by the prophet Jeremiah, c. 600 B.C. 330
Jeremiah 5:20–22 by the prophet Jeremiah, c. 600 B.C. 155
Jeremiah 6:16 by the prophet Jeremiah, c. 600 B.C. 105
Jeremiah 7:10–11 by the prophet Jeremiah, c. 625 B.C. 239
Jeremiah 31:15 by the prophet Jeremiah, c. 600 B.C. 37
Jeremiah 32:8–9 by the prophet Jeremiah, c. 600 B.C. 292
Ezekiel 12:1–2 by the prophet Ezekiel, c. 575 B.C. 155
Ezekiel 34:20–24 by the prophet Ezekiel, c. 575 B.C. 191
Daniel 7:9–10, 13–14; 10:5–6 by the prophet Daniel, c. 550 B.C. 333
Daniel 7:13–14 by the prophet Daniel, c. 550 B.C. 53, 290
Daniel 7:14 by the prophet Daniel, c. 550 B.C. 327
Hosea 6:2 by the prophet Hosea, c. 725 B.C. 318
Hosea 6:6 by the prophet Hosea, c. 725 B.C. 75
Hosea 10:8 by the prophet Hosea, c. 725 B.C. 299
Hosea 11:1 by the prophet Hosea, c. 725 B.C. 36
Joel 3:13–14 by the prophet Joel, c. 825 B.C. 120
Micah 5:2 by the prophet Micah, c. 740 B.C. 35, 180
Micah 7:5–7 by the prophet Micah, c. 740 B.C. 135
Zechariah 9:9 by the prophet Zechariah, c. 520 B.C. 238
Zechariah 11:12–13 by the prophet Zechariah, c. 520 B.C. 292
Zechariah 12:10 by the prophet Zechariah, c. 520 B.C. 307
Zechariah 13:7 by the prophet Zechariah, c. 520 B.C. 285
Malachi 3:1 by the prophet Malachi, c. 425 B.C. 27, 44, 102
Malachi 4:5–6 by the prophet Malachi, c. 425 B.C. 22, 163
John 6:36 by the Messiah, c. A.D. 30 287
John 12:33 by the Messiah, c. A.D. 30 294
John 17:12 by the Messiah, c. A.D. 30 287

337

SYNOPTIC INDEX

THE ADVENT OF MESSIAH — The First Christmas
In the Beginning: Luke 1:1–4; John 1:1–18 19–20
Before Jesus' Birth: Matthew 1:18–25; Luke 1:5–80..21–29
The Birth of Jesus: Matthew 2:1–18; Luke 2:1–38 31–37
The Boyhood of Jesus: Matthew 2:19–23; Luke 2:39–52 39–40

MESSIAH'S MINISTRY BEGINS — Going Out into the Harvest
The Inauguration: Matthew 3:1–4:11; Mark 1:1–13;
    Luke 3:1–4:13; John 1:19–34...43–53
First Judea: John 2:1–3:26 55–59
Then Samaria: Matthew 4:12; Mark 1:14; Luke 3:19–20; 4:14;
    John 4:1–45 61–64

THE GREAT GALILEAN MINISTRY — Acceptance and Rejection
Home in Galilee: Matthew 4:13–25; 8:14-9:8; Mark 1:14–2:22;
    Luke 4:14–5:39; John 4:46–54..67–76
The Second Passover: John 5:1–47 77–80
Back to Galilee: Matthew 10:1–4; 12:1–21; Mark 2:22–3:19;
    Luke 6:1–16 81–84
The Sermon on the Mount: Matthew 5:1–8:1; Luke 6:17–49 85–97
Growing Fame: Matthew 8:5–13; 11:2–30; Luke 7:1–50 99–106
First Public Rejection: Matthew 12:22–50; Mark 3:20–35;
    Luke 8:1–3; 11:14–54 107–113
Secrets of the Kingdom: Matthew 13:1–35; Mark 4:1–34;
    Luke 8:4–18; 13:18–21 115–122
The Kingdom Secrets Revealed: Matthew 13:36–53 123–125
Continued Opposition: Matthew 8:18–34; 9:18–34; 13:54–56;
    Mark 4:35–6:6; Luke 8:22–56..127–132
Final Galilean Campaign: Matthew 9:35–11:1; 14:1–12; Mark 6:6–29;
    Luke 9:1–9 133–137

TRAINING THE TWELVE — Lessons on Discipleship
Lessons on the Bread of Life: Matthew 14:13–36; Mark 6:30–56;
    Luke 9:10–17; John 6:1–71..139–147
Lessons on Leaven: Matthew 15:1–16:12; Mark 7:1–8:26; Luke 12:1–21;
    John 7:1 149–157
Lessons on Messiahship: Matthew 16:13–17:13; Mark 8:27–9:13;
    Luke 9:18–20; 9:21–36 159–163
Lessons on Responsibility: Matthew 17:14–18:35; Mark 9:14–50;
    Luke 9:37–50 165–171
Lessons on Commitment: Matthew 8:19–22; Luke 9:51–62;
    John 7:2–10 173–174

MESSIAH'S FINAL MISSIONS — The Judean and Perean Ministries
Last Judean Ministries: John 7:11-10:21 177–191
Lessons on Loving Service: Luke 10:1-11:13 193–196
Accusations and Warnings: Luke 12:22-59 197–200
Repent or Perish: Luke 13:1-17; John 10:22-39 201–203
Principles of Discipleship: Luke 13:22-17:10; John 10:40-11:54 205–217
To Jerusalem: Matthew 19:1-20:28; Mark 10:1-45; Luke 17:11-18:34 219–228

JERUSALEM — The Final Countdown
Seventh Day before Passover: Matthew 20:20-34; Mark 10:46-52;
    Luke 18:35-19:28; John 11:55-57 231–234
Sixth Day before Passover: John 12:1-11 235
Fifth Day before Passover: Matthew 21:1-11; Mark 11:1-11;
    Luke 19:29-44; John 12:12-19 237–239
Fourth Day before Passover: Matthew 21:12-19; Mark 11:12-19;
    Luke 19:45-48 241–242
Third Day before Passover: Matthew 21:20-26:5; Mark 11:19-14:2;
    Luke 20:1-21:38; John 12:20-50 243–263
Second Day before Passover: Matthew 26:6-19; Mark 14:3-16;
    Luke 22:1-13 265–266

LAST DAYS OF MESSIAH — The Weekend that Changed the World
The Day Before Passover: Matthew 26:20-27:34; Mark 14:17-15:23;
    Luke 22:14-23:31; John 13:1-19:17; Acts 1:18-19;
    1 Corinthians 11:23-26 269–299
Six Hours on the Cross: Matthew 27:35-56; Mark 15:24-41;
    Luke 23:32-49; John 19:18-37 301–307
Passover Sabbath, Messiah's Burial: Matthew 27:55-66; Mark 15:42-47;
    Luke 23:50-56; John 19:31-42 309–310
The First Day of the Week, The Resurrection & Easter Sunday
    Matthew 28:1-16:12; Mark 16:1-18; Luke 24:1-32; John 20:1-18 311–315
The Second Day of the Week, The Next Day and the Next Week
    Matthew 16:13; Luke 24:37-49; John 20:19-31 317–319
From Galilee to Glory — The Ascension: Matthew 28:16-20;
    Luke 24:50-53; John 21:1-25; Acts 1:3-14; 1 Corinthians 15:1-8 321–325
Messiah Glorified: Acts 7:55-56, 59-60; 9:1-22; 26:12-17;
    Philippians 2:5-11; Revelation 1:9-18; 5:1-13 327–333

SCRIPTURE INDEX

GENESIS
28:12–13.................53

EXODUS
12:46....................306
20:8–10.................310

LEVITICUS
12:8......................32

NUMBERS
9:12......................306
24:17....................36

DEUTERONOMY
1:1.......................180
1:3.......................18
18:15..............141, 180
18:17–18..........141, 180
19:15...................170

2 SAMUEL
7:12–16.................24

1 CHRONICLES
17: 12–14...............25

PSALMS
2:7–8................47, 304
2:13–18.................304
7–8......................17
13–18....................17
16:9–10.................325
16:10....................314
22:1.....................305
22:1–2...................17
22:18....................302
31.......................17
31:5.....................305
34:20....................307
35:19....................279
38:11....................307
41:7–9...................270
41:9–10..................284
42:1–6...................254
69:4.....................279
69:21...............299, 305
72:10–15.................34
78:1–2...................122
89:3–4...................180
91:11–12.................51
109:25...................303
110:1....................289

ISAIAH
6:8–10...................119
6:9–10...................155
7:14.....................24
8:11.....................103
8:13–15..................103
9:1–2....................70
9:2......................27
9:6–7....................333
29:18–19.................103
35:5–6...................103
40:1–5...................44
42:1.....................162
42:1–4................47, 83
42:6.....................29
44:6.....................332
45:22–24.................328
46:13....................29
49:6.....................29
50:6.....................291
53:1–12..................335
53:3.....................163
53:4.....................72
53:7.....................294
53:9.....................310
53:12...............273, 301
60:6.....................34
61:1.....................103
61:1–2...................69
66:22–24.................169

JEREMIAH
1:5–8....................330
5:20–22..................155
6:16.....................105
7:10–11..................239
31:15....................37
32:8–9...................292

EZEKIEL
12:1–2...................155
34:20–24.................191

DANIEL
7:9–10...................333
7:13–14.........53, 290, 333
7:14.....................327
10:5–6...................333

HOSEA
6:2......................318
6:6......................75

10:8.....................299
11:1.....................36

JOEL
3:13–14..................120

MICAH
5:2..................35, 180
7:5–7....................135

ZECHARIAH
9:9......................238
11:12–13.................292
12:10....................307
13:7.....................285

MALACHI
4:5–6................22, 163
3:1...............27, 44, 102

MATTHEW
1:1–17...................50
1:18–25..................25
2:1–12...................35
2:13–18..................36
2:19–23..................39
3:1–6....................44
3:7–10...................46
3:11–12..................46
3:13–17..................46
4:1–11...................51
4:12.................61, 64
4:13–17..................69
4:18–22..................71
4:23–25..................73
5:1–12...................86
5:13–20..................87
5:21–48..................90
6:1–18...................92
6:19–34..................93
7:1–5....................94
7:6–12...................95
7:13–27..................97
7:28–8:1.................97
8:2–4....................73
8:5–13...................100
8:14–17..................72
8:18.....................127
8:19–22..................174
8:23–27..................127
8:28–34..................129
9:1–8....................74
9:9–13...................75

9:14–17	76	19:1–12	223	27:37	302
9:18–26	131	19:13–15	224	27:35–37	302
9:27–34	131	19:16–30	226	27:39–44	303
9:35–38	133	20:1–16	227	27:45–50	305
10:1–4	84	20:17–19	227	27:51–54	306
10:1–42	135	20:20–28	228	27:55–56	307
11:1	136	20:29–34	231	27:57–60	310
11:2–19	102	21:1–7	237	27:61–66	310
11:20–24	104	21:8–11	239	28:1	311
11:25–30	105	21:12–17	242	28:2–4	311
12:1–8	82	21:18–20	241	28:5–8	312
12:9–14	82	21:20–22	243	28:9–10	312
12:15–21	83	21:23–27	244	28:11–15	313
12:22–37	109	21:28–32	244	28:16	322
12:38–42	110	21:33–46	245	28:16–20	324
12:43–45	112	22:1–14	246		
12:46–50	113	22:15–22	247	**MARK**	
13:1–3	115	22:23–33	248	1:1–6	44
13:3–23	119	22:34–40	249	1:7–8	46
13:24–30	121	22:41–46	249	1:9–1	46
13:31–32	121	23:1–12	250	1:12–13	51
13:33–35	122	23:13–36	252	1:14	61, 64
13:36–43	124	23:37–39	252	1:14–15	67
13:44–46	124	24:1–51	260	1:16–20	71
13:47–53	125	25:1–13	260	1:21–28	71
13:54–58	132	25:14–30	261	1:29–34	72
14:1–2	136	25:31–46	262	1:35–39	73
14:3–12	137	26:1–5	263	1:40–45	73
14:13–14	139	26:6–13	265	2:1–12	74
14:15–21	141	26:14–16	266	2:13–17	75
14:22–23	141	26:17–19	266	2:18–22	76
14:24–33	142	26:20	270	2:23–28	82
14:34–36	142	26:23–25	271	3:1–6	82
15:1–9	150	26:26–29	272	3:7–12	83
15:10–20	151	26:30	276	3:13–19	84
15:21–28	152	26:31–35	284	3:20–30	109
15:29–31	152	26:36–46	286	3:31–35	113
15:32–38	153	26:47–56	287	4:1–2	115
15:39–16:4	154	26:57–58	288	4:3–25	119
16:5–12	155	26:59–68	289	4:26–29	120
16:13–20	159	26:69–75	291	4:30–32	121
16:21–26	160	27:1	291	4:33–34	122
16:27–28	161	27:2	294	4:35–41	127
17:1–8	162	27:3–10	292	5:1–20	129
17:9–13	163	27:11–14	294	5:21–43	131
17:14–21	166	27:15–18	295	6:1–6	132
17:22–23	167	27:19	295	6:6	133
17:24–27	167	27:20–23	296	6:7–11	135
18:1–5	168	27:24–26	298	6:12–13	136
18:6–14	169	27:27–30	298	6:14–16	136
18:15–20	170	27:31–34	299	6:17–29	137
18:21–35	171	27:38	301	6:30–34	139

341

6:35–44	141
6:45–46	141
6:47–52	142
6:53–56	142
7:1–13	150
7:14–23	151
7:24–30	152
7:31–37	152
8:1–9	153
8:10–12	154
8:13–21	155
8:22–26	157
8:27–30	159
8:31–37	160
8:38–9:1	161
9:2–8	162
9:9–13	163
9:14–29	166
9:30–32	167
9:33–37	168
9:38–50	169
10:1–12	223
10:13–16	224
10:17–31	226
10:32–34	227
10:35–45	228
10:46–52	231
11:1–7	237
11:8–11	239
11:12–14	241
11:15–19	242
11:19–26	243
11:27–33	244
12:1–13	245
12:13–17	247
12:18–27	248
12:28–34	249
12:35–37	249
12:38–40	250
12:41–44	252
13:1–37	260
14:1–2	263
14:3–9	265
14:10–11	266
14:12–16	266
14:17	270
14:20–21	271
14:22–25	272
14:26	276
14:27–31	284
14:32–42	286
14:43–52	287

14:53–54	288
14:55–65	289
14:66–72	291
15:1	291
15:1–5	294
15:6–10	295
15:11–14	296
15:15	298
15:16–19	298
15:20–23	299
15:24–25	302
15:26	302
15:27	301
15:29–32	303
15:33–37	305
15:38–39	306
15:40–41	307
15:42–47	310
16:1–3	311
16:4	311
16:5	312
16:6–8	312
16:12	315
16:13	318

LUKE

1:1–4	19
1:5–25	22
1:26–38	23
1:39–45	26
1:46–56	27
1:57–80	29
2:1–7	31
2:8–14	32
2:15–20	32
2:21–24	33
2:25–35	34
2:36–38	34
2:39–40	39
2:41–50	40
2:51–52	40
3:1–6	44
3:7–14	46
3:15–18	46
3:19–20	61
3:21–23	46
3:23–28	48
3:31	69
4:1–13	51
4:14	61, 64
4:14–15	67
4:16–30	69

4:31–37	71
5:1–11	71
5:12–16	73
5:17–26	74
5:27–32	75
5:33–39	76
6:1–5	82
6:6–11	82
6:12–16	84
6:17–26	86
6:27–30	90
6:32–36	90
6:37–42	94
6:43–49	97
7:1–10	100
7:11–17	100
7:18–35	102
7:36–50	106
8:1–3	107
8:4–18	119
8:19–21	113
8:22–25	127
8:26–39	129
8:40–56	131
9:1–5	135
9:6	136
9:7–9	136
9:10–11	139
9:12–17	141
9:18–20	159
9:21–25	160
9:26–27	161
9:28–36	162
9:36	163
9:37–43	166
9:43–45	167
9:46–48	168
9:49–50	169
9:51–56	174
9:57–62	174
10:1–16	194
10:17–24	194
10:25–37	195
10:38–42	195
11:1–13	196
11:14–23	109
11:24–28	112
11:29–36	110
11:37–54	112
12:1–3	155
12:4–12	156
12:13–21	157

12:22–34.............................198
12:35–48.............................199
12:49–53.............................199
12:54–59.............................200
13:1–5................................201
13:6–9................................202
13:10–17.............................202
13:18–19.............................121
13:20–21.............................122
13:22–30.............................206
13:31–35.............................206
14:1–6................................207
14:7–14..............................208
14:15–24.............................208
14:25–35.............................209
15:1–32..............................211
16:1–13..............................212
16:14–18.............................213
16:19–31.............................214
17:1–10..............................215
17:11–19.............................219
17:20–37.............................221
18:1–14..............................222
18:15–17.............................224
18:18–30.............................226
18:31–34.............................227
18:35–43.............................231
19:1–10..............................232
19:11–28.............................234
19:29–36.............................237
19:36–44.............................239
19:45–48.............................242
20:1–8................................244
20:9–19..............................245
20:20–26.............................247
20:27–39.............................248
20:41–44.............................249
20:45–47.............................250
21:1–4................................252
21:5–36..............................256
21:37–38.............................256
22:1–6................................266
22:7–13..............................266
22:14................................270
22:19–23.............................272
22:21–23.............................271
22:24–30.............................271
22:31–34.............................273
22:35–38.............................273
22:39................................276
22:40–46.............................286
22:47–53.............................287

22:54–55.............................288
22:56–62.............................291
22:63–65.............................289
22:66–71.............................291
23:1–5................................294
23:6–12..............................294
23:13–17.............................295
23:18–19.......................295, 296
23:20–23.............................296
23:24–25.............................298
23:26–31.............................299
23:32–34.............................301
23:34................................302
23:35–43.............................303
23:38................................302
23:44–46.............................305
23:44–47.............................306
23:48–49.............................307
23:50–56.............................310
24:1.................................311
24:2.................................311
24:3–5...............................312
24:6–8...............................312
24:9–11..............................313
24:13–32.............................315
24:37–49.............................318
24:50................................324
24:50–53.............................324

JOHN
1:1–18...............................20
1:19–28..............................46
1:29–34..............................51
1:35–51..............................52
2:1–12...............................55
2:13–22..............................56
2:23–25..............................56
3:1–21...............................58
3:22–36..............................59
4:1–4................................61
4:5–26...............................63
4:27–38..............................63
4:39–42..............................64
4:43–45..............................64
4:46–54..............................68
5:1–9................................77
5:9–16...............................78
5:17–47..............................80
6:1–4................................139
6:5–14...............................141
6:15.................................141
6:16–21..............................142

6:22–59..............................146
6:39.................................287
6:60–71..............................147
7:1..................................150
7:2–9................................173
7:10.................................174
7:11–52..............................180
7:53–8:11............................181
8:12–20..............................182
8:21–30..............................183
8:31–59..............................186
9:1–41...............................188
10:1–21..............................190
10:22–39.............................203
10:40–42.............................205
11:1–44..............................217
11:45–54.............................217
11:55................................219
11:55–57.............................232
12:2–11..............................235
12:12................................237
12:12–19.............................239
12:20–50.............................254
12:33................................294
13:1–20..............................270
13:21–30.............................271
13:31–38.............................273
14:1–31..............................276
15:1–27..............................278
16:1–33..............................281
17:1–26..............................284
17:12................................287
18:1.................................284
18:2–11..............................287
18:12–14.............................288
18:15–16.............................288
18:17................................291
18:18................................288
18:19–24.............................288
18:25–27.............................291
18:28–38.............................294
18:39–40.............................295
18:40................................296
19:1–3...............................296
19:4–6...............................296
19:7–12..............................297
19:13–15.............................297
19:16................................298
19:16–17.............................299
19:18................................301
19:19–22.............................302
19:23–24.............................302

19:25–27..........................304
19:28–30..........................305
19:31–37..........................306
19:31–42..........................310
20:1.................................311
20:2.................................312
20:3.................................312
20:3–10............................313
20:11–18..........................314
20:19–23..........................318
20:24–25..........................318
20:26–31..........................319

21:1–12 322
21:13–19 322
21:20–23 323
21:23–25 325

ACTS
1:3–8 324
1:9–14 324
1:18–19 292
7:55–56 328
7:59–60............................328
9:1–22..............................330

9:12–17 330
9:26.................................330
26:12–17..........................330

1 CORINTHIANS
11:23–26 272
15:1–8..............................325

PHILIPPIANS
2:5–11 327

REVELATION
1:1–18..............................332
5:1–13..............................332

SUBJECT INDEX

Alpha (the) and the Omega 13, 330–331

Abomination of Desolation 258

Abraham ...10, 27–28, 45, 48, 50, 99, 184, 186, 202, 206, 213–214, 232, 248

adultery.................88, 151, 181, 213, 223–224

advocate 275–276, 278–279

Ananias 329

Ancient of Days.............................53, 290, 333

Andrew 52, 70–71, 84, 140, 252, 257, 324

Angel of the Lord 21, 25, 31, 36, 39, 77, 311

angel/angels...............21–23, 25, 31–32, 36, 39, 50–53, 77, 123–124, 156, 161, 169, 210, 213, 247, 253, 258–259, 262, 285, 287, 311–312, 314–315, 331–332

Anna 7, 34

Annas.....................................11, 43, 287–288

anointed..........8, 11, 52, 68–69, 103, 105–106, 136, 215, 235, 303

Aramathea..309

ascension 5, 7, 12, 173, 321, 323–325, 340

authority 8, 11, 56, 71, 74, 79–80, 84, 97, 99, 133, 156, 177, 183, 185, 190, 194, 203, 228, 243–244, 246, 249, 254, 274, 280, 297, 323–324, 328

baby 23, 25–26, 28, 31–33, 36

Babylon..49–50

banquet...............10, 55, 74, 137, 198, 207–208

baptism 7, 43, 46, 102, 199, 228, 244

baptize..45–46, 51

Barabbas....................................12, 295–296, 298

Bartimaeus 231

Batholomew..84, 324

Beatitudes 8, 85

Beelzebub................................8, 107–108, 134

believe 15, 19, 22, 52, 57–58, 62, 64, 67, 79–80, 108, 117–118, 131, 143–144, 146, 166, 168, 183, 185, 187–188, 203, 216–217, 243–244, 252–254, 256, 258, 270, 274, 276, 279, 281–283, 291, 303, 306, 313, 315, 317–319, 325

believes......57–59, 79, 144–145, 166, 179, 216, 243, 254, 275

Bethany...........10, 46, 205, 215–216, 235, 237, 239, 241–242, 265, 323

Bethlelem 31–32, 34–36, 179–180

Bethsaida....9, 52, 104, 139, 141, 157, 193, 252

betrayed 84, 166, 227, 255, 286, 291

blaspheming....................................74, 203, 289

blessed..........26, 33, 85–86, 101, 112, 117, 140, 153, 159, 194, 198–199, 206, 208, 238, 252, 262, 270, 289, 299, 319, 324

blind 8–11, 68, 77, 93–94, 100–101, 103, 107, 131, 151–152, 157, 186–188, 190, 208, 216, 231, 241, 250–251, 329

blood...111–112, 130, 145, 159, 201, 251–252, 272, 285, 291–292, 297–298, 306, 332

boat 70–71, 73, 83, 115, 127–129, 139, 141–143, 153–154, 321

bones........12, 17, 251, 303–304, 306–307, 317

born again 57

branches 121, 238, 259, 277

bread 9, 50, 81, 91, 95, 102, 139–141, 143–147, 149, 152–155, 196, 208, 263, 265–266, 270–272, 284, 315, 317, 322, 339

Bread of Life.....9, 139, 141, 143–145, 147, 339

bridegroom 55, 59, 75, 260

bridesmaids 11, 260

Caesar 12, 31, 43, 247, 293, 297

Caesar Augustus 31

Caesarea Philippi..159

Caiaphas 11, 43, 217, 263, 287–288

Calvary..299, 301

Cana 8, 55, 67, 321

Capernaum 8–9, 55, 67–69, 71, 73, 99, 104, 139, 141, 143, 146, 167, 194

centurion.............8, 12, 99–100, 305–306, 309

Cephas 52, 325

ceremonial washing 55

chaff 46

chief priest.................11, 217, 287–290, 328

children of God........................20, 86, 217, 247

children of Light 212

Chosen One.........9, 47, 83, 161–162, 180, 303

circumcised 28, 33

City of David 31

Cleopas 315

colt 11, 237–238

comfort 44, 69

Commandments 87, 150, 224, 248, 275, 277

condemned 58, 82, 93, 109, 181, 251, 280, 289, 291, 335

covenant..................27, 29, 44, 102, 180, 272

cross 12, 112, 127, 135, 141, 160, 209, 213, 298, 301–307, 327, 340

crown of thorns 296, 298

crucify 12, 227, 251, 295–298

345

crucify him..............................12, 227, 295–298

cup.......110, 135, 168, 228, 251, 272, 285, 287

cup of sorrow 228

Damascus...328–330

Daniel 53, 258, 290, 327, 333, 338, 342

David.............................11, 17, 23–25, 28, 31,
48–50, 81, 107, 131, 151, 179–180, 191,
231, 238, 242,249, 270, 279, 284, 289,
299, 302–305, 307, 314, 325, 331, 333,
336–337

Day of Judgment...................11, 104, 134, 262

Day of the Lord..............................22, 120, 163

deaf 101, 103, 152, 166

death...........5, 9–10, 17, 27, 29, 67, 69–70, 79,
129, 134, 136, 150, 161, 166, 174,
185–186, 215–217, 227, 235, 244–245,
253, 255, 257, 263, 265, 272–273, 285,
289, 291, 293, 295, 301–304, 315, 322,
325, 327, 331, 335, 352

demons 72, 96, 107–108,
128–129, 131, 133–134,
136, 168, 194, 206

denarius 105, 140, 171, 226–227, 247, 265

desert 43–44, 50, 103, 128, 143, 217

devil 50–51, 117, 123, 147, 185, 262, 269

dice.......................................17, 302, 304

divorce 10, 88, 213, 222–223

dominion 53, 290, 327, 333

donkey 11, 202, 237

dove 46, 51

drink 61–62, 92–93, 145, 157, 168, 179,
198–199, 215, 228, 259, 262, 271–272,
285, 287, 299, 304–305, 329

Egypt 7, 36, 39

Elijah...............9, 22, 45, 68–69, 102, 136, 159,
161–163, 304–305

Elizabeth 7, 21–23, 26–28

Emmaus......................................12, 314, 317

eternal life 15, 57–59, 62–63, 79–80,
143–146, 194, 203, 224, 226, 253–254,
262, 282

evil.........58, 74, 79, 83–86, 89, 91, 95–96, 100,
107, 109, 112, 117, 123–124, 128–129,
151, 154, 168, 173, 196, 206, 245, 283,
296

evil one..............................89, 91, 117, 123, 283

evil spirit 109, 128, 151

expected one...100

eye......................88–89, 92, 94, 110, 169, 225

Ezekiel...........................155, 191, 338, 342

faith 8–11, 20–22, 74, 93, 99, 106, 127,
130–131, 142, 151–152, 166, 198, 214,
219, 221, 231, 243, 257, 273, 329

Feast of Tabernacles 9, 173, 177

feet........17, 29, 70, 89, 94, 105–106, 128–129,
134, 151–152, 168, 193, 195, 211,
215–217, 219, 235, 249, 269–270, 304,
312, 314, 317, 329, 331, 333

Festival of Booths 173

Festival of Unleavened Bread 263, 265–266

fire..............................45–46, 95, 123, 165–166,
168–169, 174, 199, 220, 246, 262, 277,
288, 290, 322, 331–332

fish..........70, 95, 124, 140, 153, 167, 196, 317,
321–322, 329

fishermen 70

five thousand......9, 11, 140–141, 154, 260–261

flogged 295–296, 298

"Follow me!" 52, 71, 74, 135, 160, 174, 203,
209, 225, 253, 273, 322–323

forty days 50, 321, 323

four thousand...................................9, 153–154

fruit.........45, 95, 109, 118, 201–202, 241, 245,
272, 276–277

Gabriel 22–23

Galilee..8, 12, 23,
31, 39, 43, 46, 52, 55, 61, 64, 67–73, 75,
81, 83, 128, 137, 139, 149, 152, 166, 173,
179–180, 219, 222, 239, 252, 284, 294,
307, 312, 321, 323–325, 339–340

gate...........77,95, 100, 159, 189, 213, 237, 259,
288, 290, 307, 310

Gehenna 88, 134, 156, 169

Gennesaret 9, 70, 142

Gentiles...............29, 33, 69–70, 83, 90–91, 93,
133–134, 227–228, 256, 270, 329

Gerasenes 128–129

Gethsemane 11, 276, 285

glorify...............32, 70, 74, 100, 186, 219, 231,
253, 272, 280, 282, 322

Golgotha...............................12, 298–299, 301

good news 22, 31, 46, 67–69, 72, 103, 106,
133, 136, 243, 325

Good Shepherd 10, 189–190

harvest.............7–8, 42, 63, 120–121, 123, 133,
193, 233, 244, 339

heal...............67–68, 82, 84, 99, 117, 133, 193,
207, 253

hearts 46, 74, 82, 117, 119, 142,
149, 154–155, 163, 167, 213, 256, 274,
276–280, 315, 317

heaven...........10, 29, 32, 43, 46, 51–53, 57–59, 69, 85–87, 89–92, 95–96, 100–101, 104, 107, 113, 120–122, 124–125, 133, 135, 140, 143–146, 152–153, 159, 167–171, 174, 194, 197–198, 210–211, 213, 220, 222–226, 233, 238, 244, 246–247, 250–251, 253, 259–260, 282, 285, 289–290, 311, 323–324, 327–328, 331–333

Herod 10–11, 21, 35–36, 39, 43, 61, 107, 136–137, 154, 206, 246, 294–295

Herodias..61, 136–137

Holy One........................71, 103, 146, 314, 325

Holy Spirit 13, 21, 23, 25–26, 28, 33, 46, 50–51, 108, 156, 194, 196, 257, 276, 318, 323–324, 328–329

Hosea.......................36, 75, 299, 318, 338, 342

humble.....26, 85, 103, 105, 168, 214, 237, 262

hypocrites................90–91, 149, 200, 202, 247, 251, 259

hypocritical 250–251

I Am......................9, 17, 22–23, 33, 45–46, 58, 63, 70, 73, 77–79, 99, 101, 105, 119, 131, 134, 142, 144–145, 159, 162, 170, 173, 177–179, 181–183, 185–187, 189–190, 193, 196–197, 199, 203, 208, 210–216, 222, 224, 227–228, 233, 244, 248, 253, 255, 257, 269–270, 272–279, 281–284, 286–287, 289–291, 293–294, 296–297, 303–304, 314, 318, 321, 323, 328–332

Immanuel..24–25

in remembrance of me...................................272

Isaiah..............12, 24–25, 27, 29, 34, 43–45, 47, 68–70, 72, 83, 103, 116, 119, 149, 155, 162–163, 169, 253, 273, 291, 294, 301, 310, 328, 332–335, 337, 342

Iscariot 84, 147, 235, 265, 269, 271, 275

Israel 22–23, 27–29, 33, 35–36, 39, 51–52, 57, 68–69, 99, 103, 131, 133–134, 152, 180, 225, 238, 248, 271, 292, 303, 315, 324, 329, 332

James.......71, 84, 130–131, 161, 174, 227–228, 257, 285, 307, 311, 313, 324–325, 343

Jehovah Sabaoth 27, 44, 102

Jeremiah........37, 105, 155, 159, 239, 292, 330, 337, 342

Jericho..................................11, 195, 231–232

Jerusalem....................7, 10–11, 33–35, 39–40, 44–45, 50, 56, 62, 64, 73, 77, 83, 85, 89, 103, 107, 149, 160–161, 173–174, 178, 195, 201–202, 205–206, 216, 219, 221, 223, 225, 227, 230, 232–234, 237–239, 241, 243, 252, 255–256, 294, 299, 307, 314–315, 317–318, 323–324, 328–329, 340

Jews.........10, 21, 35, 45, 56, 61–62, 77–78, 99, 139, 144, 149, 173, 177, 179, 183–190, 203, 215–217, 232, 272, 288, 293, 295–298, 302–303, 306, 309, 313, 317, 330

Joel...120, 338, 342

John the baptizer.............7, 9, 28, 43, 100–102, 136–137, 159, 163

Jonah................................8, 109–110, 154, 342

Jordan 10, 43–44, 46, 50, 58, 69–70, 73, 83, 180, 205, 222

joy............21, 26, 31, 35, 59, 86, 103, 118, 124, 210–211, 277, 280–281, 283, 312, 317, 324

Judas Iscariot 84, 235, 265, 275

Judea 8, 21, 26, 28, 31, 35, 39, 43–44, 55, 57–59, 61, 67–68, 72–73, 83, 85, 100, 149, 173, 215, 222, 255, 258, 294, 309, 324, 339

judge 10, 58, 79, 88, 93–94, 156, 178, 182–183, 185, 191, 200, 221, 233, 254, 293

Kidron 284

King Agrippa...328

King David .17, 24–25, 49, 270, 279, 284, 289, 299, 302–305, 307, 314, 325, 336–337

King of the Jews 21, 35, 293, 295–296, 298, 302–303

King Solomon 34, 336

kingdom of God 57, 67, 72, 101, 107–108, 116, 119, 121–122, 133, 139, 161, 169, 174, 193, 206, 208, 213, 219–220, 224–225, 244–245, 249, 256, 272, 309, 323

kingdom of heaven............................10, 43, 69, 85–87, 96, 100–101, 120–122, 124–125, 133, 159, 167–168, 171, 223–226, 233, 246, 250, 260

kiss..106, 286

lamb..............7, 32, 51–52, 266, 294, 331–332, 335

Lamb of God 7, 51–52

lame 77, 101, 103, 152, 208, 241

Last Day (the) 144–145, 217, 254, 268, 287

Law.................8, 10, 20, 32–33, 36, 40, 52, 71, 73–74, 77–78, 81–82, 87, 95, 97, 101–102, 107, 109, 111–112, 125, 149, 160, 163, 165, 177–179, 181–182, 194,

203, 207, 209, 212–213, 227, 248, 251, 253, 263, 265, 278, 286, 288, 291, 293, 297, 303, 317, 336

law of Moses 32, 36, 178, 317, 336

Lazarus...........10, 213, 215–217, 235, 239, 242

lepers...69, 101, 133

leprous men 219

Levites..45

light 9, 19, 27, 29, 33, 58, 69–70, 79, 86–87, 92, 105, 110, 118, 134, 181, 187, 210, 212, 215, 253–254, 328–329

lion...17, 303, 331

Lord of Hosts 27, 44, 102–103, 285, 332

Lord's supper...11, 272

Lot...220

love......46, 80, 89–92, 106, 111, 162, 185, 195, 212, 215, 224, 248–250, 257, 269, 272, 275–278, 284, 322

love one another..272

loving one another.................................277–278

Magi 7, 35–36

Malachi 22, 27, 44, 102, 163, 338, 342

Malchus 286

manger...31–32, 202

Martha 10, 195, 215–217, 235

Mary 7, 10–12, 23, 25–27, 31–36, 39, 48, 50, 107, 131, 195, 215–217, 235, 304, 307, 309, 311, 313–314, 324

Mary of Magdala..........107, 307, 309, 311, 313

Matthew.....................7–8, 13, 25, 35–36, 39, 44, 46, 50–51, 61, 64, 69, 71–76, 82–84, 86–87, 90, 92–95, 97, 100, 102, 104–105, 109–110, 112–113, 115, 119, 121–122, 124–125, 127, 129, 131–133, 135–137, 139, 141–142, 150–155, 159–163, 166–171, 174, 223–224, 226–228, 231, 237, 239, 241–250, 252, 260–263, 265–266, 270–272, 276, 284, 286–289, 291–292, 294–296, 298–299, 301–303, 305–307, 310–313, 322, 324, 339–340, 342

Micah.............................35, 135, 180, 338, 342

mina...233

miraculous sign 56, 68, 109, 141, 143, 205

moneychangers....................................56, 241

morning 72, 142, 153, 181, 226, 241, 243, 256, 260, 291, 293, 306, 311, 315

Mosaic law 33, 102, 194, 248

Moses.......................................20, 32, 36, 52–53, 57, 73, 80, 141, 143, 150, 161–162, 170, 177–178, 180–181, 188, 214, 222–223, 247–249, 306, 310, 315, 317, 336

mother of Jesus...............................55, 309, 324

Mount of Olives.................181, 237–238, 257, 276, 324

Mount Olivet 237, 256, 324

mustard seed 8, 121, 166, 214

nard...35, 265

narrow door 10, 205

Nathan.................................24–25, 48, 336

Nathaniel 52, 84, 321

Nazarene 39, 286, 312

Nazareth.................7–9, 23, 31, 39–40, 46, 52, 68–69, 71, 131, 231, 239, 290, 302, 315

neighbor.................89, 135, 195, 224, 248–249

nets...70–71

New Commandment 272

New Covenant 272

Nicodemus................................56–57, 179, 309

ninety-nine...169

Noah 48, 220, 259

Olivet Discourse...................................11, 257

one (the) 22, 51–52, 80, 111, 123, 135, 143, 145, 168, 178, 183, 185, 189, 194, 217, 221, 238, 270, 278, 331–332

Palm Sunday 237

parables 10, 108, 115–117, 122, 125, 209, 221, 245–246

paradise 303

Passover.......8, 11–12, 39, 56, 77, 79, 139, 219, 231–233, 235, 237–239, 241, 243, 245, 247, 249, 251–253, 255, 257, 259, 261, 263, 265–266, 269, 271–273, 275, 277, 279, 281, 283, 285, 287, 289, 291, 293, 295, 297, 299, 306, 309, 339–340

Patmos 330

peace 10, 29, 32–33, 106, 130, 134–135, 169, 193, 199, 209, 238–239, 276, 281, 317–318, 333–334

peace on earth 32, 199

pearl...8, 124

penny...............................11, 88, 134, 156, 252

Peter.............8–9, 11, 52, 70–71, 84, 130, 140, 142, 146, 151, 159–162, 167, 170, 199, 225, 243, 257, 266, 269, 271–273, 284–286, 288, 290–291, 311–313, 321–325, 343

Philip 43, 52, 84, 136, 140, 252, 274, 324

Pharisee.........................10, 105, 110, 221–222

physician 68, 75

pigs...8, 94, 128, 210

Pilate's wife...12, 295

Pontius Pilate 43

possible 13, 51, 63, 166, 178, 225, 258, 285

Potter's Field..292

Praetorium 293, 297–298

pray......................73, 84, 89–91, 141, 161, 196,
221–223, 243, 258, 283, 285

prison..........58, 61, 69, 88, 100, 103, 136–137,
171, 262, 273, 295, 298

prodigal son 10, 209

proverb...68

purification 33, 55, 58, 149

rabbi...................52, 56, 58, 63, 143, 186, 215,
250, 286

Ramah 36–37

repent..................10, 43, 67, 69, 104, 136, 168,
201, 203, 214, 340

repentance....................43, 45–46, 75, 210, 318

resurrection 5, 7, 9–11, 79, 160, 166, 208,
216, 227, 235, 247–248, 305, 340, 352

Resurrection (the).........160, 166, 216, 227, 305

return......9, 22, 88, 90, 94, 112, 116–117, 119,
129, 134, 155, 162, 193, 195, 198–199,
208, 219, 233, 237, 241, 256, 258–259,
261, 274, 323, 325

rooster..........................260, 273, 284, 290–291

ruling priests 35, 160, 178–179,
217, 227, 232, 235, 241, 243, 245, 263,
265, 286–288, 291–297, 302–303, 310,
313, 315, 328–330

Sabbath 8, 10, 12,
68, 71, 77–78, 81–82, 131, 169, 178, 187,
202, 207, 258, 306, 309–311, 324, 340

Sadducees.......................45, 153–155, 247–248

salt 86, 169, 209

Samaria 8–9, 61, 63, 173, 219, 324, 339

Samaritan 8, 10, 61, 185, 194–195, 219

Sanhedrin.......................87, 217, 288, 291, 309

Satan 50–51, 108, 117, 160, 194, 202, 265,
271, 273, 329

Saul...328–330

saved 28, 55, 58, 79, 106, 117, 134, 205,
225, 257, 325, 328

Savior 5, 25–26, 28, 31, 64, 254

scribes 35, 71, 74, 82, 87, 97,
107, 109, 112, 149, 160, 163, 165, 209,
227, 241, 243, 248–251, 263, 286, 294

Scriptures 5, 13, 50–51, 56, 80, 179, 238,
241, 245, 247, 251, 255, 270, 283, 287,
302, 304, 306, 313, 315, 318, 325

Sea of Galilee............................69–70, 139, 152

seed...........8, 24, 115, 117–121, 123, 166, 214

sepulcher...12, 309–310

sheep 10, 31, 56, 77, 82, 95, 133–134, 139,
152, 169, 189–191, 203, 209–210, 214,
262, 284–285, 294, 322, 334–335

shepherds 7, 31–32

shroud..12, 309, 313

Sidon 69, 83, 85, 104, 151–152, 193–194

Siloam 187, 201

Simeon.......................................7, 33–34, 48

Simon 52, 70–72, 84, 105–106,
132, 140, 146–147, 159, 167, 265, 269,
271–273, 285–286, 288, 298, 311, 313,
317, 321–322, 324

slave 9, 99–100, 134, 170–171, 184, 199,
208, 212, 214–215, 228, 277, 327

Sodom.................................104, 134, 193, 220

soldiers 12, 45, 99, 286–287, 294, 296, 298,
301–303, 306, 310, 313

Solomon.....34, 49, 93, 110, 197, 202, 336, 342

son of David......11, 25, 48, 107, 131, 151, 231,
238, 242, 249

Son of God............9, 15, 23, 48, 50–52, 58, 72,
79, 83, 142, 161, 203, 215–216, 289, 291,
297, 302–303, 306, 319, 329

Son of Man 9–10, 52–53, 57, 74, 79,
82, 86, 102, 108–109, 123, 134, 143,
145–146, 155–156, 159–163, 166, 174,
183, 188, 198–199, 220–221, 225,
227–228, 232, 252–253, 256, 258–259,
262–263, 271–272, 286, 289–291, 312,
328, 331, 333

sorrow 10, 199, 228, 279, 285

sower...63, 115, 117

sparrows 134–135, 156

Spirit 13, 21, 23, 25–26, 28, 33,
46–47, 50–51, 57, 59, 61–63, 67–69, 71,
74, 83, 103, 108–109, 112, 128, 131,
134, 146, 151, 153, 156, 162, 165–166,
174, 179, 194, 196, 202, 216, 249, 257,
271, 275–276, 278, 280, 285, 305, 318,
323–324, 328–331

Spirit of Truth 275, 278, 280

star...35–36

stone 9, 50–51, 55, 95, 103, 181, 203,
215–217, 239, 244–245, 252, 255, 257,
285, 297, 310–311

stones, ...45, 50, 128, 186, 203, 206, 238,
255, 257

sword 34, 135, 256, 273, 285–287, 331

synagogue..........8, 68–69, 71, 82, 99, 129–131,
146, 188, 202, 279, 288

Syria.......................................31, 73, 151

talents 171, 260

tax...............9–11, 45, 74–75, 84, 89, 102, 167,
170, 209, 221–222, 232, 244, 246–247

tax collectors 45, 74–75, 89, 102, 209, 244

349

teacher of the religious Law 125

teachers of the Law......40, 73–74, 97, 107, 181, 209, 263, 265, 288, 291, 303

temple 7–9, 11, 21–22, 27–28, 33–34, 39, 44, 50, 56, 78, 81, 102, 167, 177–179, 181–182, 186, 202, 222, 232, 239, 241, 243, 249–251, 255–257, 265, 287–289, 292, 302, 305, 324

temptation 7, 50, 196, 285–286

Thaddaeus 84

thanksgiving...26, 254

third day 11, 55, 167, 206, 227, 243, 245, 247, 249, 251, 253, 255, 257, 259, 261, 263, 310, 312, 315, 318, 325, 340

thirsty....................................62, 179, 262, 304

Thomas 12, 84, 216, 274, 318–319, 321, 324

three days 40, 56, 109, 153, 160, 167, 227, 289, 302, 310, 329

tomb 12, 137, 216, 239, 309–315, 335

touch me 130, 317

transfiguration...9, 161

transgressions 91, 243, 334–335

treasures 35, 92, 125

tree.......................10–11, 45, 52, 95, 109, 121, 201–202, 214, 232, 241, 243, 256, 259

triumphal entry 7, 11, 238

truth...................20, 45, 52, 57–58, 62–63, 68, 78–79, 87–88, 90–91, 101, 117, 130, 134–135, 143, 145, 154, 161, 166, 168–169, 177, 184–185, 189, 198–199, 224–225, 248, 255, 257, 259–260, 262, 265, 270–275, 278–281, 283–284, 293, 303, 305–306, 322

Twelve (the) 84, 107, 116, 133, 136, 138, 140, 146–147, 154, 168, 227, 239, 242, 265, 269, 271, 286, 318, 325

unclean spirit...........................71, 112, 128, 166

upper room 11, 266, 274, 324

vinegar 299, 303–305

vineyard 10, 201, 226, 244–245

virgin...23–25

vision 12, 22, 162, 315, 328–330

walking on the water 142

water 9, 17, 46, 51, 55, 57–58, 61–63, 67, 70, 77, 106, 115, 128, 135, 141–142, 165–166, 168, 179, 202, 213, 266, 269, 297, 303, 306, 323

Way (the) 274, 329

wedding 11, 55, 102, 198, 207, 246, 260

weeds 8, 120–121, 123

well.................8, 15, 21, 61–63, 68, 72, 77–78, 83–84, 86, 89, 92, 107, 111, 120, 129–130, 136, 146, 153, 178, 190, 194, 198–199, 202, 207, 216, 219, 231, 233, 248, 260–261, 269, 278, 306, 313, 351

wept 216, 239, 291

wheat 46, 120–121, 212, 252, 273

wilderness........29, 43–45, 50, 57, 73, 101, 103, 128, 143, 145, 180, 217, 258

wine 21, 55, 67, 76, 102, 120, 195, 299, 303–305

woe............8, 86, 104, 110–112, 168, 193, 214, 250–251, 255, 271

wolves 95, 134, 193

womb..................21, 26, 33, 57, 112, 223, 330

Word (the) 15, 19–20

Word of God...........43, 70, 112–113, 117, 150, 203, 330

worry 10, 93, 134, 197, 257

worthy.............46, 99, 134–135, 193, 210–211, 247, 331–332

yeast 122, 154–155

Zacchaeus...11, 232

Zacharias......................................21–22, 26, 28

Zebedee...........................71, 84, 227, 285, 307

Zechariah 43, 112, 238, 285, 292, 307, 338, 342

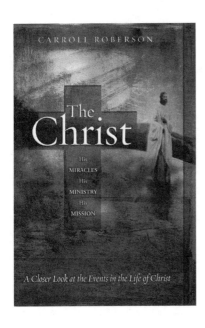

The Christ

His Miracles,
His Ministry,
His Mission

by
Carroll Roberson

Southern Gospel singer/songwriter Carroll Roberson reveals more of his talent as he examines the main events in the life of Christ. Recalling Old Testament prophecies, relating manners and customs of the Jewish people, and utilizing his knowledge of the Hebrew and Greek languages, Roberson unfolds an account of Christ like no other in an easy-to-follow format. Many illustrations and historic photos of the Holy Land are included, as well as a CD of 17 songs by Carroll specifically recorded to go with this unique book. Having many facets, this book can be used on many different levels: as a commentary, a devotional, a study guide, a reference book, or simply a book to be enjoyed as a leisurely read.

ISBN: 0-89221-610-7 • $14.99
288 pages • paperback • 6½ x 9

New Leaf Press

Another exciting title from New Leaf Press!

365 Fascinating Facts about Jesus

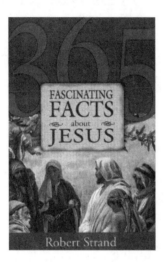

by
Robert Strand

The political, cultural, and religious times in which Jesus lived are brought to life in this terrific book. Fact by fact, the history of His birth, life, death, and resurrection are recounted along with the rich traditions and customs of His people. The interesting information also includes fascinating articles about many things related to Christ, such as the wise men who visited Him after His birth, Da Vinci's Last Supper, the Via Dolorosa, the calendar, the Wailing Wall, and much more.

ISBN: 0-89221-488-0 • $10.99
224 pages • paperback

Available at Christian bookstores nationwide!

New Leaf Press